CLASSICS

MAJOR AND MINOR

Da Capo Press Music Reprint Series

GENERAL EDITOR

FREDERICK FREEDMAN

VASSAR COLLEGE

CLASSICS
MAJOR AND MINOR

With Some Other Musical Ruminations

By Eric Blom

DA CAPO PRESS • NEW YORK • 1972

Library of Congress Cataloging in Publication Data

Blom, Eric, 1888-1959.
    Classics: major and minor.

    (Da Capo Press music reprint series)
    1. Music—Addresses, essays, lectures.
I. Title.
ML60.B664 1972   780'.8   74-166098
    ISBN 0-306-70293-2

This Da Capo Press edition of *Classics, Major and Minor* is an un-
abridged republication of the first edition published in London in
1958. It is reprinted by special arrangement with J. M. Dent & Sons
Ltd.

Published by Da Capo Press, Inc.
A Subsidiary of Plenum Publishing Corporation
227 West 17th Street, New York, N.Y. 10011

CLASSICS: MAJOR AND MINOR

By the same author

A MUSICAL POSTBAG
EVERYMAN'S DICTIONARY OF MUSIC
MOZART *(Master Musicians)*

ERIC BLOM

CLASSICS

MAJOR AND MINOR

with some other
MUSICAL RUMINATIONS

LONDON
J. M. DENT & SONS LTD

To All My Grandchildren

Preface

DARE I confess that I found a certain cow-like, placid, idle and reminiscent satisfaction in the process of ruminating a sizable cud and retasting, at my publishers' request, some of my browsings of long ago —over thirty years in one case? If I may hope to communicate some of that sensation to others, late as it is, I shall be happy enough to feel that the publication of these essays in a more permanent form has been justified.

The term 'rumination' has a non-literal meaning, and is intended to apply to mental, not digestive activity. Whether this book will stimulate many readers to exercise this remains to be seen. They will not find in it much of that philosophical criticism which is now fashionable in certain quarters, nor any of that psychological probing which tries so aggressively to establish itself and denies or at any rate ignores the value of historical views. These, however, continue to interest me, as I hope the following essays will show even where they are largely analytical in a technical sense. It has always seemed to me, and still does, that analysis plus history add up to an aesthetic total from which something of positive value is to be gained, provided the approach is right and the treatment adequate.

Where I analyse masterpieces, or music which, for some reason or other, I like sufficiently to wish to share my pleasure with others, I am afraid I do it very much in the way now dismissed with derision and obloquy by the musical psychologists as merely telling people what is there for them to hear in performance or to see in a score. To which I can only reply that this is after all the kind of exegesis that has always been found valuable as criticism of all the arts, provided only that it is well done, which in my case I must leave to others to judge. For the critic may legitimately assume that many things, however clearly audible or visible, remain unperceived unless they are pointed out by him, or that, even if others do perceive them, his individual apprehension of them may be of interest, if only because it differs from theirs. Analytical criticism of the visual arts does not seem as yet to have come in for the contemptuous treatment meted out to that of music, possibly because by going to absurd lengths at times in 'merely telling people what is plain for them to see,' it may show that its often over-exuberant use of jargon and metaphor does in fact tell them *how* to see things.   By analogy, musical criticism of a similar kind can teach the public—let us hope with as little jargon as possible—not merely to hear, but to listen.

With psychological quests, or inquests, I could not hope to interest my readers, for the simple reason that I find them desperately tiresome and uninteresting when they are undertaken, however skilfully, by others.   That is one objection; the other, to my mind, is that to find hidden thematic connections between one section or movement and another of a composition is fatally easy if one has made up one's mind beforehand to do it with the idea of proving a work a masterpiece.   I am convinced that as a matter of fact it can be done with any piece of music, good, bad or indifferent; but, of course, those who set out to prove greatness in that way are anything but anxious to try their method on what they deem inferior, lest it should lead them to dis-coveries of correspondences exactly similar to those which have induced them to see greatness where they want to see it.   Not that it is not perfectly easy to hush up such inconvenient disclosures, if they awkwardly insist on invalidating preconceived notions.

In any case, even if thematic correspondences were found only in great works by great composers, produced unconsciously (let us say by Mozart) or consciously (e.g. by Schoenberg), why should that give us a greater thrill than sheer spontaneous inventiveness?   The answer is, I am sure, that they satisfy only the critics for whom nothing will do but 'serial' music, of which twelve-note music is now seen to be by no means the only manifestation.   It seems to give them strange com-fort, to soothe their consciences, so to speak, to prove to their own satisfaction, if to nobody else's, that all great composers were serial composers, that in fact serial composition is the only valid sort of composition.   It is no doubt pleasant to confront sceptics with ocular proof (much more ocular than aural) that Mozart justifies Schoenberg —though in the other arts nobody is foolish enough to want Shake-speare to justify Ibsen or Raphael Picasso.   Unfortunately for critics of the new school their arguments are only too apt to turn topsyturvy and to force them into the ridiculous situation of appearing to be anxious to show that Schoenberg has at last justified Mozart.

It is only fair to give warning that I shall be unimpressed by any complaints of my having failed to exercise a sort of criticism for which I have no use.   Whether I have succeeded in my own kind is for others to say, and I am prepared to face any reproach but that of having failed in what I did not attempt, or wish to attempt.   I may not have done the best that can be done on my own lines; but I think I may at least claim, not for myself, but for technical criticism in general, that when-ever it is exercised with love for and interest in its object, it rarely turns

out to be concerned solely with dry matters of technique and incidentally with historical aspects, but sets in motion reactions of taste and
feeling to which the reader may respond in kind.

It only remains for me to say that, after due verification, I found
little occasion to correct mistakes or to alter opinions (the latter,
indeed, I often left unchanged even at the risk of their no longer quite
representing my present views); and to acknowledge, most gratefully,
the kind permission to reprint the material in this book by those who
first published it.   They are the following:

The Governors of the Sadler's
    Wells Foundation   The Music of *Figaro*
                                          The Music of *Così fan tutte*

The Gramophone Company Ltd
    (Beethoven Sonata Society)   Beethoven's Diabelli Variations
The Editors and/or Publishers of
    Music & Letters   Schubert's Favourite Device
                                          The Minuet-Trio
                                          Verdi as Musician
    Musical Opinion   The Prophecies of Dussek
                                          Vincent d'Indy's 'Enigma'
    The Chesterian   John Field
    The Monthly Musical Record   The Happy Ending
    The Musical Quarterly   The Literary Ancestry of *Figaro*
    The Musical Times   Key Heredity
                                          Phrase-lengths
    The Sackbut   A Disgraceful Career

                                                        ERIC BLOM.

London, *September 1958*.

Contents

Mozart's 'Figaro'

THE LITERARY ANCESTRY

(The Musical Quarterly, October 1927)

DURING the First World War, when Sir Thomas Beecham brought out a lavish production of *The Marriage of Figaro* in London, he or the producer, Nigel Playfair, hit upon the happy idea of scrapping the part of Don Curzio and assigning the tenor voice in the sextet to Basilio. Musically this arrangement proved satisfactory from every point of view, and not least so from that of the impersonator of Basilio, who never has enough to do in the opera. Da Ponte's libretto, too, to which as much as possible of the original Beaumarchais dialogue had been restored, was easily accommodated to the justifiable liberty taken with it. The idea of making the Count appoint the most servile creature of his household to act as counsel in a case in which his own interests make the judgment a foregone conclusion, added a touch of piquancy to the aristocrat's unscrupulous wielding of the *droit du seigneur* that would doubtless have delighted Beaumarchais himself. To have his scorn of a corrupt society thus intensified by a deft twist in the situation would have consoled him for the loss of the stuttering blockhead of a lawyer, a character introduced for no better purpose than that of propping up the trial scene. Bridoison in the comedy and Curzio in the opera, indeed, are neither essential nor particularly amusing, while Basilio can easily appear to be both. The substitution of knave for fool decidedly adds spice to the scene. Of course, Basilio did not stutter in the Beecham version, but the very absence of this feature led one to reflect how little Beaumarchais was justified in resorting to so childish a device, and why in the name of common sense Da Ponte should have transferred it to his Don Curzio. There is no dramatic reason whatever for it, and it strikes a decidedly false note in Beaumarchais, who knew his business better than to introduce such superficialities into a comedy except by a slip; into a comedy, moreover, where plot and character are otherwise so closely and logically interdependent down to the smallest detail. The drunkenness of the gardener, for instance, is demanded by the situation, whereas the impediment in the lawyer's speech is merely a gratuitous effort to amuse, a decorative excrescence upon the polished surface of the play.

Driven by this instance to search the two comedies of what might be called the 'Almaviva trilogy' [1] for other redundancies of this kind, one comes upon the somnolent servant in *The Barber of Seville* and discovers that there is no need at all for him to be a sleepyhead. He is more than stupid enough even when wide awake to be fooled to the top of his bent by Figaro whenever the latter desires to effect an entry for the Count into Dr Bartolo's house. What was Beaumarchais about?

The obvious answer is that we are here confronted by some of those conventional flourishes which insinuate themselves into the substance of a work of art in an unguarded moment. It requires but a slender literary culture to know that the characters in the two comedies are merely a presentation in a new guise of the stereotyped figures of the Italian impromptu comedy, and it is here that one naturally looks for the source of such irrelevant details as the stammering judge and the gaping servant, only to discover how much more than one had suspected, before the retracing of two unimportant points had led one to make an exhaustive study of the whole question, Beaumarchais and (it is always understood in the course of this study) the paraphrases of Da Ponte and Sterbini are indebted to the *commedia dell' arte*.

Beaumarchais, in truth, contrives nothing new beyond details of invention and workmanship; in their broad outlines the comedies are complacently traditional. The stories of the tricked guardian and of the erring lover reformed by the ruse of turning jealousy into repentance are as little the French author's own as the characters who enact them. The fact is that he did his purloining of the ready-made tricks and petrified idiosyncrasies of the Italian stock characters so thoroughly that here and there, almost mechanically, he was bound to make use of things which had not the least bearing on his dramatic development.

Bridoison (Don Curzio), then, stutters for no better reason than Beaumarchais's neglect to dress up the traditional Italian figure of Tartaglia in a semblance of new fashion, as he did to a greater or less extent in the case of practically all his other characters. Tartaglia was simply taken over wholesale and stuck into the French comedy without so much as an attempt to plane him down until he fitted in with the rest. The Italians made use of Tartaglia whenever the plot needed an

---

[1] The third part, 'La Mère coupable,' is a serious drama, where the familiar characters become involved in psychological complications that mark the end of classical French comedy and the dawn of the modern problem play. But Beaumarchais is not happy in that vein and, in any case, this piece does not concern the musician.

auxiliary figure, and he never appeared in more than one scene of any comedy, which is exactly what happens with Bridoison. In order to make him appear something more than a mere padding, he had to be amusing, and the stammering fool served the purpose well enough to make any further creative effort on behalf of this minor personage unnecessary for all time. Most often the utility role filled by Tartaglia was that of a notary, an advocate or a judge (of course no opportunity to ridicule the law was missed), and lo! in *Figaro* he becomes something like solicitor, counsel and judge all rolled into one. Bridoison is a very composite, a canned preserve, of Tartaglia.

The yawning servant in the *Barber* is quite simply the accessory figure of Peppe-Nappa, a Sicilian character from which the French Pierrot or Gilles took its origin. Peppe-Nappa has a faculty for sleep equal to any situation. He will nod while taking his master's orders or receiving a sound cudgelling, and snore whenever his vigilance is especially required.

As with the characters, so with the plots. Innumerable details are adopted by Beaumarchais from the Italian scenarios, the so-called *ossature*, mere skeletons of the action upon which the comedians based their scenes, inventing their dialogue with incredible readiness of wit and repartee as they went along. The same scenario could be seen over and over again with renewed pleasure because of the ever-varying freshness of the players' improvisations. The inevitable consequence was that novelty of plot lagged considerably behind inventiveness in the contrivance of situation. The characters too, being the creation of generations of actors and never minutely prescribed by the scenic framework, remained unaltered in the main outlines for centuries. Only a comedian of quite exceptional histrionic genius could now and again fundamentally change an old type or create an entirely new one. Thus Lucio Burchiella invented the Bolognese doctor, the prototype of Bartolo, in 1560, and Harlequin was changed from a zany into an astute, lively, witty and sometimes philosophical valet by Domenico Biancolelli in the second half of the seventeenth century.[2]

Directly the influence of the *commedia dell' arte* on the French theatre, to which I shall revert presently, is understood, there can be no matter for surprise in the fact that Beaumarchais was in his turn tempted to parade the familiar figures upon the familiar scenes. He does so more especially in *The Barber of Seville*. The Doctor's

[2] Domenico affords an interesting example of the longevity of characteristic features gradually accumulated by the outstanding representatives of the *commedia dell' arte*. He had a vocal defect that gave a parrot-like quality to his speech. This is doubtless the origin of the traditional Punch voice, whose screech is still occasionally heard piercing through the street noises of London.

tyranny over and amorous inclination towards his ward, the subterfuges on Figaro's part in smuggling the lover into the house, the
trickery hidden under the girl's demure and docile attitude, are themes
enacted again and again by the puppet-like casts of the Italian comedians.   There is a French comedy in the Italian manner in Evaristo
Gherardi's collection of scenarios [3] actually bearing Beaumarchais's
subtitle of 'La Précaution inutile,' where the principal characters are
Bartolo, Rosina, Almaviva and Figaro to the life under different
names, Figaro's intrigues being undertaken jointly by Mezzetin and
Arlequin.   Moreover, this play contains a scene where the heroine,
having fibbed herself successfully out of a predicament, feigns indignation and sorrow at having been unjustly suspected, which is exactly
the trick to which Rosina is to resort when she has become Countess
Almaviva.

Beaumarchais's dependence on the Italian theatre is simply to be
ascribed to the fact that the history of French comedy is largely that
of the *commedia dell' arte*.   A brief outline recapitulating the invasion
of France—or of Paris, which in matters of culture is the same thing
—by Italian companies on and off for nearly two centuries before the
inventor of Figaro [4] was born [5], will show how ineradicable the
influence had become by the time Beaumarchais had reached his
artistic maturity.   Nothing less than a revolution could uproot it,
together with so many other deep-seated conventions, and not even
the Revolution could quite kill French love for the charmingly
artificial figures of Harlequin and Columbine, of Pantaloon and Lelio
and Isabella, which may assume names like Figaro and Susanna, like
Bartolo, Almaviva and Rosina, but remain ever the same fundamental
types.

When Italian comedy began to invade France, the drama there was
still in its preliminary stages of religious mystery plays and trestle
theatres at the fairs, and there was no clear division between the
ingenuousness of pious beliefs and superstitions and that of profane
grotesquerie and coarseness.   In 1548, when the city of Lyons
received Henry II and Catherine de' Medici, some Florentine mer-
chants settled there brought Italian comedians to perform in France
for the first time.   Paris, however, had no experience of the *commedia
dell' arte* until 1570, when one Juan Ganassa, a hispanicized Italian
who had been at the court of Philip II, introduced his company to the
capital.   The personages of the improvised comedy were soon all
the fashion.   At a masked ball that preceded the massacre of St

[3] A series of fully written-out comedies by French authors closely modelled on Italian
patterns, first published in 1692.
[4] The name only, not the character itself.
[5] 24 January 1732.

Bartholomew's Day [6], Catherine appeared as Columbine, her son, Charles IX, as Brighella, the Duc de Guise as Scaramouche, the Duc d'Anjou as Harlequin and his Eminence the Cardinal de Lorraine as Pantaloon! So early did these comedy characters acquire in France that curious admixture of the grisly and the tragic of which they were quite innocent at home. Meanwhile the company known as *I Comici confidenti* and its rival troupe, *I Comici gelosi*, were touring through the French provinces, amalgamating in 1574 under the name of *I Comici uniti*. But in 1576 they separated again and the *Gelosi* were now headed by Flamminio Scala, a collection of whose scenarios was published in 1611. This company was summoned by Henry III first to Blois and afterwards to Paris, where it arrived in 1577.

Now began an interminable period of intermittent successes and withdrawals, of constant bickering by the established French theatres, retreats under their attacks, triumphant returns under the protection of a public whose affection for the Italians was not to be alienated. The troubled years after the accession of Henri IV until his final renunciation of Protestantism drove the Italians from France, and the building of the Théâtre Français in 1592 was not calculated to make Paris a more fruitful field for them; but after the Peace of Savoy and Henry's marriage to Mary de' Medici in 1600, the king recalled them. The first quarter of the seventeenth century not only consolidated their re-establishment, but made them an integral part of Parisian life. French comedians now began to pay them the sincerest form of flattery by assuming their costumes and much of their traditional stage business. Becoming thus naturalized, Italian comedy in its original form again lost credit, but it was not to be more than temporarily extinguished. Both Louis XIII and Cardinal Mazarin ordered Italian companies to Paris, and in 1660 such a troupe was established at the Théâtre du Palais Royal concurrently with Molière's company. By this time the great dramatist-comedian himself had begun his career as an author with farces closely modelled on the Italian scenarios and peopled by their stock characters. [7] The original versions of *Le Médecin malgré lui*, of *Les Fourberies de Scapin* [8] and of *Georges Dandin* were Italian plays in all but language [9], written before his first dramatic satire, *Les Précieuses ridicules*, which appeared in 1659. In his reaction against the lofty mythology and declamatory rodomontade of the purely French stage before him, it was natural for Molière to turn to the truthfully human situations and the realistic dialogue of

---

[6] 24 August 1572.
[7] It has been asserted that Molière actually embraced a dramatic career because of his enthusiasm, from early childhood, for the Italian comedians, and that he always imitated them in the comic parts he acted.
[8] Scapino is a figure of the *commedia dell'arte*, a mixture of Harlequin and Brighella.
[9] *L'École des Maris* was based on a scenario of 1667, entitled *La Hotte*.

the Italian comedy.   For in spite of the rigid framework upon which the *commedia dell' arte* was built, the actors, giving free rein to their invention, must have represented life as they saw it.   No doubt they exaggerated, but then actuality is rendered more forcible, rather than less, when adroitly caricatured.

In proportion as the French stage encroached upon the Italians' dramatic patrimony and thus threatened to replace their comedies by a similar type of entertainment in a language understood by all, the latter found it necessary, in order to retain something of their hold on the public, to begin to use the French tongue themselves.   But the comedians were not all equally versatile linguists and their plays were now enacted in an absurd jargon of mingled French and Italian, into which morsels of Spanish were strewn in the case of traditional characters like the blustering and cowardly Captain, who was generally represented as a Spaniard.   Indigenous actors in their turn again retaliated by poaching more shamelessly than ever on the Italians' preserves.   What the legitimate theatre left untouched was eagerly snatched up by the tumbling comedians at the fairs.   The characters whom they presented under French names and, it is true, with some additional French idiosyncrasies, such as Turlupin, Gros-Guillaume, Jodelet, Fracasse and Gilles, were merely acclimatized Italians.   This competition was the more serious for the genuine Italians because the theatrical booths at the fairs were by no means patronized by the populace only.   The nobility, the courtiers, for all their fastidiousness and culture, loved the *théâtres de la foire* and the adventurous sense of naughtiness and open-mindedness a visit to so disreputable and coarse an entertainment doubtless gave them.   Gentlemen at first went alone; ladies more spotless of garb than of name next ventured to approach these histrionic mud-shoals with a great deal of circumspection; finally the *grandes dames* of the most sheltered reputations would draw their hooped skirts about them and, with endless misgivings and precautions, allow themselves to be drawn into a timorous enjoyment of such forbidden pleasures.   The performances on the trestles of a fair-theatre, even at their worst, were physically drastic rather than immoral, filthy rather than indecent, and as the patronage of the great increased, they gradually acquired a certain polish and relied more on wit than on grossly comic situation.   Propriety was observed to a greater extent and morality adjusted to that of the court, which meant merely a change from honest dirt to refined prurience. Towards the end of the seventeenth century authors of standing no longer disdained to write for the fair-theatres, and among the first to do so we find such eminent men as Regnard and Lesage.[10]   The link

---

[10] A collected edition of whose comedies of that type was published in 10 volumes under the title of *Le Théâtre de la Foire* in 1737.

between the *commedia dell' arte* and French comedy was thus established and the intimacy between them was to last for a century.

The more the French fair actors attracted the exalted patrons of the established stage, the more violent grew the latter's defence of its prerogatives. The Comédie Française and the Opéra succeeded time and again in persuading the Magistracy that their rights were being infringed by their freebooter-rivals and in securing their temporary suppression; but the public's romantic love of these piratical entertainments always triumphed in the end and the *forains* were rapturously applauded every time they contrived to evade the prohibition. Their trickery and cunning only endeared them the more to the *canaille*, in whom revolutionary opposition to tyranny of any sort already smouldered. The authorities might forbid plays in dialogue to be given anywhere but at the licensed theatres: the *forains* would immediately present on their illegitimate stages comedies entirely in monologue, one personage retiring behind the wings while the other spoke his lines to the audience. Spoken plays of any sort might thereupon be expressly interdicted: the actors would soon retort with a ridiculous entertainment in dumb-show with the words written on a placard and suspended over their heads. All through the early eighteenth century this struggle continued. Intrigue on one side and subterfuge on the other kept the balance tilting now one way, now the other. When complete suppression of the fair-theatres appeared quite hopeless, a means was found of keeping at least the upper classes away from their entertainments: by regulation prices had to be kept so low that the nobles, if they wished to be present, were forced to mix with the rabble, a blow before which most of them capitulated.

The Italians, in the meantime, had been forced to retreat once more. In 1716, however, the famous Luigi Riccoboni and his more famous wife, Flamminia, who was a scholar and a wit as well as an astonishing actress, arrived with their company and established themselves at the Hôtel de Bourgogne with the coarsest of repertories 'in the name of God, the Virgin Mary, St Francis of Paola and the Souls in Purgatory.' Once again the plays were given in Italian, but the public soon began to clamour for the vernacular and to complain of the grossness of many of the jests, which offended audiences corrupt in morals but refined in manners. It was the age of Mme de Maintenon, a royal mistress so scrupulous as to outward appearances that owing to her influence the Italian comedians, who were openly and candidly indelicate on the stage, but on the whole morally vastly superior to the French actors of the time in private life, had to quit Paris again and could only return after her death in 1719. Meanwhile no less an author than Marivaux had begun to write comedies in the Italian manner. In 1716 he wrote for Antonio Vicentini, who called himself

Thomassin and played in French.   Gradually his comedies became subtilized, philosophical, satirical—in a word, Frenchified—but plots and characters remained Italianate [11] and many of the plays were written for the Comédie Italienne, a theatre now in the hands of French actors and to be united in 1762 with the Opéra-Comique. By the middle of the eighteenth century Italian was no longer spoken on any Parisian stage and the few Italian actors who remained all performed in French.   When in 1780 the Opéra-Comique took the name of Théâtre des Italiens, there was not a single Italian left.   Just as many authors of repute had written for the *théâtres de la foire* in the preceding century, so now men of similar standing, following the example of Marivaux, wrote for the Comédie Italienne.   Eminent among them was Sedaine, another whose success is still remembered was Favart, and even Diderot enjoyed writing comedies in the Italian style in spite of his view that social conditions rather than interplay of character should sustain the interest of a play.[12]

Enough has been said in this sketch to show that the connection of Beaumarchais with the *commedia dell' arte* rests on a solid historical foundation.   Like Molière, like Marivaux, he thought the pseudo-classical drama barbarous, and its divinities, heroes and monarchs had no interest for him.   'What are the revolutions of Athens and Rome to me?' he asked.   But, significantly enough for the nature of French comedy, in discarding the classical tradition he fell like his predecessors into that of the Italian impromptu comedy.   We have already seen his indebtedness to Italian plots and traced the descent of two of his minor characters.   The chief figures of his two comedies are in their main outlines as plainly unchanging types derived from the *commedia dell' arte*.   What is French about them (they appear in Spanish guise merely for the sake of picturesqueness and perhaps from political prudence) is the endeavour to make them true to life by chiselling finer and more personal traits upon the rough-cast of the traditional features.   Types have become characters; plots and situations which in the *commedia dell' arte* have no other aim but to amuse [13], have acquired a satirical moral or political significance.   It is interesting to note, however, that in Marivaux, for instance, love often finds obstacles in the character of the lovers itself, not in the purely external opposition of parents or guardians, to which Beaumarchais reverts. The creator of Figaro is therefore more closely allied to the Italians than Marivaux, and certainly more so than the mature Molière.   In

[11] *Arlequin poli par l'Amour* is a typical title.
[12] It was this dictum that induced Beaumarchais to try his hand at a play which had the Lyons silk trade for its theme.   This was *Les deux amis*, his second dramatic effort, and an early example of the social drama.
[13] At any rate as far as the author of the scenario is concerned.   The actors were doubtless prodigal with scorn and topical allusions according to their personal gifts.

other words, the influence had lost nothing of its force by the time it reached Beaumarchais.

Let us now examine the ancestry of the chief characters in *The Barber of Seville* and *The Marriage of Figaro* one by one.   Figaro is the offspring of Harlequin.   It is true that the original Arlecchino was a zany, a simpleton, an ill-used servant employed to do any dirty work and rewarded with slender pay and profuse blows and kicks. The true descendant of this type is not Figaro, but Leporello, and one might be inclined to trace the former back to the cunning Brighella, were it not for the goodness of heart which alone prompts him to intrigue and lie and manœuvre, a quality in which Brighella is entirely deficient.   Figaro may be as crafty as Brighella, but he is anything but hypocritical and sycophantic.   He is the Harlequin as converted by Domenico Biancolelli for the benefit of the French public, who did not care to have a great actor's talent wasted on the parts of dunces and dullards, but liked to see him in more spirited, witty and adroit roles.   A character who employed his astuteness and readiness of wit in the cause of good, as Brighella employed his in that of evil, was an immense asset to the *commedia dell' arte*, and in the hands of its creator it rose at once to a leading place in the cast, just as it is the mainspring of Beaumarchais's two comedies in the guise of the barber-valet.

Harlequin was always the lover, and generally became the husband, of Columbine.   It would follow that, Figaro being Harlequin, Susanna must be Columbine, which is certainly confirmed by her character and her place in the plot of the second comedy.   Whether called by the most common name of Columbina, or bearing a rustic one like Betta, Gitta or Nina, or again a more sophisticated one like Fiammetta, Pasquella or Diamantina, the type remains always essentially the same: that of a *servetta*, a serving-maid, sometimes worldly-wise and philosophical, sometimes corrupt and cynical, always in the heroine's confidence and proffering her advice with unfailing assurance either for good or ill, most often with an admirable gift of compromising between the two.   In many of the scenarios she stands for little more than a recipient of confidences which are in reality addressed to the audience or a *seconda donna* conveniently used to complete the conventional double set of happy lovers at the close.   In opera the character survived with especial tenacity in this subordinate function for the additional reason that it offered a good excuse for the introduction of the contralto voice required in the concerted numbers, and this is perhaps why it is so frequently represented as middle-aged on the lyric stage.[14]   That she should exchange the role of confidante

[14] Even Magdalena in *The Mastersingers* is little more than a Columbine grown staid, and at the risk of being accused of sacrilege, one might point out that even Brangäne's chief function is that of acting as transmitter of Isolde's explanations to the audience and supplying a change of vocal colour.

for that of duenna was by no means unusual even in the Italian comedies, which with Gilbertian cruelty made the tragedy of approaching age a matter for jesting.[15]   Thus Marcellina, who is unscrupulous as well as old and ridiculous, presents the elements of Columbine which are lacking in Susanna.   The latter, although playing the part of soubrette, in reality resembles more the variant of Columbine in the part of younger sister to the heroine, a pert, precocious, amorous and pretty foil to the more serious and high-principled leading lady.[16]

That lady, whose most usual name in the *commedia dell' arte* is Isabella, is a type perfectly represented by Rosina—her tutelage and her evasion of its stringencies is perhaps the most steadily recurrent subject in the impromptu comedies—and still maintained when she has become Countess Almaviva.   In the latter part, it is true, the character is deepened and emotionalized, but not more so than was the custom in the finest of the earlier French comedies derived from Italian models, and probably not more so than was done extemporaneously by a great representative of the original type like Isabella Andreini, engaged for the *Gelosi* company in 1578, a beautiful, virtuous and intelligent actress and a poetess and musician to boot, or Françoise Biancolelli and Giovanna Benozzi in the late seventeenth and early eighteenth centuries respectively.

The Count, especially in *The Barber*, is a typical representative of Lelio, whose name was also frequently Flavio or Cinthio.   The figure was that of a gentleman of the world with 'a leg' like Sir Willoughby Patterne's, generally the accepted lover of Isabella, frequently involved in ridiculous situations, but never undignified.   If we remember that there was Orazio, a variant of Lelio, who was also something of a Don Juan, we have the character of Almaviva in all its essentials.

The Italians had, however, yet another character of the Lelio type, generally called Leandro, who until the eighteenth century, when he became a strutting and foolish dandy, was a boyish and ingenuous lover who constantly (or rather inconstantly) fluttered around the ladies with the alternate shyness and boldness of adolescent devotion. Leandro was a youthful disciple of Lelio just as Cherubino is a butterfly of the Almaviva species at the point of emerging from the chrysalis stage.   But Cherubino has also a strain of Pedrolino, the Italian archetype of Pierrot, an unrequited lover who hankers after petticoats throughout the play, only to be ignominiously snubbed or ridiculed at the end.

Dr Bartolo already bears that very name in some of the Italian written comedies, the *commedie sostenute*.   He is, of course, faithful

---

[15] Gozzi, in whose dramatic fairy-tales the *commedia dell' arte* reaches it final apotheosis with an appropriate touch of fantasy, is fond of introducing this type.

[16] The two sisters of these types reappear in Mozart's *Così fan tutte*, which also has its Columbine in Despina.

to the tradition of the Bolognese doctor, Graziano or Baloardo (often Balouard in France), and that figure again is no other than that of Cassandro or Pantalone.   He is sometimes the father of unmanageable daughters who refuse to marry the suitors chosen by him, and sometimes the guardian of a girl whom he annoys not more by his vigilance than by his amorousness and jealousy.   He is always old and ugly, rheumatic or asthmatic, a pedant and a miser, always duped and mocked, but, to do him justice, generally accommodating to the inevitable in the end.   The only feature of the character not enlarged upon by Beaumarchais is his incurable habit of airing badly digested learning and spouting incomprehensible Latin; otherwise the copy is faithful even to his wearing the Louis XIV periwig in the period of the pigtail, a convention adopted by French comedy to accentuate his age and his obsoleteness.

Basilio's ancestor is no less manifest: he is Brighella, a servile flatterer and tale-bearer, hypocritically polite to those above him and ironically so to those below, always ready with ingenious sophistries to corrupt people to his master's advantage and, as Basilio tells in Mozart's aria, to wear the humble ass's skin in order to save himself from the claws of a disdainful lion.

Such originality as is left in Beaumarchais, then, is confined entirely to the refining and elaborating and pointing of raw material that lay ready to his hand.   But when all his indebtedness is reckoned up, enough of topical allusions, niceties of shading in character-delineation, political and social quips, adroitness in sally and repartee, and countless charming details of situation still stands to his credit for him to be honoured for all time as a genius.   Nevertheless, one wonders whether even in such matters he was greater than the best of the Italian impromptu actors, of whose performances, in the nature of things, we can unhappily never know more than what rumour has left us.   Theirs is a lost art and we can but dimly imagine to-day what an unselfish spirit of teamwork must have reigned among them, what prodigious feats of ready wit they must have performed in their rejoinders and their *lazzi*, and with what delightful malice they must often have challenged each other to incredible dexterities in the handling of unforeseen and knotty situations.

THE MUSIC

(Sadler's Wells Opera Books, 1948)

ASKED to describe the music of *Figaro* in a single word, one cannot fail to think at once of the inevitable one—perfection.   One may make certain reservations on second thoughts, if only to find, on third thoughts, that they have nothing to do directly with Mozart.   The construction of the third act is not faultless, and obviously the fault is the librettist's, or at any rate the composer's only in so far as he did not insist on a better shape and on the avoidance of letting the curtain rise on a bald recitative.   Furthermore, the bunch of arias at the beginning of the fourth act, including at least one that is musically inferior, can be said to have been due to the custom of Mozart's time, which was to defer to singers in a way composers no longer think it necessary to do.   Two of the characters, Marcellina and Basilio, had been given no aria up to that point, and show-pieces for them had thus to be pushed in somewhere before the end.   If Mozart, the diplomat, had no objection, it is plain enough that Mozart, the artist, jibbed, though perhaps quite unconsciously.

There is something a little amiss, then, even musically speaking, with the form of *Figaro* as a whole.   The third and fourth acts have not the immaculate shape the first and second make together, and this in spite of the fact that the third concludes with a piece which is at least nominally a finale, whereas the first-act curtain comes down on a mere aria.   But we need not quarrel with that.   The reasonable thing to do is to regard the whole opera as a work in two parts, each crowned by an astonishingly extended and well-organized set piece.

To call almost everything in the work musically perfect is to repeat a critical commonplace.   But one may be trite in the interests of truth. The craftsmanship, elegance, style and contemporaneous appositeness of the idiom, the never-ending flow of ideas and of beauty, the un-failing shaping of musical forms satisfactory in themselves to the exigencies of every dramatic situation, the amazing insight into human character exhibited with endless resource and variety within the strict limits of a ripe and settled personal style: all this and more is—once again, since tautology is not to be eschewed—perfection.

OVERTURE

The overture passes by in a flash.   It was not always meant to do so.   Mozart originally interrupted it with a slow movement, as he did the *Seraglio* overture; but his instinct seems to have told him that there was a difference between a play with music, which permits a looser assortment of tunes, and an opera, which, for him in his full maturity at any rate, was a matter of close organization.   (I almost wrote closely reasoned organization, but nobody knows where the line of demarcation lies between reflection and intuition in a great artist's mind.)

Programme annotators are fond of saying, because it is an easy thing to say, that the *Figaro* overture is full of laughter.   That is as may be, or again, there is laughter *and* laughter. Mozart's 'gaiety' is always deceptive. May not those stealthy figures at the outset, that explosive outburst immediately after, those rushing scales a little farther on, strike this or that listener with dismay, not as things only of sound, but of fury? The second subject, after the first has been nailed down with the conventional cadence establishing the new key, certainly chuckles, but it may be found to do so as if in derisive response to those peevish *sforzandi*; and those pacing figures presently, with a wrenching modulation, may they not represent Count Almaviva venting his spleen on his dependants? But there, we cannot be sure. One evening the *Figaro* overture seems full of the rebellion stirred up by Beaumarchais's play; another time it will just be a perfect interpretation of his alternative title, *La Folle Journée*. We may doubt whether Mozart himself knew if he was concerned merely with a noble household's mad day or with the social maladies of a period. It is certainly fatuous to represent him as a revolutionary or a reformer. He was an artist and had, in as high a degree as any artist ever had, the kind of universal understanding that does not take sides because it can grasp things all round, an understanding which, being perhaps not more than half conscious, could at the same time see everything with absolute personal detachment.

The overture is in D major, the principal key of the whole opera and therefore of the last-act finale. The whole orchestra, such as it is for a comic opera that is almost chamber music, is used here, as it is not again until the first finale is reached at the end of the second act: flutes, oboes, clarinets, bassoons, horns, trumpets and kettledrums in pairs, in addition to strings. That is all: Mozart had no need in this wonderful conversation-piece of even such extras as the 'Turkish' percussion of *The Elopement from the Harem* (to give *The Seraglio* its almost literal English title [1]), the trombones of *Don Giovanni* or the basset horns and chime-bells of *The Magic Flute*.

ACT I

1. Duet: *Allegro*, G major (F. S.). [2] Even before the curtain has risen we can almost see the two people on the stage: Figaro pacing the room and taking its measure to musical figures expressive of the action; Susanna trying on a new hat and expressing her joy in a blithe phrase

---

[1] The strictly literal equivalent of 'Entführung' would be 'Abduction,' but this is flight with an unwilling woman, and in Mozart's opera the heroine is anxious to run off with her lover.

[2] The names of the characters are thus abbreviated, so far as is necessary: A., Count Almaviva; B., Don Basilio; C., Cherubino; D., Dr Bartolo; F., Figaro; G., the Gardener (Antonio); J., the Judge (Don Curzio); M., Marcellina; R., Countess Almaviva (Rosina); S., Susanna.

burst into by giggling violin figures. Note the sly basses creeping in off the beat in the first example:

Ex. 1 a   Allegro

Ex. 1 b

Technical points worth noting here as typical of Mozart's refinements of workmanship are a curtailment by two bars where the transition between these two subjects is repeated, the lightening of the texture where they are transferred to the voices and, for compensation of their abridgement, the extension of the introduction into an instrumental peroration at the end of the duet.   It may as well be borne in mind at once that the composer's care for such balance of design will be found at work throughout the opera.   I have just called *Figaro* a musical conversation-piece.   In the matter of design, indeed, it resembles the best work of the English master of that species of painting, Arthur Devis.   But in the matter of portraiture Mozart immensely surpasses Devis, not to mention any other exponent except Hogarth, for in the conversation-piece, which Hogarth transcended when he touched it, the deliberate convention is to show likenesses without betraying character.   Mozart, like Hogarth, does betray it: in fact he revels in his amazing gift of delineating human beings unerringly, not only as they look, but as they behave in any situation; and the major wonder is that it is all done without seeming to have been attempted at all. Indeed, there are people who never see it; but we need not trouble to assure the short-sighted that there are marvels beyond the range of their vision, if they are not prepared to believe us.   Here, then, for those who have, not eyes to see but ears to hear, are Susanna and Figaro, two real people, each in love with the other and each in a definite state of mind: he preoccupied with domestic plans, she happily confident in her ability to order her life to her own satisfaction—and his.

2. Duet: *Allegro*, B♭ major (F. S.).   But the intervening colloquy (in recitative or dialogue—and one hopes the former, for reasons to be given presently) has sown the seeds of doubt in Figaro's mind.   The smugness of the little tune that forms the main subject of this second duet, its interruptions in the voice-part while it goes on smoothly in the orchestra, the pretty and not too realistic imitations of the Countess's bell (high flutes and oboes) and the Count's knock (low bassoons and horns)—for after all they are only referred to, not actually heard —all this is sheer grace and charm.   Susanna's revelations of the Count's dishonourable intentions turn bright B♭ major into darker G minor.   Gradually the music gathers up into a climax, but it remains beautifully urbane to the end and in spite of gnawing doubts neither Susanna nor Figaro shows any sign of losing a sense of proportion.   But then Mozart himself never does, and *Figaro* is civilized art in its most exquisite flowering.   This duet, by the way, contains a good example of one of those minute points which yield a delight out of all proportion to their apparent unimportance: the two little sighs for oboe and bassoons in three octaves which intrude into a phrase at the second time only of its appearance and add to it an extra speck of chromatic harmony which, small as it is, has the effect of showing the whole picture in a different light:

3. Cavatina: *Allegretto—presto*, F major.   Figaro's first song is preceded by a recitative that is half-way between a *recitativo secco* and a *recitativo accompagnato*.   The string basses play rhythmic figures between the vocal phrases, but the whole is of course to be supported by the usual chords on a keyboard instrument.   For the cavatina the orchestra is reduced to oboes, bassoons, horns and strings, the flutes,

which took part with these instruments in the first two numbers, being dropped. Mozart is always careful to gain variety of colour by reducing his orchestra to various combinations for each number and keeping the full forces only for a very few points of climax. This piece begins in triple time, as simply as a song in a ballad opera. The prominent horn parts over an accompaniment of plucked strings are a delightful illustration of Mozart's wonderfully varied use of the horns in his operas, despite the severe restrictions they suffered before the invention of the valves that gave them a full chromatic scale. Their rapping octaves at the point where the song becomes more highly organized and dramatic further emphasize this observation. The change of tempo to *presto*, 2–4, shows that Figaro's schemes quickly begin to form in his fertile brain, and it also does duty in rounding off the song after a repetition of the original tune and thus giving Figaro an effective exit.

4. Aria: *Allegro con spirito*, D major. Bartolo's plotting of revenge, though futile, is far more pompous. Mozart therefore brings back the trumpets and drums for his aria, as well as the flutes. The doctor was old-fashioned even in his earlier days, in *The Barber of Seville* (Figaro being, of course, the barber then), when he was the jealous guardian of Rosina, now Countess Almaviva. He is old-fashioned now and therefore begins and ends his aria with conventional flourishes and brings it to an even more conventional climax. But of course Mozart does not allow him to present himself as he thinks he is. The composer takes a hand in the portrait. He pokes fun at the dry old stick and his legal quibbles by little sly digs of sudden accentuation off the beat and loud outbursts as a new idea seizes on the doctor's mind. A sudden rush into patter, as though Bartolo could not reveal his schemes fast enough, is irresistibly comic.

5. Duet: *Allegro*, A major (M. S.). A picture of feline flattery bubbling up into rage is here combined with incomparable grace and beauty. The catty squabble which develops between Susanna and Marcellina, after an exchange of purring politeness, begins in the wrong key, E major, for the piece is decidedly in A major. Now this would be an unheard of thing to do, for Mozart, or indeed for any composer of his time, if we could not find a good reason for it. Needless to say we can, but only on condition that we consider recitative an indispensable ingredient of Mozart's Italian operas, though in his German ones spoken dialogue is the rule. Very well: the colloquy between Susanna and Marcellina begins, not with the duet, but with a recitative that leads from the D major of Bartolo's aria to the A major of the duet by way of the latter key's dominant, E major, and the concluding cadence of the recitative is, in turn, on that key's dominant, B major. The simple explanation of an apparently monstrous

irregularity is, therefore, that the first two orchestral bars of the duet are a transition making perfect sense in a performance in which the recitatives are sung, but becoming nonsense if they are replaced by dialogue. The conclusion is obvious: *Figaro* without the recitatives is incomplete.

6. Aria: *Allegro vivace*, E♭ major. For the first time since the overture the clarinets, the sentimentalists of Mozart's orchestra, are brought in for Cherubino's first song. Here is palpitating adolescence, enchantingly idealized yet as true as any commonplace turned to poetry can be. The little page, brought up in an atmosphere of luxurious dalliance, very much in love though with no one in particular, expresses his feelings in urgent phrases and catches his breath in stumbling over a cadence to which he has to go back a second time:

And at the point where Cherubino babbles of water, flowers, the wind, the echo and other phenomena of nature, a breath of the open country is wafted in with a little extra tune for the violins, not enough to disturb the exquisite eighteenth-century artificiality of the picture, but enough to reveal the touch of a master who can penetrate to the truth of things below the polished surface of his music:

7. Trio: *Allegro assai*, B♭ major (A. B. S.). This is one of the great concerted pieces in *Figaro* which advance the drama as well as expose character. So far, with the exception of No. 2, we have had only

portraits of the people who have appeared up to this point, though portraits shown with wonderful plasticity on the background of certain moods or situations.   Susanna and Marcellina in their duet, for instance, were for the moment musically treated in exactly the same way, neither singing more than a phrase or two that is not given to the other.   But now the voices of the Count, Basilio and Susanna enter one by one with themes not only sharply contrasted musically, but immediately delineating three entirely different people in three very different frames of mind.   The Count is angry and dictatorial, Basilio cringingly apologetic yet secretly delighted at the mischief he has made (his phrase is the classic musical expression of hypocrisy) and Susanna is clearly frightened to death.   The marvel is that, when the voices are interlocked into wonderfully smooth part-writing, each still retains its special character.   Only for a moment do the two men unite in the same music—Basilio taking the lead a bar ahead—when they offer to get the faltering Susanna a chair.   But the chair, unfortunately, is that on which Cherubino has been concealed, and Susanna has to take refuge in protesting indignantly that she has no need for it.   Her pretended fury gives rise to new musical ideas, and then the whole material is woven into a kind of working-out section followed by a return to the opening like a sonata-form recapitulation when the Count discovers the cowering Cherubino.   The music lapses for an instant into accompanied recitative, only to shape itself the more firmly into a few astounding pages that blend the elements of recapitulation, development and coda.

8. Chorus: *Allegro*, G major.   This is a perfectly straightforward, very pretty and very graceful piece.   It called for no subtlety from the composer, who therefore—he is subtle enough even for that—lavished none on it.   But his artfulness remains.   The contractions of the main theme near the end, as though the young people did not quite believe in their perfunctory homage to the Count and were anxious to be done with it and away, are a point of technical if not psychological interest.

9. Aria: *Allegro vivace*, C major.   Figaro's 'Non più andrai' hardly needs description.   It is the most familiar number in the opera, and was so from the first, for it is said to have been whistled by the errand-boys of Prague after the production of the work there and was popular enough by the following year for Mozart to quote it in *Don Giovanni* with no other explanation than Leoporello's remark: 'Now then, that there I know but too well, sir.'   The clarinets are dropped, but trumpets and drums are brought back to underline Figaro's allusions to the military life in which Cherubino is going to be so unwillingly engaged.   The piece is in fact a military march, and it winds up the act with a lengthy orchestral peroration with trumpet

fanfares and the conventional musical clichés by which eighteenth-century composers suggested cannon-fire. This brings down the curtain festively and compensates sufficiently for the lack of a long-developed finale.

10. Cavatina: *Larghetto*, E♭ major. We are introduced to the Countess by means of one of the loveliest musical women's portraits ever painted by Mozart—and that is to say by anybody. The music forms one of the very few slow movements in the opera. Although a lament from the Countess's point of view, it is full of tenderness and consolation rather than distress. Mozart in his operas could never bear to see a woman in trouble without wanting to lavish on her the most beautiful music even he could possibly devise. Ilia in *Idomeneo*, Constanze in *The Elopement*, Elvira in *Don Giovanni*, Fiordiligi in *Così fan tutte*, Pamina in *The Magic Flute*, all have their share in this glorious bestowal of compassionate and indulgent affection, and the Countess in her two arias has more than her fair share of it. The cavatina has an extended orchestral introduction to prepare for the rise of the curtain, and it has shown us a picture of the Countess, Gainsborough-like in its fusion of grace and characterization, before we have so much as set eyes on her and before she has uttered a note. The mild tones of clarinets, bassoons and horns combine with the exquisite interlacing of their parts in producing an impression by deliberate artifice converted into the purest art:

11. Canzone: *Andante con moto*, B♭ major. Cherubino's second song (composed by himself) is accompanied by Susanna on a guitar, according to da Ponte's prescription, which Mozart faithfully follows by using plucked strings throughout. A delicious commentary is added by a small wind team of one flute, one oboe, one bassoon and both horns, an unusual procedure for Mozart, who as a rule subtracts

certain wood-wind colours entirely for a whole number rather than using them thinned out.   The song, 'Voi che sapete,' is of course one of the two or three best-known things in *Figaro*, but familiarity has bred an increased love for it.   No music has ever conveyed a boyish mixture of shyness and ardour with such grace and poetry.   The gliding back into the main theme and key, after an excursion into C major, A♭ major, G minor and F minor in close proximity, is enchanting.   So is the very simple close, which brushes the song aside with a little chuckle of wood-wind.

12. Aria: *Allegretto*, G major.   The next air, during which Susanna dresses up Cherubino as a girl, is even more exquisite, if possible, but it is less well known because as an 'action song' it is unsuited to concert performance.   Susanna's tender little pats and giggles are perfectly outlined:

Ex. 6

and a special feature of this number is the breaking up of the voice-part in a variety of ways to give pauses for action, while the orchestra continues to spin out the music into a satisfying form.

13. Trio: *Allegro spirituoso*, C major (A. R. S.).   The plot has thickened into a tense situation.   Mozart is more than capable of dealing with it: this number is another of those great concerted pieces in which each character retains a distinct personality, at the same time expressing each twist and turn of the action, while the music builds itself up into a flawless symphonic shape in spite of the fact that it takes into account every detail of the dramatic circumstances.   Mozart's arias are often reflective and, therefore, dramatically static (though we have just found a striking exception in No. 12); in the concerted numbers the stage action is advanced while the music develops in a way suited to it and never unsuited to the demands of composition as such.   One would have to show the whole of this trio in music-type in order to demonstrate how the three characters show themselves as individuals—the Count jealous and angry, the Countess injured and indignant, Susanna anxious—while blending their voices into wonderful euphony and weaving their parts into intricate polyphonic patterns. A brief example must suffice:

Ex. 7   Allegro spirituoso

ca - pis - co   qual - che   co - sa
Ah, now   I   un - der - stand it

bru - tis - si - ma   è   la   co - sa
Too hor - ri - ble   is this mo - ment

chia - ri - ssi - ma è la   co - sa
'Tis   all   too plain, the rea - son

Apart from such agitated entanglements, special points are made when the Countess's voice rises urgently to A, when the Count suddenly lowers his tone for a threatening turn into the remote key of A♭ major, when the music loses its rhythmic control and dissolves into two bars of timeless recitative, only to break dramatically into the *allegro* again, and when Susanna twice soars up to high C, as though at a loss where to turn next.

14. Duet: *Allegro assai*, G major (C. S.).   This little duet, in which Cherubino resolves to jump out of the window and Susanna anxiously tries to prevent him, was originally ten bars longer than it is now.   It may be difficult to believe that a cut saving some eight seconds could make any appreciable difference, but the fact is that the duet, left as it stood at first, would delay the action by just an excessive fraction of time and make the music, which relies almost wholly on the use of two rhythmic figures, too repetitive.   As we know it, the piece is exactly right.   It not only takes precisely the time the little incident will bear, but presents an inimitable picture of two young things in a flutter of apprehension.

15. Finale: *Allegro, etc.—prestissimo*, E♭ major (A. B. D. F. G. M. R. S.).   If this is not Mozart's greatest finale in every way, it is certainly formally his most perfect and dramatically his most amazingly cumulative.   As a musical composition it is a symphonic movement in E♭ major on a scale so vast as to involve of necessity lengthy excursions into other keys, which take the form of a chain of long intermediate sections, each with its own scheme of pace and basic rhythms.   But E♭ is certainly the principal key, established in a long, dramatically agitated duet between the Count and Countess and finally consolidated in an equally long septet beginning at the entry of Marcellina, Basilio and Bartolo.   Vocally seven parts make the final climax, for although eight characters are involved in the finale, they never all sing together, the gardener, Antonio, having disappeared

C

before the entry of the nefarious trio who provide the counter-plot. Not only the structure, the scoring as well is designed to provide a climax.   Oboes, clarinets, bassoons, horns and strings alone are used at the beginning; the orchestration is then changed from time to time until trumpets and drums enter with the three plotters to bring the orchestra to full strength.

The quarrel between the noble couple at the beginning is as dramatic as any violent scene between two well-bred people could fittingly have been made and as true to life as the aristocratic art of immaculately polished music would allow.   It is, in fact, the ideal artistic compromise.   That the music is surpassingly beautiful need hardly be said by this time, but attention may be drawn to the ingenious way in which the spacing of the vocal parts is varied to heighten the dramatic effect at every point: they sometimes allow each character to hear what the other has to say and sometimes tumble over each other in a dispute which, needless to say, preserves ideal harmony from a musical point of view.   The Count's louring passage in F minor, with menacing accents on each first beat, is almost terrifying, and his low threat to kill the page, with runs for clarinets and bassoons in thirds above it and the Countess's imploring interruptions in between, is both musically and dramatically thrilling.

The placidly graceful music in B♭ major, *molto andante,* where Susanna saves the situation temporarily by appearing where Cherubino was expected, brings delicious relief as a faultlessly managed moment of high comedy.   The following trio, *allegro,* in the same key, is the first example of a special way of ensuring musical continuity by the persistent use of one or two figures which Mozart exploits with immense skill in this finale as well as that of the fourth act.   What he can make of two simple things like the following:

Ex. 8

has to be heard to be believed.   What remains almost beyond belief is that this slender material can serve to underline the expression of anxiety, reassurance, repentance, pleading, roguish admonition, reproach and forgiveness, all by varied manipulations of the same musical elements.

Figaro's intrusion, being quite unexpected, jerks the music cheerfully into G major and 3–8 time, *allegro con spirito.*   But it begins to tie the plot into a further twisty knot.   The *andante* section in C major and 2–4, where the Count confronts Figaro with the compromising letter, begins to make corresponding entanglements in the vocal part-writing, and at one point a little canon answers the Count in the cellos and basses, as though Figaro's thoughts were trying to keep pace with those of his interlocutor:

Note also the very simple tune in the top stave of the following example and the various counterpoints to it that make it a thing of perennial delight:

At Antonio's entry a new section starts off *allegro molto*, in F major. It is thematically almost featureless, being based on one of those repetitive figures mentioned above, this time one of very animated triplets:

On this background, constantly enlivened by variants and by subtleties of orchestration, the action goes forward at such a pace that in the theatre we have hardly time to realize what a leisurely study of the score reveals: the ceaseless succession of dramatic felicities in the disposition of the voice-parts. It is the same with the next section, *andante*, 6–8, B♭ major (the dominant of the main key of E♭ for the return of which this prepares [3]).   Here again a single small figure is almost continually employed, again the voices are made to combine and part with the minutest attention to the action—the uncomfortable discovery of Cherubino's lost commission—and at the end, Antonio having been sent about his business, the remaining voices unite in a quartet of exquisite beauty and gaiety.

With the entry of Marcellina, Basilio and Bartolo begins the great culminating piece in the main key forming the matchless climax of this finale, and indeed of the whole opera.   There is so much to admire that the music almost lapses into the fault of a bewildering over-richness in admirable qualities.   There are the tremendous verve and spirit of the invention; a structure as rounded and solid as that of any symphonic movement; character revealed now individually and now in two contrasted groups, each of three people, with the Count placed in a central predicament where he belongs to neither party; and details of wonderful beauty or of exhilaratingly comic effect, such as the accusations brought by the three intruders, beginning at a normal pace and then falling over themselves in an excited gabble.   The speed grows faster and faster, the villains break into sneaking little phrases of their own, the others twist and turn in runs and syncopations, and the whole thing winds up brilliantly in a precipitate coda.

ACT III

The third and fourth acts may be a little more briefly dealt with, not only because many points that might be made in connection with their music have already arisen in the discussion of earlier numbers, but also because the interest is no longer quite so continuously sustained. There are things as great, or greater, among the later pages of *Figaro*, but there is no longer quite the same consistency in the quality of invention and structure, though the workmanship remains flawless to the last.   Mozart need not be blamed; perhaps even da Ponte must not be held altogether responsible, since he only followed custom in supplying words for those extra arias which hold up the fourth act,

---

[3] This is a convenient place to draw attention to the surprisingly consistent key-scheme of the second act as a whole.   B♭, which in the finale leads back to E♭ for the concluding section, had led away from the opening of the act in the latter key by means of 'Voi che sapete,' which is in its dominant, B♭.   We then had an aria in G, a trio in C and a duet in G again.   In the finale, too, B♭ succeeds E♭ and is in turn followed by G and C.   If the little duet for Cherubino and Susanna had been in F instead of G, the finale would have followed exactly the same changes of key as the separate numbers in the act—and one almost wishes it had been, for symmetry's sake.   However, these numbers being intersected by recitatives with their own modulations, the irregularity is hardly disturbing, and it is obvious that F major was the proper key to lead from C major to B♭ and E♭ in the finale in a progression of key-signatures with flats increasing one by one.

while the fatal happy ending [4] was prescribed by Beaumarchais. The second big finale in *Figaro* is inferior only in comparison with the first, which is in any case incomparable formally. The opera certainly ends gloriously in a musical sense, though it cannot in the nature of its plot end dramatically. But there is too much 'happy ending' about the whole of the second part of the work, and it cannot be doubted that the comparative lack of interest we find towards the close of the third act is due not merely to the absence of a proper finale (for the splendid first act is even more deficient in that respect), but simply to the fact that it is concerned with preliminary wedding festivities which unduly relax the dramatic tension too long before the actual close of the opera. But let us resume our voyage of discovery, which is after all to lead us to many wonders yet.

16. Duet: *Andante*, A minor and major (A. S.). This little colloquy, in which Susanna feigns to make her assignation with the Count, is one of the only three minor-key pieces in the whole opera, which of course modulates frequently into minor keys incidentally. Even here the minor turns into the major after a short time, with the specially lovely effect that was so dear to Schubert but is much rarer in Mozart.[5] Tenderness and comedy are mingled in this duet like smiles and tears in a child's face. Susanna has her fun and at the same time thinks of her true love—Figaro; the Count wavers between illegitimate hopes and only too well justified doubts. The passages where Susanna very nearly gives herself away by returning the wrong answers to her would-be lover's alternating questions are surely the high spot of high comedy in all music. Her contrapuntal phrases mingling with his exultantly happy tune combine the finest imaginable workmanship with the greatest imaginable beauty.

17. Recitative and Aria: *Maestoso, etc., Allegro maestoso—allegro assai*, D major. It is curious that Mozart seems to be studiously avoiding the main key of *Figaro*, D major, during the course of the work, between the overture and the last finale. It had so far occurred only once, in Bartolo's pompous aria of revenge in the first act, and we are not to meet it again after the present aria until the end of the fourth act. But here it is, in another aria that introduces the pomp of trumpets and drums, another concerned with vengeance. What is curious, too, is that the music here becomes relatively conventional, as in Bartolo's case, and, though full of character and admirably descriptive of the thwarted amorist's annoyance, does not on the whole make one of the most engaging numbers in the work. It is rather too obviously a piece for virtuosic display—deserved, it must

---

[4] See the concluding essay in this book.
[5] An exception as striking as this duet is the finale of the D minor piano Concerto (K. 466). For Schubert see the essay on p. 79.

be said, by the only one among the main personages in the opera who has not so far been given a solo number and is not to have another for the rest of the evening. The recitative is scored for oboes, bassoons, horns and strings; flutes, trumpets and drums come in for the aria.

18. Sextet: *Allegro moderato*, F major (A. B. D. F. J. S.). This is one of Mozart's very greatest concerted pieces, wonderfully contrived technically, outlining several characters simultaneously in contrasting moods and furthering the action very considerably during its progress. Marcellina's maternal gushings, Bartolo's surprised conversion to fatherly affection for Figaro, the latter's comic dismay, Susanna's warm womanliness turning into a fit of temper, the Count's impotent fury as he finds himself thwarted by yet another turn of events, all this is sheer delight. Figaro's phrase:

Ex. 12

is as much a classical quotation as 'Full fathom five thy father lies.' Only Don Curzio remains a dim figure musically, a mere tenor voice used to fill in the vocal texture satisfactorily. True, he has as good a part to sing as any of the others, so far as it goes, but he merely echoes this or that phrase sung by this or that character. Well, perhaps that is part of his nature after all, and in any case he is so unimportant, apart from being required for the business of this one scene, that to make him stand out more clearly would have been to waste a great musical dramatist's art.

19. Recitative and Aria: *Andante, etc. Andantino—allegro*, C major. If, as I showed at the beginning of this book, we find connections of great interest with earlier theatrical history in *Figaro*, we may also find some with musical history. The Count's aria, we have seen, showed a certain tendency to relapse into an earlier convention. So does the present aria, the Countess's famous 'Dove sono.' It too is preceded by an accompanied recitative (strings only), and in the moderately paced opening section followed by a brilliant *allegro* that does not disdain the display of *bravura* and even contains the conventional shake near the end-cadence of the voice-part, we may find a formal design never encountered in the course of the first and second acts, which are, truth to tell, much more modern than the later two, and correspondingly more dramatically alive. But 'Dove sono,' in which tradition is used with such mastery and beauty, silences complaint. What more can we ask for? The voice swallowing half a phrase, as though choked with pain for a moment:

and later pausing in the middle of another as the thought arises that perhaps happiness may yet be recoverable after all, the turn into the minor as doubt stirs anew, the soaring figure that rises twice near the end like a wave of overwhelming tenderness—what else could be imagined to describe the Countess and her state of mind better? Since we get all this, shall we protest against being given a magnificent concert piece into the bargain?

20. Duet: *Allegretto*, B♮ major (R. S.) The familiar letter duet is not musically very eventful, but its very slight scoring for one flute, one bassoon and strings as well as its moderate pace make a cool and quiet contrast. One seems to feel the coming fall of evening as the Countess dictates to Susanna a letter of assignation, to be kept in the summer garden of the fourth act. The broken-off sentences, repeated in part by the writer, are managed with a superb art of timing.

21. Chorus: *Grazioso*, G major. This little homage paid to the Countess by country girls (among whom is Cherubino in disguise) is slight but incomparably graceful. A most subtle technical point deserves attention: the overlapping of the metrical accents between the violins and the voices half-way through:

22. Finale: *Marcia, allegretto, andante, allegretto*, C major, etc. (A. F. R. S. and chorus). The piece that opens the comparatively perfunctory third-act finale, which indeed is better not counted as such at all but just considered a final concerted number, is not so much a

wedding march as a pre-nuptial one.   Although scored for the full orchestra, it is light and tripping, and the little bleating wood-wind turns, scattered all over it, have an effect of delicious irony.   A curious fact is that the march begins on a chord of G major; the explanation of this 'wrong key' is, of course, that already given in connection with the first-act duet for Susanna and Marcellina (No. 5).   If the recitatives are used, we see that here are two orchestral bars of dominant preparation connecting the proper key of C major with the preceding G major phrase of the recitative.

The march is succeeded by a chorus of congratulation, which appears twice in the main key of C, intersected by a dance in A minor that is the only piece of music in the opera in which Mozart shows any awareness of the Spanish setting of Beaumarchais's comedy (a purely French comedy, nevertheless, and in spite of its conventional Italian figures).   Also the only piece not of Mozart's own invention, for this fandango is actually a Spanish folk dance, or rather a slow variant of it, from the Basque country.   Mozart obtained it at two removes, for it was used, with considerable differences, by Gluck in his *Don Juan* ballet, and it was this version which the younger master wrote down, probably from memory, and very thoroughly amplified, refined and elaborated.   There is no hint in Gluck, for instance, of those exquisite little sighing figures of semitones for flute, oboe and bassoon which give the dance a curiously melancholy atmosphere, indeed almost one of sinister forboding.   There is a brief accompanied recitative for the Count before the chorus is resumed to bring down the curtain.

ACT IV

23. Cavatina: *Andante*, F minor.   Barbarina's tiny song, accompanied by muted strings only, is the third piece in a minor key after the two in A minor we have encountered in the third act.   The plaintive tone, not unmixed with trepidation, is wonderfully caught, and the question at the end, leading straight into C major for the recitative over a chord of the German sixth, is the very *locus classicus* of musical interrogation, at any rate until we come to Schumann's *Warum?*:

24. Aria: *Tempo di minuetto—allegro*, G major. Marcellina's aria, which is always cut nowadays, needs no detailed description. It is a conventional piece of writing with opportunities for old-fashioned vocal display of the most lavish kind, harking back to Mozart's early comic-opera manner of about the time of *La finta giardiniera*, and it does nothing to advance our knowledge of Marcellina's character, which has already been indelibly drawn for us, although she has had no solo number to sing.

25. Aria: *Andante—tempo di minuetto—allegro*, B♭ major. Basilio, who has been given similar short shrift, also had to have his aria somewhere, and this is sometimes sung when a particularly good exponent of the part is available. It has much more quality and is indeed a capital piece of ironic characterization; but it does delay the opera unduly at this late stage, especially as its three sections take up more than a subordinate character's fair share of time.

26. Recitative and Aria: *Andante. Moderato*, E♭ major. The cuts often extend even to Figaro's great aria, which, however, is a masterpiece it is difficult to resign oneself to doing without. In the whole range of comic opera there is only one thing to compare with it as an expression of jealousy—for we must not bring the tragic jealousy of Verdi's Othello into the argument—and that is Ford's monologue in the same master's *Falstaff*. But there we have the perfect picture of a jealous man in a rage, whereas here is an equally perfect one of a lover with a sense of humour who takes his supposed defeat at the hands of Cupid ruefully, but, on the whole, philosophically. It does not matter if this is not so much Figaro's view as the product of Mozart's superior instinct as an artist, an artist great enough to view every human concern, as only one other equally great one did, with a boundless compassionate indulgence. Need it be said that the other is Shakespeare? The aria is very far from conventional and it dispenses with the traditional *bravura* at the end, being quite sufficiently brilliant already in its suggestions of gesture and speech-inflection. The threefold horn fanfare at the close may or may not be a musical pun, alluding to the instrument's name, which is also that of the traditional symbol for the betrayed male.

27. Recitative and Aria: *Allegro vivace assai. Andante*, F major. Susanna's 'Deh vieni' enwraps us in that nocturnal summer-garden atmosphere which had been cunningly foreshadowed in the letter duet (No. 20). We also find something like it in the middle movement of the F major piano Concerto of 1784 (K. 459), where some fifteen months before *Figaro* Mozart seems to have tried his hand at a kind of study for 'Deh vieni,' though a very finished and much more extended one. Open-air music, at which Haydn was such an adept, is not often to be thought of as one of Mozart's achievements. Art

—or if we like artifice, but divine artifice—not nature is his concern. But here we do breathe the warm air of a summer night out of doors, though we must admit that we are not in the midst of a country land-scape, but in that of very formal horticulture and topiary.

28. Finale: *Andante, etc.*, D major (All and chorus).   The opening section of the 'second' finale, as we have agreed to call it, since it is the only great set piece in the opera at all comparable in structure with that of the second act, is among the most lovely things in the work.   The dramatic shudder that comes over it as the Countess utters her first frightened words, the way in which the voices are set across the instru-mental rhythms in the most natural declamation, as here:

Ex. 16

and the gradual gathering into a concerted climax—all this and much else that cannot be told conspires in stirring in the hearer, tired as he may be of solo numbers by this time, the expectation of further events to come.

The following section, in F major, *con un poco più di moto*, follows the method of the first finale in exploiting at length similar material in a great variety of treatment for the furtherance of the action and to give the voices every opportunity to make the dialogue natural and the personages musically characteristic.   As to the latter, we may note that the Countess disguised as Susanna sings music that is neither in keeping with her own usual dignity nor quite successful in simulating her maid's skittishness.

After a short monologue for Figaro in E♭ major, *larghetto*, the process of making much of little material is again followed in the duet in the same key, *allegro molto*, between Figaro and Susanna, the latter in the Countess's clothes.   The syncopated and interwoven sequences that lead to the main cadential point show the impeccable beauty of Mozart's workmanship.

After a change to *andante*, B♭ major, the plot gradually begins to smooth itself out into charmingly placid music interrupted only by two fiercely rising scales, like the drawing of a sword, where the Count finds himself fooled.

The music turns without preparation into G major, *allegro assai*, where he calls for help and all the characters rush upon the stage to hear explanations, witness all-round forgiveness and sing the brilliant final pages in concert with the full orchestra, trumpets, drums and all —indeed one almost sees the fireworks.   But this does not happen until Mozart has lavished yet one more lovely slow melody, *andante*, G major, on the characters whom he has long come to love impartially, and in whose future happiness he shows a most touchingly warm-hearted belief, though we in the audience may have our doubts and Beaumarchais, indeed, showed something very different in the final play of his trilogy, *La Mère coupable*, posing a problem that may almost be said to anticipate Ibsen.   This brief slow tune is taken up by all the characters in a page of wonderful part-writing, and the music then modulates to the central key of D major for the final boisterous winding-up.

(*Note.*—The English words in the music examples are taken from Edward J. Dent's translation.)

The Music of Mozart's 'Così fan tutte'

(Sadler's Wells Opera Books, 1945)

COMPARED with that of Mozart's three other surpassingly great operatic masterpieces, *Così fan tutte* may be found to lack something of the humanity of *The Marriage of Figaro*, the tension and atmosphere of *Don Giovanni* and the far-ranging variety of *The Magic Flute*; so that probably the listener will be struck first of all by the formal perfection and elegance of the score. He will be right in admiring this, even if he does so purely instinctively, and although it is but one of the many aspects of Mozart's superiority.

This perfection manifests itself not only number by number, but in the scheme and balance of the whole. To begin with, an opera by Mozart is a work in a particular key, just as a sonata or quartet or symphony would be. Thus *Figaro* is an opera in D major; *Don Giovanni* one in D minor and major; *The Magic Flute* one in E♭ major. *Così* is in C major, with a first act ending in a D major finale, just as the exposition of a movement in sonata form would end in a key other than that of the tonic. It might, in fact, almost be said that *Così* is a sonata movement on a huge scale with the exposition ending in the key of the supertonic and the development after the double bar (in this case at the beginning of the second act) turning to the dominant of the home key: for that act opens with an aria for Despina in G major. The tonic (C) is then avoided for the next six numbers, which go through the major keys of B♭, E♭, D, F, B♭ and E, whereupon the dominant of the home key, G major, returns in Guglielmo's aria 'Donne mie' ('Ladies have such variations,' No. 26) [1], and we reach the tonic through its minor mode, but very soon clearing into major, in Ferrando's cavatina, 'Tradito, schernito' ('Her falsehood and treason,' No. 27). After that we have only, as it were, incidental modulations to an aria in B♭ and a duet in A before a kind of transitional arioso, Alfonso's 'Tutti accusan le donne' ('Man accuses the woman,' No. 30) re-establishes C major, which is confirmed by the second finale with the same emphasis as the first laid on D major.[2]

Now I have no desire whatever to discover subtleties which Mozart may never have intended, even subconsciously. At the same time it is important to realize that an opera of his is not just an array of so

---

[1] Words quoted in this chapter are those of Lorenzo da Ponte's Italian original, followed by the English translation by Marmaduke Browne, revised by Edward J. Dent.

[2] It need hardly be pointed out that each finale goes through a number of sections in a variety of keys, just as, on a smaller scale, an extended coda of a symphony or sonata movement would do.

many pieces following each other in a haphazard selection of different keys that happened to take his fancy.   It may be an accident that the last three numbers before the D major finale of the first act are in keys (G and A) forming the bass of a formal cadence of D, to name only one instance of several ingenuities of this kind that might be pointed out; but it is surely too much to take it as a coincidence that all the incidental keys [3] in the work, on being counted up number by number and (in the finale) section by section, are found to balance each other with mathematical exactitude (18 sharp and 18 flat).

So much for the general formal aspect of the score.   Before we proceed to a consideration of details, its entire contents must be surveyed from two or three other points of view.   One of them is that of the orchestration.   The scoring is, of course, not spectacular, in the sense that Wagner's is, for example.   But we must remember, first of all, that we have no business to expect an eighteenth-century master to indulge us in luxuries that were not imported into music until the nineteenth, and also that spectacular scoring is not characteristic only of a great composer like Wagner, but also of lesser ones like Spontini or Meyerbeer.   In other words, its absence from *Così fan tutte*, though not a positive merit, is not in itself a defect.   What does amount to a merit, indeed to an overwhelming proof of supreme artistry, is the extraordinary subtlety with which Mozart uses a small orchestra of flutes, oboes, clarinets, bassoons, horns, trumpets and kettledrums in pairs in addition to strings, as in *Figaro*, with no extras of any sort.   His way of securing variety of tone-colour is to regard each separate number as a piece to be scored, as it were, on its own merits, in a scheme or instrumental combination determined beforehand and retained throughout.   Trumpets appear in few of them, drums in fewer still, and the wood-wind couples are used by turns in various combinations, rarely all coming together except in the overture and each finale.

The great quality of Mozart's orchestration in *Così* is the wonderful economy with which he obtains the most limpid and exquisite effects and the utmost imaginable eloquence and justness of expression without often going out of his way to draw any attention to the scoring at all.   Not that he hesitates to do so when it suits his purpose: only the most inattentive hearer could fail to notice the beautiful, very low trumpet figure in 'Come scoglio' ('Firm as rock,' No. 14) [4], which

---

[3] That is, excluding C major, which is the tonic key of the whole work and the D major of the first finale, which constitutes, as it were, a symphonic movement in itself.   (The 'round' in the second finale, where the lovers drink each other's health, is, of course, in A♭ major, although written with a key-signature of three flats.   Flats are added to the D's casually as they occur.)

[4] The repeated use of the trumpets as if they were horns, and in place of the horns, is a quite distinctive feature of the *Così* score.

seems to illustrate the granite firmness with which Fiordiligi compares—unjustifiably, as it turns out—her fidelity to Guglielmo. And in her second aria, the rondo 'Per pietà' ('Ah, my love, forgive my madness,' No. 25), there is an *obbligato* for the two horns that almost amounts to a little concerto.[5] The treatment of those drudges of the classical orchestra, the violas, also deserves attention: they are often divided to enrich the harmony and given many interesting things to do. In the overture they stand out with a beautiful sustained inner part here and there, and in Alfonso's agitated, mock-tragic 'Vorrei dir' ('Could I tell,' No. 5) they draw a pathetic two-part thread through an otherwise merely accompanying texture.

A general feature of style in eighteenth-century opera that must be mentioned is its division into separate numbers. These, particularly the arias, which were usually reflective and therefore dramatically static, had somehow to be connected by verbal matter designed to advance the action. Except in the *finali*, and occasionally in large-scale concerted numbers earlier in the acts, little provision was made by the librettists up to near the end of the century for musical treatment in set pieces of what may be called the mere mechanics of a plot. These were got over as quickly as possible, either by means of recitatives or, as in French comic opera, English ballad opera and its later descendant, the German *Singspiel*, in spoken dialogue. This persisted in Germany for quite a long time and remained a feature of even such serious works as Beethoven's *Fidelio* and Weber's *Freischütz*. Mozart's German operas also had spoken dialogue: indeed *The Seraglio* is a typical *Singspiel* that happens by accident to have been furnished with great music, and so is, regarded from that point of view, even *The Magic Flute*. But Mozart's Italian operas connect their set numbers by recitative.

The Italian convention was that recitative should be accompanied by a harpsichord played from a part amplified harmonically according to the theory of thorough-bass. What the composer actually wrote was nothing but a string bass part, which might or might not actually be played below the harpsichord part by cellos and double basses. Unless the player skilfully exercised his fancy, that harpsichord part consisted of mere dry chords, some sustained, some detached, forming good harmonic progressions, leading from the key of one set number to that of the next and usually concluding with a conventional full close in or near the latter's key. The singers delivered the dialogue

---

[5] This aria is in E major, and so is Leonora's 'Abscheulicher' in Beethoven's *Fidelio*, which also has elaborate horn parts. It is impossible not to regard the latter as being directly modelled on 'Per pietà,' though very likely Beethoven was unaware of the fact that subconscious memory dictated certain features of his aria. Other cases in music seem to prove that similarity of key often engenders reminiscences of this kind in composers. *See* 'Key Heredity,' p. 184.

in musical notes above these harmonies, as a rule very quickly and often in a half-spoken tone, certainly never with full deployment of their vocal powers, which were reserved for the musical numbers. This sort of recitative, no doubt because of its dry chords, was called *recitativo secco.* But there was also another kind, called *recitativo accompagnato* or *stromentato*, accompanied by the orchestra, and this was always musically and often dramatically more important.

Mozart, of course, refines upon these practices, which in the common run of Italian opera composition were mere expedients. It is the way of genius to turn the mechanics of art into positive virtues, and this is what Mozart does with the conventions of 'dry' and accompanied recitative. In his hands a purely artificial opera like *Così* becomes a musical organism arranged on a series of different levels of intensity, in such a way that an interplay of climax and anticlimax finally works up, at the end of each act, into long and complex dramatic scenes and symphonic music. A *secco* recitative is the lowest level: almost spoken dialogue, but not so much so as to drop the musical thread altogether. A finale is the highest, and so is an overture. Accompanied recitatives are a step above those of the *secco* type, and then come, progressively, arias, duets and concerted pieces. But Mozart achieves many finer gradations. A concerted piece of his may be a more or less static number, like the quartet 'La mano a me date' ('Now give me your hand,' No. 22) in Act II, which does next to nothing to further the action, or it may be a great piece of dramatic writing like the sextet in Act I, which differs from a finale only in length, as do the similar numbers for six characters in *Figaro* and *Don Giovanni*. Also, he does not always proceed from one plane to the next with a jerk. There are many instances of almost imperceptible transitions, especially from *secco* to accompanied recitative. There may be a clean cut with one of those stereotyped cadences everybody knows, from Bach and Handel, if not from Mozart and old Italian opera, as at the end of the recitative preceding the first quintet in Act I:

Ex. 1

A - mi - ci   en - tra - te!
Come   in   now,   I've told them!

Elsewhere he may slip straight from a *secco* into an aria, without a full

close, and by letting the end of a vocal phrase coincide with the opening of an aria accompaniment:

A further point of interest may be mentioned: Mozart's special use
of thematic references in *Così*.   One need not talk of his anticipating
the Wagnerian *Leitmotiv*, although that is what he and several other
composers did do.   He certainly introduced what may be called a
musico-dramatic 'motto' theme into the present work.   It is a phrase
that goes with the actual words *così fan tutte*, and Mozart very wittily
sets it to what amounts to one of the commonest cadences to be found
in eighteenth-century Italian opera, with a progression in the bass that
was used over and over again by Cimarosa, Paisiello, Sarti, Zingarelli,
and dozens of others, himself by no means excluded.   In the arioso
just before the second-act finale already mentioned, 'Tutti accusan le
donne,' Alfonso exclaims, and at last succeeds in getting the lovers to
confirm, that

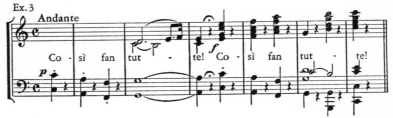

('That's what they all do!'), the feminine *tutte* meaning 'all women.' But Mozart's choice of this very conventional turn of cadential phrase adds a jest of his own to the librettist's: his musical epigram not only expresses *così fan tutte le donne*, but also *così fan tutti i compositori*. What is more, Mozart writes the title of his opera over the score in musical notes, as it were, by introducing this theme twice into the overture—which, incidentally, is one of the reasons, apart from the untranslatability of the feminine plural, why the opera cannot very well be called by any but the original title in English-speaking countries.

Other thematic references are to be found in the second finale, where they are intimately bound up with the plot. First we have a restatement of the military march which had accompanied the lovers' pretended departure when they make their return towards the end. Later, the lovers and Despina reveal themselves as the former impersonators of imaginary characters by music that reverts to earlier incidents in the score. Ferrando's phrase, it is true, is nowhere to be found there, as the work stands at present, but is very obviously a quotation of something that was later cut by the composer.[6] Guglielmo returns the miniature portrait in the locket to Dorabella to the music of the charming duet during which she gave it to him (*see* Ex. 7); Despina is revealed as the absurd witch-doctor of the first finale to the accompaniment of the comic passage with the prolonged shake already heard there (*see* Ex. 6).

Other points of general interest may be left to arise during a brief—all too brief—analysis of the opera number by number that must now be attempted.

OVERTURE

Invention is deliberately restrained here to make no more of the overture than a kind of decorative curtain. It is just an arrangement of recurrent patterns, but ideally suited in style to the opera and steeped in that quite peculiar atmosphere that pervades the whole work. *Così* is unique: nothing in it can be imagined transferred to Mozart's other great stage works without sounding like a solecism in style. It is not his greatest operatic music, but perhaps his most original, and in its own environment of preposterously artificial comedy it is enchanting. The 'motto' or title-theme (Ex. 3) occurs

---

[6] Among the separate concert arias by Mozart there is one catalogued by Köchel as No. 584 (*Così* being 588), the words of which, 'Rivolgete a lui lo sguardo,' are known to have been originally in Da Ponte's libretto; but it does not contain this phrase, or any reference to 'a gentleman from Albania' (as the original has it), so that at least one other cut must have been made. K. 584 was assigned to Guglielmo, and evidently stood originally in the place of his shorter 'Non siate ritrosi' ('O vision so charming') preceding the laughing trio in Act I, for it finishes with the same kind of half-close.

D

twice in the overture, at first in the short slow introduction and again near the end of the extended *presto* movement, where its notation is augmented to twice the original length, so that, on account of the greater speed, its actual pace remains much the same.

ACT I

1. Trio: *Allegro*, G major (Fe. G. A.).[7] The three men, on the edge of a quarrel about the ladies' reputation, shape their argument into a kind of little concerto—as all Mozart's stage situations are shaped into perfect musical forms—beginning and ending with the same orchestral ritornello (abbreviated the second time).   While the two lovers and their opponent exhibit their characteristics to perfection, the vocal writing often becomes beautifully interlaced into ideal patterns of musical composition.   A quotation may here be shown to serve as a single example of such incidents, though they could be cited by the hundred (voices only: the orchestra adds further independent matter):

Ex. 4

2. Trio: *Allegro*, E major (Fe. G. A.).   The recitative-dialogue has let the music travel smoothly over the considerable distance between G and E major, a matter the reader is asked to take for granted hereafter.   Alfonso's gaily cynical tune is followed by a

[7] The names of the characters are thus abbreviated: Fi., Fiordiligi; Do., Dorabella; Fe., Ferrando; G., Guglielmo; A., Alfonso; De., Despina.

plain cadential bass similar to the *così fan tutte* quotation (Ex. 3), and this turns up again at the conclusion.   Alfonso's music is wheedlingly persuasive, the lovers' confidently assertive.

3. Trio: *Allegro*, C major (Fe. G. A.).   The first bar finishes off in the orchestra a G major cadence started by the recitative before the music modulates to C major—a point which spoken dialogue would obliterate.   Festive strains with trumpets and drums confirm the wager made by the men and at the same time brilliantly close the first scene.

4. Duet: *Andante—allegro*, A major (Fi. Do.).   A complete change of key and character (clarinets for the first time since the rise of the curtain).   The two ladies sing more slowly and sentimentally, with a sort of kittenish gentleness that leaves room for doubts in the hearer and for self-conscious displays of elaborate vocal vanities by the singers.   The change to a quicker pace gives greater energy to affirmations of eternal fidelity, but a certain frivolous skittishness keeps the hearer sceptical while musically it yields incomparable delight.

5. Aria: *Allegro agitato*, F minor.   Alfonso begins to act his part. The exaggerated agitation with which he proclaims his grief at the lovers' pretended call-up to war, in a vocal line broken up by sighs, is so obviously insincere in the present context that this very short piece amounts to a brilliant parody of certain types of tragic operatic aria.

6. Quintet: *Andante*, E♭ major (Fi. Do. Fe. G. A.).   The first of the great concerted pieces, with wonderfully interlaced voice-parts which individually express to perfection the different feelings of the three groups of characters: the pretended sorrow and suppressed exultation of the lovers, the despair of the ladies, and Alfonso's secret triumphant amusement.   One voice or another emerges from the texture here and there with lovely, creamy strains: the music is, in fact, at least as glorious to sing as to hear.

7. Duet: *Andante*, B♭ major (Fe. G.).   A simple, soldierly little song of farewell, cheerfully expressing belief in a speedy reunion. Each voice has just one bit of smooth ornamentation towards the end, while the other stands still.

8. Chorus: *Maestoso*, D major.   The military march, with voices added to what is mainly an instrumental piece, made martial with trumpets and drums, but kept well within the artificial make-believe style of music suited to a plot the composer intends nobody to take seriously.   The noises of trump, fife and gun-fire are musically illustrated much as in the aria, 'Non più andrai,' with which Figaro sends Cherubino on his way to the regiment.

9. Quintet: *Andante*, F major (Fi. Do. Fe. G. A.).   In voices broken by sobs, and in Alfonso's case by laughter, the last farewells

are said, the lovers now and again forming sustained phrases in which
pain and tenderness are most poignantly blended, while the throbbing
violin accompaniment continues to suggest hearts trembling with
sorrowful agitation or—for such is the ambiguity of the world's great
art of comedy, to which *Così* belongs—shaking with suppressed mirth.
The violas again play beautifully drawn-out phrases.   An abrupt
change back to the distant key of D major, with a renewed outburst
of the march, rudely reminds the lovers that they must part instantly.

10. Trio: *Andante*, E major (Fi. Do. A.).   The male lovers having
departed by water, the three characters left behind sing what is one of
the most miraculously beautiful and perfectly fashioned pieces in all
opera, and indeed in any music.   They adjure the winds to be gentle
and propitious, and muted violins paint quietly lapping waves in
semiquaver thirds.   A sudden stab of pain is produced by the discord
copied, intentionally or subconsciously, by a later composer, Mendelssohn, at the age of seventeen, in the *Midsummer Night's Dream*
overture (in the very same key)[8]:

This scene is rounded off by a short *secco* recitative for Alfonso
followed by an accompanied one in which he moralizes—or perhaps
one might say immoralizes—on the subject of feminine fickleness, of
which he is by now sure that he will find magnificent specimens in
Fiordiligi and Dorabella.   This passage goes in strict time and
therefore almost becomes an arioso, but it concludes with a typical
recitative cadence of the kind of Ex. 1.

The next scene introduces Despina with a recitative soliloquy on
the plaguy life of chambermaids.   She is surprised by her two mis-
tresses and told by Dorabella in a tragic outburst of accompanied

[8] See also 'Key Heredity,' pp. 184-7.

recitative to keep out of the way if she does not wish to be a witness to a fury of despair.   This is followed by:

11. Aria: *Allegro agitato*, E♭ major (Do.).   The first full-scale aria in the work, a grand dramatic piece with words in the manner of Metastasio containing classical references to the Eumenides (in the original) and music so evidently exaggerated that one is at once aware of a parodistic intention.   This number thus keeps quite legitimately within the framework of comedy.   Mozart, in fact, laughs not only at operatic conventions, but at himself, for there is no escaping the impression that the aria is a skit on Donna Elvira's 'Mi tradì' in *Don Giovanni*, which it resembles closely in many ways (the key is the same).   But for all its fun, it is a superb piece of music and of vocal declamation.   As usual, Mozart's genius manages to have things both ways.   What is more, he begins at this point to show the ladies and their lovers as quite distinct individuals: it is especially in their solo pieces that their different characters become sharply defined.

12. Aria: *Allegretto*, F major.   This is Despina's first air and shows her as the direct descendant of all the pert chambermaids of the Italian *commedia dell' arte* and of Neapolitan comic opera.   Her musical idiom throughout the work proves that Mozart's characterization includes a sense of class distinctions—praiseworthy in art if merely expedient in life.   Only once does one of the ladies fall into Despina's musical idiom, and then for a definite purpose, as will be seen later.

13. Sextet: *Allegro—allegro* (3–4)—*molto allegro*, C major (All).   This great centrepiece of the first act is divided into three sections or movements, each faster than the last, so that even from a purely musical point of view it makes a climax quite apart from the fact that the number begins as a quartet, the ladies not entering until the second section is reached.   The dramatic situation has by this time come to the crucial point at which the ladies first meet the supposed strangers and begin by indignantly rejecting their advances.   This situation is built up by Mozart into a composition on a large scale which is formally as flawless as it is scenically apt, not to mention the fact that even so he still finds opportunities for psychological strokes that help to outline the characters and their gradual changes of attitude.   The polyphonic interplay of the voices and the orchestral colour are once again sheer perfection.

14. Aria: *Andante maestoso—allegro—più allegro*, B♭ major.   Fiordiligi's first great aria (with the trumpet figure already mentioned) is also in the nature of parody.   It makes fun of the so-called metaphor or parable aria, for she likens her constancy extravagantly to a rock in a tempestuous sea, and both the accompanied recitative and the aria itself musically keep to the grand manner with a kind of quizzical

exaggeration. This shows itself particularly in the very florid treat-ment of the voice-part which, moreover, contains those characteristic wide skips written specially for Ferrarese del Bene, whom Mozart rather despised, but who happened to be able to 'sing both high and low' with extrordinary facility. Fiordiligi's character, like Dora-bella's, has now becomes clearly outlined. She is proud of her correct behaviour and anxious to be thought the perfect lady; the latter has a dash of frivolity as well as of the spitfire in her make-up.

15. Aria: *Andantino*, G major. This short air serves to define Guglielmo more clearly. He is found to be rather a gay dog and not inclined to see more in the test of the two ladies' fidelity than a good joke. Indeed, for the moment even the more serious and sentimental Ferrando is overcome by the comic absurdity of the situation. The aria is followed without a break by:

16. Trio: *Allegro molto*, G major (Fe. G. A.). Here the two lovers fairly split their sides with laughter, heedless of Alfonso's warn-ing that before long it may turn to anger and sorrow. The gay and vivacious music, with its springy rhythm, its chuckling violin figures and the metre going out of control near the end, draws the audience irresistibly into the fun.

17. Aria: *Andante cantabile*, A major. Ferrando recovers his seriousness and gives expression to his continued confidence in Dora-bella in a love-song of exquisite form and sensibility, charming colour (clarinets, bassoons, horns and strings with muted violins) and perfectly controlled ornamentation of vocal phrase.

18. Finale: *Andante, etc.—presto*, D major, etc. (All). We have now reached the vast and carefully built-up musical climax that crowns the first act. It is divided into a number of sections, beginning with a lengthy duet in which the ladies deplore the loss of their lovers. But the lament is a kind of peaceful twittering, quite free from any note of distress: we begin to suspect that the loss is not going to prove irreparable. Sure enough, when there is a dramatic interruption, the lovers bursting upon the scene to poison themselves, followed by Alfonso, the ladies are quite prepared to take this absurd pretence seriously. A great mock-dramatic quintet develops, which turns into a sextet as Despina enters. She is sent off to fetch a doctor, while the ladies show signs of softening into pity, if not yet into love.

Despina's arrival in the guise of an absurd witch-doctor, in which she makes topical fun of Mesmer's magnetism, deceives nobody but the two ladies. But this very transparent masquerade was acceptable to eighteenth-century audiences because they were still quite used to artificial male sopranos, whose tradition has, in fact, survived to this day in such parts as Octavian in Strauss's *Rosenkavalier* and, in a debased form, in the English pantomime boy. All is well, therefore,

when Despina begins to work wonders to strains which leave no
doubt in the hearer that Mozart intends caricature of the broadest
kind:

Ex. 6

A lovely sextet in E♭ major with richly interwoven parts follows
where the lovers revive, pretending to think themselves in some
classical realm of the blessed, and the ladies melt for a moment into
tenderness; and the act finishes with an amazingly brilliant *strepitoso*
movement of a musical quality on a level with the finale of any Mozartian symphony, but with the spirit of comic opera reigning supreme.

ACT II

The second act is often considered inferior to the first, and it must
be admitted that, apart from the finale, it lacks the wonderful climaxes
of concerted pieces in which the first is so rich.   This criticism, however, must be countered by the assertion that the second finale contains
far more great music than the first, which does show some rather arid
patches.   Also, for all that it is preceded, with a single exception, by
nothing but arias and duets, these complete the gradual building-up
of the characters in a way that may be said to have been achieved,
during centuries of development in the art of the stage, by very few
great dramatic creators, and that at the head of these stand Shakespeare
and Mozart.   The figures of Fiordiligi and Ferrando in particular
come to be seen in the round through their second-act arias (dis-
regarding emergency cuts).

19. Aria: *Andante*, G major.   Despina's second song, on the other
hand, adds nothing new to her picture; nor does it contain anything
of special musical value, so that its omission need not be regarded as an
irreparable loss.

20. Duet: *Andante*, B♭ major (Fi. Do.).   This number, however,
no lover of *Così* would willingly miss, nor would any conductor or
producer sacrifice it for any purpose but that of shortening an abnormally long work.   It has a deliciously feline grace and a particular
kind of sly humour with which the composer ironically comments on
the situation that has now developed: the ladies compare notes as to
which of the two strangers each would choose, *if* it were a question of

choosing.   And we, of course, know that it soon will be.   This number is full of ingredients that go to the making of the peculiarly subtle *Così fan tutte*-ish flavour : the florid passages in thirds for the voices, the return of the first theme in canon (indicating impatience to speak), the hugging of the tonic in the bass with dominant harmony above, the extra dash of spice of a passing C♯ in the orchestral peroration, and so on.

21. Duet and Chorus : *Andante*, E♭ major (Fe. G.).   This, it must be confessed, would make a very fitting opening for the second act, if one could resign oneself to cuts preceding it, much better than the original recitative with which Despina opens it.   Flutes, clarinets, bassoons and horns alone play a delicious piece in the manner of the best of Mozart's serenades and divertimenti for wind instruments ; the voices, with only a very short choral passage at the end, join in without adding anything essential.   There is some lovely wedding music to come later, and this piece at once sets its tone, which has just enough warmth, but also a certain playfulness and artificiality that warns us not to take any of the impending happenings too much to heart.

22. Quartet : *Allegretto grazioso—presto*, D major (De. Fe. G. A.). The only concerted number for more than two voices occurring before the finale must be admitted to be by no means on the level of those in the first act, and it is not a real quartet, for the four voices never sing together.   But it has its place in the scheme, for it falls into a tone of frivolous gaiety which shows that the character who has by this time begun to assert a considerable influence is Despina.   Her and Alfonso's very quick patter at the end is most amusing ; so are the trumpets, which add a special touch of perkiness to this piece.

23. Duet : *Andante grazioso*, F major (Do. G.).   The music here returns to the bland tone and graceful banter of No. 20, with a note of tenderness added from the very beginning :

Ex. 7

Il co · re vi do -no, bell' i · do · lo mi · o.
This heart that I give thee, I pray thee to trea- sure

Dorabella is the first to exchange new love for old, and she does it characteristically in a mood of playfulness, into which Guglielmo enters.   One hesitates to say, though it is true, that the music is exceedingly pretty, lest this should confirm in anyone the infuriating notion that Mozart is merely a composer of 'dainty' music.   The plain fact is that he can suggest prettiness when it is wanted as well as he can suggest anything else in the whole range of human experience.

24. Aria : *Allegretto—allegro*, B♭ major.   Ferrando is in no mood

to enter into any game.   In the accompanied recitative preceding this aria he fiercely woos Fiordiligi, who can resist his plea only by running away from him.   This does for a moment amuse him, and he sings this difficult and brilliant solo with much gaiety to begin with; but suddenly a stab of despair comes into the music, and in the quicker final portion he shows that things threaten to turn serious, for him as well as for Fiordiligi, and that he will not only lose his wager, but suffer the pangs of conscience for having challenged Alfonso's riper wisdom.

25. Rondo: *Adagio—allegro moderato*, E major.   Fiordiligi re-enters, and in an orchestral recitative reveals that for her the situation has become desperate indeed.   She knows she is in love with the stranger, yet blames herself bitterly for finding her heart so much less steadfast than she had proudly declared it to be.   The slow portion of the aria is a heart-rending lament because of its beauty rather than its tragedy, and the faster one is full of dramatic agitation without falling short of that ideal tone of classical serenity which pervades the whole of this miraculous piece.   The concertizing horns have already been mentioned; flutes, clarinets, bassoons and strings alone go with them.

A recitative between Ferrando and Guglielmo becomes too agitated for the *secco* accompaniment and runs over into the orchestra.   It merges into:

26. Aria: *Allegretto*, G major.   Guglielmo tries to laugh off his predicament by adopting Alfonso's philosophy, which the music expresses to prefection.   A martial note comes into it (trumpets and drums) where he remembers ruefully how gallantly he used to defend women against such cynical views.

27. Cavatina: *Allegro*, C minor-major.   Ferrando's reaction is quite different.   In his accompanied recitative he expresses bitterness and despair; the short air paints indignation, mixed with thoughts of love that will return in spite of all, by means of a kind of condensed sonata movement with two subjects, the first a tragic C minor out-burst, the other a tender phrase that appears in the keys proper to a second sonata subject, at first in the relative (E♭) and then in the tonic (C) major.

28. Aria: *Allegretto vivace*, B♭ major.   This is Dorabella's song already referred to as falling into the manner of Despina's music. The less class-conscious of the two sisters has come so much under her maid's influence that she expresses in strains appropriate to a chamber-maid rather than a lady the view that it is useless for women to struggle against Cupid's rogueries.

29. Duet: *Adagio—allegretto—larghetto—andante*, A major (Fi. Fe.).   This is the most extended concerted piece preceding the

second-act finale.   It finishes the complex portraits of the two
characters, to which each of the four sections has something new to
contribute by making points in a purely musical way which would
not emerge so clearly from the libretto alone.   Mozart is, in fact, like
a great actor in whose handling words and stage-directions develop
their full meaning, including a good deal that never came into the
author's mind.

30. Arioso: *Andante*, C major (Fe. G. A.).   This, an air with a
refrain for two additional voices rather than a trio, is a very short
but important piece.   It re-establishes the fundamental key of the
whole opera, preparing it for the second finale, and sums up Alfonso's
views of women, which now assume a new note of mellow indulgence
and in which the lovers at last acquiesce as they join into the motto
(Ex. 3) *così fan tutte.*

31. Finale: *Allegro assai, etc.—allegro molto*, C major, etc. (All
and Chorus).   The great crowning piece of the whole work is now
gradually built up with cumulative orchestration as it passes through
a number of sections in different keys.   Despina, supported by the
chorus and joined by Alfonso, supervises the final preparations for a
wedding breakfast.   The key then changes to E♭ major for some of
that special kind of serenade music as the chorus welcomes the lovers,
now reassorted, as the ladies think, into new bridal pairs.   Their
quartet incident, with richly interlaced parts, is particularly beautiful.
The chorus recapitulates and is followed by a new episode, a feature of
which is a gurgling accompaniment for second clarinet of a kind
exploited by Mozart as a new orchestral device of a quite peculiar
charm.[9]   This leads to the quartet 'round' in A♭ mentioned earlier,
the slow and expansive melody of which is stated by Fiordiligi,
Ferrando, Dorabella and again Fiordiligi, in turn, each voice continuing with contrapuntal matter as the next enters with the theme.
Guglielmo does not take up the tune, but pursues his own vengeful
thoughts in an aside.   The primary reason for this is that a bass voice
cannot encompass the theme laid out in the first place for two sopranos
and tenor; but Mozart, as usual, makes a virtue of a limitation by
enriching the situation and the musical texture with a contrasting
element.

A sudden change to the distant key of E major brings on Alfonso,
with Despina disguised as a notary.   This time she indulges in some
amusing parody of what we may take to be Mozart's idea of 'legal'
music.   Just as the marriage contract is signed the military march
with chorus from Act I is heard.   Alfonso dramatically acts consterna-
tion at the return of the old lovers, the ladies urge the new ones to hide,

[9] Not only here and in No. 21, but also in the A major (K. 488) and C minor piano
concertos, in the minuet-trio of the E♭ major Symphony (K. 543), in *Don Giovanni*, etc.

while the music apes real tragedy and manages at the same time to capture genuine beauty of the highest order.

Ferrando and Guglielmo without their disguise enter to a comfortable strain in the key of their little farewell duet in Act I (B♭ major) and in much the same vein.   But things grow dramatic again as the lovers pretend to discover their rivals and stumble by an accident well contrived by Alfonso upon the marriage contract.   The thematic references to earlier music follow, as outlined above, including Exx. 6 and 7.   Alfonso explains the wager and persuades all to subscribe to his philosophy.   Since women are all alike and human frailty is universal, why not make the best of the situation and forget and forgive all round?   This is done, and a final movement in which beauty and gaiety are enchantingly blended concludes the opera most happily and sends the hearer home with a tune ringing in his ear fit to make him dream of the loveliest of fools' paradises.   The sudden turn of this coda into F minor at one point always sends shivers of delight down one's spine, however often one may hear *Così*.   It is one of those felicities in Mozart which never lose their surprise through familiarity.

That is one of his secrets.   He has many others.   The greatest and most mysterious is his genius for finding even in so frivolous, artificial and absurd a play that real humanity all great dramatic art stands in need of and that touch of pathos which is the secret of all true comedy, from the lowest vulgarity of the music-hall comedian to the finest art of Shakespeare or Molière.   And we can only place him in the company of the greatest exponents.

Beethoven's Diabelli Variations

(The Beethoven Sonata Society, Vol. XIII)

THE VARIATION FORM AND BEETHOVEN

THOSE WHO have studied Beethoven's works in sonata form may have come to the conclusion that no other musical form had anything like the same importance for him. In a sense that is true. The other two great principles of construction in classical music, which are those of treatment by fugue and by variation, are not represented as conspicuously in his catalogue as, for example, in that of Bach and Brahms respectively. We find, indeed, only one supremely great separate work of each species in Beethoven: the *Grosse Fuge*, Op. 133, for string quartet, and the *Variations on a Waltz by Diabelli*, Op. 120, for pianoforte—the work to be discussed here. Even in these two isolated cases we know that neither work was originally intended to appear independently. The *Great Fugue*, as every musician knows, was at first planned as a finale for the B♭ major Quartet, Op. 130, while the Variations grew out of a commission to contribute to a collective work by a number of contemporary musicians.

But although Beethoven exploited neither the variation nor the fugue form much for its own sake, it would none the less be wrong to say that they were of less than enormous importance to him. It is true that he did little to develop them independently, because he happened to be taken up with the advancement of the sonata form— itself a task for a lifetime; but they served him again and again in his titanic efforts to bring about that advancement and, indeed, often induced him to burden himself with the most heroic struggles in its accomplishment. The last movements of the Sonatas Opp. 109 and 111 owe their greatness to Beethoven's superb treatment of their themes by variation, and those of Opp. 106 and 110 represent his fiercest intellectual grapplings with the fugal writing which never at any time of his life came easily to him. The slow movement of the ninth Symphony and the finale of the third Rasumovsky Quartet come to mind as other instances of his application of the variation and fugal principles, both of which appear together in the 'Eroica' Symphony. The Diabelli Variations themselves contain a fughetta and a double fugue, both of them extremely interesting examples of Beethoven's characteristic manner of tackling contrapuntal problems, and in the only other separate variation work for pianoforte that is at all comparable to Op. 120—the 15 Variations in E♭ major, Op. 35, on the theme afterwards used in the 'Eroica'—he begins the finale with an elaborate and extended fugue.

We will now abandon the question of Beethoven's fugal writing and consider his treatment of the variation form in the light of its history. We want to know what it is that Beethoven did to advance the art of varying a musical theme. The question will be asked whether the advance was purely technical—in other words, such an advance as another composer would have been sure to make sooner or later even if Beethoven had never existed; the answer is that Beethoven's achievement was such as no other composer, not even one endowed with genius comparable to his own, could possibly have reached in just the same way and that, it follows, it was by no means purely technical, in fact not conspicuously so at all.

It has been pointed out by scholars that Beethoven's important contribution to the variation form from a technical point of view is his clear recognition of the fact that a theme may be modified almost without limit in detail, so long as the structure of any variation keeps closely to the structure of the theme itself at the critical points. These critical points are not melodic but harmonic or, to put it more clearly, modulatory. If a theme is so planned, for instance, as to modulate to the dominant in the middle and to return to the tonic at the end by way of the subdominant, then, according to Beethoven, almost any modification can be made incidentally, provided that these modulatory landmarks of tonic, subdominant and dominant are retained as the main pivots on which a variation turns. Thus Beethoven was able to gain an immense amount of freedom of melodic and (incidentally) harmonic treatment without any loss of consciousness on the hearer's part that the music still rested on its thematic foundations, however fantastic the superstructure. But it would be a mistake to regard this as a discovery of Beethoven's simply because he *was* Beethoven, unless one likes to imagine that without his appearance in musical history the classical sonata form would not have developed as it did; for it is a discovery inseparable from that development, rooted in the conception of the distribution of harmonic periods over a given surface of musical form. It is idle to speculate what would have become of the sonata if Beethoven had never appeared; but we may be pretty sure that, even as it was left by Haydn and Mozart, it would have taught the variation principle as he had the genius to see it to some other musician. The greatness of his achievement, of course, remains undiminished by this recognition of the fortuitousness of musico-historical events.

For the rest, Beethoven retained the principles that had guided makers of variations ever since instrumental music began to be written down—and even then they were inherited from vocal music, which had in various ways embellished both plainsong and folksong by ornament and counterpoint. These principles were two distinct ones: variation of the tune and variation of the bass. Melodic variation, which originally arose from a desire to enliven the mere repetition that was once the only means of carrying on a composition of any length, quite early in the history of the form divided into two different modes of treatment. In the one case the tune remained unchanged or practically unchanged, while the accompaniments were gradually elaborated in the course of a composition, as in William Byrd's presentation of *Sellinger's Round*; in the other the melody itself was ornamented and modified, without losing its essential outline, as in *The King's Hunting Jig* by John Bull. These and other early English virginalists, by the way, laid down the lines of development for melodic variation for all time. The airs with 'doubles' we encounter in the works of Couperin, Rameau and Bach are less rather than more developed examples of the same thing, and the masters in whose hands it came to its culmination—Haydn and Mozart—still worked in very much the same way, as indeed did later composers, whose melodic variations were sometimes an exquisite application of decorative art, but more often an exhibition of degenerate and tasteless fancy-work, so much so that Mendelssohn protested against all this frivolity with a set he purposely entitled *Variations sérieuses*.

The second principle, which is that of basing variations on the bass or on the harmony implied by the bass, and which originated in two dance forms, the *ciacona* and the *passacaglia*, at first found its application in the 'divisions on a ground' of the seventeenth century, in which the ground basses remained unmodified but the superstructure of melody, harmony and counterpoint could vary in a number of ways limited only by the composer's skill. But although the bass here remained rigidly unchanged, if a work was written in the *ciacona* manner, according to the precedent of the *passacaglia* it could be temporarily transferred to one of the upper parts and ornamented at will. In this, tune and bass become to a certain extent interchangeable, and since the bass could for a moment become the treble melody, later composers saw no reason why the process should not be reversed. Thus we find in the finale of Brahms's Variations on a theme by Haydn that the melody has been turned into a ground bass, and some composers of variations give preference to tunes which happen to make good basses, if required.[1]

[1] e.g. Stanford's choice of *Down among the Dead Men* for a set of variations for piano and orchestra or Dohnányi's of *Ah, que dirai-je, maman* for his 'Variations on a Nursery Tune.'

The chief attraction of variations on a bass to composers later than Corelli and Purcell was that the superstructure no longer needed to be set on a *bass line* that remained inflexible whether it actually remained in the *bass position* or not, but that all it was necessary to retain was the succession of harmonic progressions implied by the bass. This greater latitude allowed composers to construct much larger works on the basis of the ground-bass principle without running the risk of monotony. One of the longest works ever written for the keyboard, Bach's Goldberg Variations, is founded entirely on a bass that is not heard in its primitive form throughout.[2]

In the Diabelli Variations Beethoven very strikingly united these two distinct historical variation principles, as indeed he had already done conspicuously in the 'Eroica' Variations, both in the Symphony itself and in the set for pianoforte, Op. 35. Although, as will be seen presently, he had no great opinion of Diabelli's tune, he must have welcomed it for the peculiarity that such interest as it has is evenly divided between the treble and the bass, the latter yielding him, for instance, his jocular allusion to Mozart's 'Notte e giorno faticar' (Var. XXII).

But, it may now be asked, if the Diabelli Variations are still so deeply rooted in historical precedent, wherein consists the startling novelty, the greatness and originality that has been so often claimed for them? How, in other words, did Beethoven advance the variation form? The answer has already been anticipated to some extent: the advance is not to be measured by mere technical examination of the music, though that reveals, for one thing, a striking development of the coda. Even that is not technically his exclusive conquest, however. Mozart, when he happened for once to use the variation form for more than merely decorative or entertaining purposes, as in the clarinet Quintet or the G major Variations for piano duet, was quite capable of devising a coda that rounded off a movement in that form to perfection. No, the answer to our question must be completed by the assertion that Beethoven added a spiritual quality to his greatest variation sets—including the coda, of course—which is the personal secret of his genius. It may be said that whereas earlier composers —and later ones, too, if it comes to that—*transformed* their themes more or less ingeniously, he *transfigured* his in his best variation works. What this transfiguration into fantasy and poetry and wit is cannot be told by verbal analysis, so that the annotations which follow will still seem like an expounding of mere transformations, mere technicalities. But to listen to a performance of the Diabelli Variations is like reading between the lines, and so the present lines may, perhaps, be of some

[2] Beethoven's own 32 Variations in C minor, published in 1807, still keep closely to this procedure, as does the finale of Brahms's fourth Symphony.

little use, if only as a kind of stave into which the hearer must fill notes of his own imagining.

In conclusion, we may ask ourselves why the variation form suited Beethoven so uncommonly well. It was Parry who hit upon the explanation most satisfactorily, perhaps, when he made the searching observation that Beethoven's creative procedure as a whole was in a sense a process of evolving by variation the themes he incessantly sketched and elaborated. But it is no less true that the principle of variation cannot fail to be the very breath of inspiration to any musician who creates on something larger than miniature scale, since it is the basic principle of all music that depends on construction. In the last resort the variation form suited Beethoven because it suits any composer, whether he writes successful separate sets of variations or not. Also, it is the most purely and absolutely musical of all. Many of the simpler forms, such as the scherzo, derive obviously from the dance, and the song derives from verse; the fugue has its analogues in decorative design and the sonata has features in common with the drama. For variations one can find no comparison in any other art, unless it be Claude Monet's series of landscapes showing the same subject under different aspects of light, temperature and weather. But these are hardly more than studies. Variation works such as Beethoven's on Diabelli's theme are among the world's monumental masterpieces.

THE HISTORY OF OP. 120

In the *Wiener Zeitung* of 19 June 1824 appeared an advertisement of which the following is a translation:

> At the house of Ant. Diabelli & Co., Art and Music Dealers, Graben No. 113 (Successors to Cappi & Diabelli), is newly published and to be had: *Vaterländischer Künstlerverein*, Variations for the Pianoforte on a given Theme, composed by the foremost Tone-Poets and Virtuosi of Vienna and the Imperial and Royal Austrian States. Part I, containing: 33 Variations by L. van Beethoven, 120th Work. Price 5 fl. 30 kr. Viennese Currency. Part II, containing: 50 Variations on the same Theme by the following Composers, viz. . . . . . . Coda by Carl Czerny. Price 10 fl. Viennese Currency. (Property of the Publishers.)

The advertisement then goes on at length to tell the reader how fortunate the new firm considers itself to begin its career with a composition unique in its kind, and likely to remain so; how fifty well-known musicians had united in writing variations on one and the same theme submitted to them for the purpose; how each of these variations most interestingly and instructively showed the ingenuity, the taste, the individuality and artistic tendency of each contributor, as well as the peculiar way of treating the keyboard instrument proper to each of them; how the work was not merely a prize competition, but at the same time an alphabetical lexicon of the 'names of such a brilliant era in our history of art,' many of which are 'already celebrated, others highly promising.'

A few of the contributors are referred to for some special reason or other. The reader is told, for instance, that the collection contains the last piece of work undertaken by Emanuel Förster (1748–1823) before his death and the first essay in composition by 'the richly gifted, eleven-year-old Liszt'; it is also pointed out that 'Mr Kalkbrenner had the complaisance to furnish a contribution during his sojourn in Vienna,' and attention is drawn a second time to the fact that Czerny had added a developed finale to the whole, apart from writing one of the variations. Schubert, on the other hand, who contributed a delightful variation (C minor, 3–4, *con moto tranquillo*), is mentioned only in the list of contributors; nor did the publishers draw attention to the fact that the name of a member of the imperial family, the Archduke Rudolph, whom history knows as a favourite pupil of Beethoven's, was among those of the collaborators, which may confirm the suspicion that possibly he did not write his contribution himself. But modesty went farther even than that: Diabelli nowhere says that the theme submitted to all these composers and would-be composers is his own.

On the other hand the advertisement makes no secret of the firm's pride in the fact that Beethoven, at first asked to contribute one variation to the club-work and afterwards expected to supply perhaps seven or eight, eventually turned out a collection which the publishers at least suspected to be one of the major works of keyboard music, then and for all time to come. For they say this:

> Earlier our great Beethoven (the Jean Paul of our time) [!] had already exhausted all the depths of genius and of art by supplying a model of original treatment in 33 Variations (published by us), which form the first part of this work.

Some of the more distinguished contributors have been mentioned; the others were, in the alphabetical order in which they appear in the *Vaterländidscher Künstlerverein* [3]: J. Assmayer, C. M. von Bocklet, E. Czapek (Čapek), Count M. Dietrichstein, J. Drechsler, J. Freystädtler, J. Gänsbacher, Abbé Gelinek (Jelinek), A. Halm, J. Hoffmann, J. Horzalka, J. Hugelmann, J. N. Hummel, Anselm Hüttenbrenner, F. A. Kanne, J. Kerzowsky, Conradin Kreutzer, Baron E. Lannoy,

[3] A copy is in the Royal College of Music. For full names, where ascertainable, see Index.

E

M. J. Leidesdorf, J. Mayseder, Ignaz Moscheles, J. von Mosel, W. A. Mozart (junior), J. Panny, H. Payer, P. Pixis, W. Plachy, P. Riotte, F. Roser, J. Schenk, F. Schoberlechner, Simon Sechter, Abbé Stadler, J. de Szalay, W. Tomaschek (Tomášek), M. Umlauf, Dion. (Dionys) Weber, Fr. Weber, F. Weiss, C. A. de Winkhler, J. Wittassek (Vitašek) and J. H. Worzischek (Vořišek).

It is not a thrilling list.   The only glorious name in it borrows its lustre from the bearer's father.   Hummel, Moscheles and perhaps Tomášek are the best remembered of all these people, many of whom are unknown even to books of reference.   Kreutzer and Schenk are still known by one work for the stage each (*Das Nachtlager von Granada* and *Der Dorfbarbier*), but almost exclusively by hearsay nowadays; Sechter and Stadler had an academic reputation in their time—the former was, in fact, the man from whom Schubert, in the last year of his life, planned to take counterpoint lessons; Leidesdorf, Hüttenbrenner and Schoberlechner appear as friends in Beethoven's or Schubert's biographies, but have no reputation of their own left; the rest are obscure, if not wholly forgotten.[4]

Many of the contributions are mere keyboard manipulations. Some bear titles indicating a special form: *Quasi Ouverture* (Drechsler), *Capriccio* (Förster), *Fugato* (Hoffmann), *Fuga* (Archduke Rudolph, ? written by Stadler), *Incitatio quasi canon* (Sechter), *Polonaise* (Tomášek).   Mozart's son wrote two variations, but only one was published, and another by G. Rieger was rejected, apparently on account of what was, for its time, a very eccentric scheme of modulation.[5]

Beethoven's own work was finished in April or May 1823 and at first published separately in the course of that year.   The connection between it and the fifty collected variations is due to Diabelli alone. Anton Schindler, who gossiped pleasantly but irresponsibly about his friendship with the great man, never mentions the latter as a published work in his story of the origin of Beethoven's set.   It is clear, however, that Diabelli had issued his invitation to other composers at least as early as to Beethoven.   Schubert's variation, for instance, dates from May 1821; Beethoven's first sketches belong to 1822.

Schindler, here as elsewhere, is not to be trusted implicitly.   There appears to be no foundation to his assertion that Diabelli paid as much as 80 ducats to Beethoven, who seems to have asked for no more than 30 to 40, according to later investigations.   Nor can the fantastic stories which try to account for the fact that Beethoven wrote no more and no less than thirty-three variations be brought into accord with

---

[4] Umlauf was not the more famous composer of that name, Ignaz, who had died in 1796, but his son Michael (1781–1842).

[5] These two rejected variations are published at the end of an article on the Op. 120 in the *Beethoven-Jahrbuch* for 1908.

what actually happened. According to Carl Holz, who, like Schindler, was a friend of Beethoven's, the latter, having asked Diabelli how many variations by other composers were ready, and being told thirty-two, said: 'I will write you thirty-three myself'; but he obviously did not know from the beginning that his variations would amount to exactly that number, or, indeed, to anything like so great a number. He refused to contribute a single one to a club-work, having no very pleasant recollection of his experiences in 1808, when he took part in a similar collective effort to set the words of 'In questa tomba oscura' as a song. But since, as we have seen, it then became a question of his writing seven or eight variations of his own, the variations evidently did not accumulate to thirty-three by premeditation, but because there was no stopping until he had said all he found to say about the subject. As for the picturesque tale that he flung the finished work at Diabelli, who had asked for one variation, with some such remark as: 'Here are thirty-three for one, take it or leave it!' there is clearly no truth whatever in it. Diabelli must have known what was coming, as the twenty-second Variation [6], which is Beethoven's humorous protest against being pestered to go on with his work, shows conclusively enough.

What one can believe of Schindler, or would like to, is that when Diabelli had asked for his collaboration Beethoven said: 'Well, he shall have some variations on his cobbler's patch [*Schusterfleck*],' or words to that effect. The theme certainly was not an inspiring one, and it has more than one fault, as will be seen presently. Still, this rather plodding waltz [7] did well enough for the basis of a great work: for it was not the subject but the discourse that mattered to Beethoven, who had previously varied themes by Handel and Mozart without finding that they yielded him great music. It made no difference to the quality of his variations whether his choice fell on masters like these or on composers of the second or third rank like Dittersdorf, Grétry, Wenzel Müller, Paisiello, Righini, Salieri, Süssmayr, Count Waldstein, Weigl, Winter and Wranizky. For a variation work or movement of real importance he had as a rule first to forge his own basic material. The slow movement of the ninth Symphony, the finale of the last piano Sonata or the *Heilige Dankgesang* in the A minor Quartet are utterly inconceivable as variations on a foreign theme.

In the Diabelli Variations, just for once, the miracle happened, however: here we have the only variation work comparable to these,

[6] See note on this, p. 71.
[7] It was called so by Diabelli, but is not, of course, a Viennese waltz as developed later in the century, mainly in the hands of Lanner and the Strauss family. It is in the nature of the more rudimentary form of the dance, the Austrian country dance known as the *Ländler*, which began to be artistically exploited in the *Deutsche* of Mozart and Schubert.

indeed the only such work by Beethoven that is to be taken quite seriously, which has a theme not his own for its foundation.   And there can be no doubt that he would never have thought of basing so vast and so grand a work on so trivial a tune had he not been induced to handle it against his better judgment.   Which only proves, as works by many other great men have done, that commissions have their value in the history of art.   Diabelli's own music has long ceased to be of the slightest use, except, perhaps, in the schoolroom; but he is, nevertheless, responsible for the production of one masterpiece for which the world has good reason to be eternally grateful to him.

The Music

THE THEME: *Vivace*—Diabelli's 'cobbler's patch' had better be shown at once in its full extent:

Ex. 1

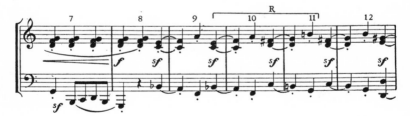

I number its bars for convenience of reference, and the reader will not
be surprised, in view of Beethoven's description of the tune, that it
works out to a multiple of four and is indeed, as ordinary tunes have
a way of being, a matter of regular four-bar phrases from beginning to
end, as well as shaped into two equal parts of sixteen bars each designed, as it were, so as to progress harmonically in opposite directions:
the first from C to G major, the second from G (with a C major
inflection) back to the tonic key again, both with a momentary excursion to F major.

Beethoven had, of course, no reason to object to all this.   A
Ländler could not well be anything more than a simple, popular tune,
and such tunes—as indeed all conventional dance tunes—are naturally
square-cut and symmetrical.   But he may well have smiled at the
clumsily repeated right-hand chords at the beginning of each section,
and we know from Schindler that he objected to the rosalias (*Schuster-
flecke*) which occur in both these sections.   The rosalia (the present
examples of which will be found marked 'R' in bars 10–11 and
26–27 of Ex. 1) is a device by which a musical phrase is repeated in a
different position—usually a whole tone higher.   It derives its name
from an old Italian popular song, *Rosalia, mia cara*, in which a flagrant
instance of it occurs.   It is a kind of sequence, but distinguished from
that much more frequently used expedient by modulating into a
different key.   The sequence is much less likely to be offensive
because, transferring a phrase to another degree of the same scale, it
produces harmonic changes without breaking the harmonic continuity,
whereas the rosalia, unless very skilfully placed, has the effect of

jerking the music violently from one key into another without any transition. I will let Beethoven himself illustrate the point by quoting the lesson in the management of such things he lost no time in giving Diabelli, for his snub occurs at once in

VARIATION I: *Alla marcia maestosa*. The whole of this, with the exception of the final cadences at the end of each section, keeps uniformly to this rhythmic scheme:

It will have been noticed that this is not a quotation of the opening, but of a passage corresponding to bars 9–12 of the theme, including the first rosalia, and it will also be seen that Beethoven does not emulate Diabelli by himself using a plain rosalia, but subtly alters the harmony a little so as to let the phrase avoid an awkward passage from plain F major to plain G major. He is not even content to turn the rosalia into a sequence, but scraps Diabelli's progression altogether, inserting a new and much more significant one. To show it for what it is worth, let us set down in music type what this incident would have looked and sounded like as a rosalia or as a sequence:

The rosalia, marked 'R,' corresponds to Diabelli; the F♮ in 'S' is strictly sequential but, it will be seen, does not make harmonic sense.

The vast superiority of Beethoven's modulation (Ex. 2) is obvious at once. But it is nevertheless a modulation that brings him to the key of G major for the close of the first section, and thus not too far from his theme. His treatment of the second section is analogous to that of the first, but describes a wider modulatory arc. It is, in fact, a flight into mysterious regions even at so early a stage of a work that is rich in suggestions of mystery. We know at once that we are in for a profound experience—and that from now on poor Diabelli is out of it.

VARIATION II: *Poco allegro*. This more vivacious movement is syncopated throughout in the following manner, though with one or two minor changes in the interplay of the hands to avoid monotony:

Ex. 4

Again I show the passage corresponding to the rosalia, as it is of the greatest interest to see how Beethoven finds more than one way of evading the triviality of this feature without actually discarding it. However, I shall as a rule leave the reader to take this for granted henceforth and draw attention to other aspects of his masterly discourse on an unpromising topic. One of these, in the present Variation, is the break in the regularity of the syncopation just referred to, as thus:

Ex. 5

A merely talented composer would more likely than not have let the preconceived rhythmic scheme of uniformly alternating quavers get the better of him; a genius like Beethoven remains in command and knows exactly when a certain device is in danger of running away with his music mechanically, and where he must intervene.

VARIATION III: *L'istesso tempo*. The pace, according to Beethoven's direction, remains the same, but this new view of the theme is entirely different in character—smooth and friendly, whereas that of

the last was capricious.   Superficially, there is a striking resemblance
to the scherzo of the early Sonata, Op. 2 No. 3 (in the same key,
be it noted).   Even the slight polyphonic working is much the
same:

Ex.6   L'istesso tempo

But there is something much more tender and yet unapproachable
about this later movement, and it is more closely packed with meaning.
In other words, it is maturest Beethoven.   It is often easier to feel
what distinguishes a master's most fully ripened art from his early
works than to say where exactly the difference lies; but one of the
signs of Beethoven's maturity on which one can lay one's finger with
some certainty is his ability to express something of significance all the
time, even simultaneously with the mere business of getting over the
ground and spacing out the music, whereas in his early works
the hearer has more often to wait for the next idea while the music
marks time and merely covers spaces necessary to the composer's
constructive plan.

The theme in the third Variation, as indeed throughout the work,
will be seen to be by no means literally adhered to, but adumbrated
in a free manner.   Strict conformity would in any case have been
impossible throughout the whole course of thirty-three variations,
even if Beethoven had still believed in varying a theme purely melodically, as he did that of the 'Andante favori,' for instance, or that of the
A♭ major Sonata, Op. 26, in the first, second and fifth variations.
For Diabelli's waltz is not simply a straightforward tune—in fact, it
is hardly a tune at all in any ordinary sense.   In the first eight bars of
each section it is mainly the bass that is melodic, though the treble adds
a salient feature in its up-beats, of which Beethoven makes as much use
as he does of the bass.

In the second part of this third Variation there is a sudden drop into
a remote, sinister rumbling that lends an inexplicable ambiguity to the
otherwise serene and friendly tone of the piece.

VARIATION IV: *Un poco più vivace.*   The opening in a threefold
canon still recognizably adheres to the initial figure of the theme, but
disposes of any sort of subservience to Diabelli's bass, though its four-
bar tonic-and-dominant sections are retained:

The canon does not persist throughout, though its use is extended in the second part; but its dactylic figure gives a new rhythmic aspect to the music.

VARIATION V: *Allegro vivace*. Here the rhythm changes from dactyls to anapaests:

a change that becomes the more startling when the figures are found to be compressed in such a way as to cut across the 3–4 metre of the music:

This fifth Variation is in Beethoven's scherzo manner. The second part leads us to an interesting observation. So far each section of both the theme and the variations has been repeated; but now the second part of Variation V shows no repeat mark, the reason being, as in similar cases later on, that this section already contains the repeat within itself. Beethoven writes out the whole thing at length because he gives fresh interest to his procedures by adding a connecting link between the two statements, with an effect of lending greater cohesion and amplitude to his music. In short, he does not merely vary another man's work; he composes one of his own. This is how he does it here:

THE LINK

VARIATION VI: *Allegro, ma non troppo e serioso.* The serious matter of this Variation is doubtless that it begins as a canon. It goes on later in free imitation, which in a way is even more serious. Strict canon may be thought more difficult to write than freely imitative music, where the composer can choose whatever subterfuge he likes to relieve himself of what is the most rigorous of musical devices. That is true in a sense, of course; but the fact remains that a strict canon is a matter of luck quite as much as of judgment. It either goes or it does not, and must therefore either be carried out mechanically or else abandoned. Free imitation, on the other hand, although it certainly allows the composer to write what he chooses, imposes on him the duty to do the best he can. It does not absolve him from using his imagination, as a strict canon does, once it has been found to fit. The art of composition is, in fact, very largely a matter of skill in making subterfuges look like perfectly natural events. Beethoven's free imitation, here as elsewhere, is immensely superior to any solution of a normal contrapuntal problem because it shows at every turn his astonishing power of making formality pliant to his particular needs. A longish musical quotation must be given to show various points of his ingenious handling:

Allegro, ma non troppo e serioso

Up to and including bar 7 we have a strict canon at the octave (actually two or three octaves apart), except that the bass in bar 4 takes a slightly different turn, just to show that music, not pedantry, is the composer's concern. Then, at bar 8, the lower part suddenly becomes contracted by the omission of one beat, and the upper part follows with the same elision, which makes the passage smooth. Next come two bars filled with similar figures in the right hand, set over a bass derived from the semiquaver motion already established. But a subtle harmonic change is made in that bass by the flattening of the A the second time. The process is then reversed between the hands, the repetitions being exact this time, save for a single note (C instead of D) in the second beat of bar 12, which leads on to the restatement of the rising figure a degree higher, Beethoven still showing Diabelli how to avoid the offence of using rosalias without adapting them to a purpose. The remaining four bars tighten the rising figures rhythmically, on the analogy of Ex. 9. The first section is then repeated and a second follows which, so to speak, turns the first upside down, though again by no means merely with geometrical regularity.

But what has become of Diabelli's theme? To look at Ex. 11, it would seem to have entirely disappeared. As a matter of fact it always remains at the base of the musical structure. Comparing Exx. 1 and 11, we find that there are far more resemblances than divergences, so far as the essential structure as distinct from the mere lay-out is concerned. The shake in the upbeat of Ex. 11, for instance, is a simple transformation of Diabelli's chirpy figure in the same place; Beethoven's semiquaver arpeggios are based on Diabelli's repeated chords in bars 1–8; the harmonic change from tonic to dominant is still in the same place and the bass figure in Beethoven's fourth bar is not very different from that in Diabelli's third; nor have the latter's rosalias quite disappeared, as we have already seen.

VARIATION VII: *Un poco più allegro.* This is a vigorous piece beginning with an incisive cross-rhythm for the right hand followed by bold triplet figures. The bass is throughout in bare octaves. For the first time the composer uses an alternative ending at the repeat of the first part to lead into the second. This is not merely a link like that shown in Ex. 10, but actually a new turning taken by the composer to lead him on to what is to come. Incidentally, this shows how essential it is that all the repeats in the Diabelli Variations should be played as indicated, even where they ask for mere note-for-note repetition, if the whole work is not to be thrown out of proportion.

The bass progressions, especially in the second part, are uncommonly bold: they include diminished and augmented fourths which are made to sound even more daring by clashing against the upper harmony. Yet everything proceeds with perfect logic and resolves itself harmoniously because it moves towards the prevailing C major at the end with an unfailingly apt adjustment of the contrasting tonalities.

VARIATION VIII: *Poco vivace.* This time it is the bass that moves rapidly, while the right hand plays a sustained melody in chords. The whole atmosphere is completely changed, for although the tempo remains animated, all is gentleness and tenderness. The theme has all but disappeared, but its ghost, so to speak, hovers over the house in which it lived, whose main structural features are recognizable, though perceived as in a dream. So far there has been fantasy, wit and ingenuity; but here is poetry.

VARIATION IX: *Allegro pesante e risoluto.* Poetry vanishes again, as it should, since in a work of this kind it makes its effect most surely by coming fleetingly and unawares. It gives way to a robust and rather impatient humour. For the first time the music goes into the tonic minor key and for the second time since the first Variation into a 4-4 measure. The whole piece is based, thematically, on Diabelli's opening figure:

Ex. 12

But we are otherwise very far indeed from the 'cobbler's patch,' for this is Beethoven in his richest and ripest humour.   Where Diabelli keeps anxiously to his dominant after the conclusion of the first part, lest he should be led too far astray to turn back home to the tonic in time, Beethoven plunges recklessly into A♭ major, and then into D♭, whence, in less time than it would take his publisher-patron to venture into the next key but one, he goes all round the world of tonality by an enharmonic change from D♭ to C♯ and back again, with chromatically rising harmony above it which is not only rich and interesting in itself, but constitutes yet one more demonstration to Diabelli of how much better a genius can employ himself than in writing rosalias.

VARIATION X: *Presto.*   C major is restored.   Here is a flash of wit, going by so fast that the composer cannot find time enough to say all he has to say unless he abandons the convention of saying it all twice over.   He therefore discards repeat marks and writes out the music at full length without the exact repetition of any single feature.   Thus the new presentation of the first five bars of the theme appears as follows:

while the passage that would normally be their mere restatement takes this form:

And so on throughout the Variation.   The whole piece is purely harmonic, in the sense that each chord is a value in itself, arranged vertically, not a cross-section in a succession of horizontal parts, as in polyphonic writing.   This winged and airy scherzo is a particularly characteristic piece of keyboard writing.

VARIATION XI: *Allegretto.* Here, on the other hand, we have a distinctly polyphonic texture, with parts moving horizontally, as though played by several single-voiced instruments:

Ex. 15

The whole piece has a kind of affectionate humour. A curious and delightful feature is the contraction of the last of the regular four-bar phrases into three bars, which gives the Variation an unforeseen epigrammatic ending. The first part remains unrepeated.

VARIATION XII: *Un poco più mosso.* Here no repeats are marked at all, but actually the second part is repeated, though not quite literally, while the first is not. We thus see some glimmerings of a justification for the deliberate avoidance of the repeat in the first part of Variation XI. At any rate we may be sure that it is not due to a printer's mistake, much less to one on the composer's part. This Variation is distinguished by smoothly running quaver figures in a variety of three-note chord formations. Thematically it is kept rather featureless, and this impression is strengthened by chromatic inflections which create fascinating momentary ambiguities of key.

VARIATION XIII: *Vivace.* Here we return to greater formality again and to regular repeats. The Variation is a comic little piece, rather in the style of Beethoven's later sets of Bagatelles, based mainly on a rhythmic figure—a kind of loud postman's knock—followed by pauses and two single, more timid raps. An oddity is that the piece, although distinctly in the C major key of the theme, begins in A minor.

VARIATION XIV: *Grave e maestoso.* This is a complete contrast, almost in the nature of a funeral march. A double-dotted rhythm, as of muffled drums, accompanies interlaced figures of this type:

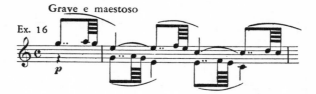

Ex. 16

which appear in plain tonic and dominant at first. But the harmony in the bars corresponding to bars 9–16 of Diabelli's tune is extremely interesting and leads, surprisingly, to E minor instead of G major,

though the second part opens in the latter key.   But what occupied
Diabelli's ninth to sixteenth bars now only takes up Beethoven's fifth
to eighth, after which the first part has arrived at its close.   The
composer has in fact halved the extent of his music to compensate for
its much longer duration at the slow pace adopted for this Variation, and
the same is done for the second part.   Both parts are, however, repeated.

VARIATION XV: *Presto scherzando.*   A succession of light cantering
dactyls, played in even *pianissimo*, represents Diabelli's bars 1–8 and
17–27, without modulation, but with slight chromatic deflections,
whereas the rest of the tune is varied by chains of crotchet chords, the
first of which describes a sharp modulatory curve and so makes a
cadence of the most enchanting harmonic beauty:

VARIATION XVI: *Allegro.*   A march-like movement with a continuous semiquaver accompaniment in broken octaves, sometimes
plain and sometimes decorated with passing notes a whole tone or a
semitone away.   I illustrate the lay-out of the whole piece by a
specimen from the second section, which also shows a very interesting
enharmonic modulation (G♯ turned into A♭):

A further quotation must be given to show how the sixteenth Variation merges directly into the seventeenth:

In the printed copies of the work the connection is not, of course, shown in this way, for each Variation appears as a separate piece; but the effect in performance must nevertheless be that there is no break between these two Variations, as the inconclusive ending of Variation XVI quite clearly shows.   And it may perhaps be reasonably argued from this particular case that no very conspicuous breaks should be made between any of the Variations, although in most other cases, though not all, the final cadence is conclusive and each section apparently self contained.

VARIATION XVII: *Allegro*.   The '*allegro*' is not Beethoven's, but the continuation of the pace of the preceding Variation is obviously intended, failing any contradiction, and the fact that no new tempo direction is given is another proof that these two Variations must be played without the least interruption between them.   But we find some other evidence that Beethoven wished continuity to be preserved throughout the whole work: whenever there is a change of key or time-signature between one Variation and the next, the necessary indication is made, not only at the beginning of the new section, but already at the end of the old one, behind the concluding double bar.

The semiquavers, it will have been seen from Ex. 19, have passed into the right hand.   The figuration is new, but the principle of semitonic deflection remains.   The rhythmic bass persists, with the dotted figures placed in various ways, and it is played in bare octaves throughout.   The music is clear in texture and harmonically uncomplicated, compared with other portions of the work.   It is as though Beethoven had purposely avoided complexity in order to make the next Variation more mysterious by contrast.

VARIATION XVIII: *Moderato.*   Diabelli is now left immeasurably behind, and we have here pure Beethoven in the manner of the late quartets rather than of the final keyboard works.   True, the formal landmarks of the theme are still discernible, but the music blends a baffling waywardness of expression with a subtle use of technical resources in a way that must have reduced poor Diabelli to a state of abject humility, unless he was so utterly devoid of perception as either to take half the credit for this piece to himself or not to understand it at all.

The Variation begins thus:

The two initial phrases in contrary motion, marked *a* and *b* above, are at once exchanged in double counterpoint, and when they recur two bars later there is something like a repetition by means of sequence or rosalia, but with a deliberate and masterly avoidance of any sort of exact reproduction.   And as if to show Diabelli once again how such pedantic restatements can be avoided by a composer of imagination, Beethoven reproduces the phrase *c* with no less than three important alterations (see end of the quotation above).   He (1) extends it by a suspension tied over the bar, he (2) changes the rising figure in the middle part to an ascending scale and (3), whereas he has screwed up the melody by a whole tone, he drops the bass by the same interval. But that is not all: when he comes to the juncture at which Diabelli introduces his rosalia, he again eschews that device in a new way, as is shown in the next musical quotation, to which I have added in brackets the kind of ordinary sequential extension a composer of no more

F

creative power than Diabelli himself would have employed to vary
the theme:

Ex. 21

VARIATION XIX: *Presto*.   We again emerge from mysterious twi-
light for a moment.   But it is only a flash: this Variation rushes past
at a great rate and does not involve itself in any refinements of new
presentation, so that Beethoven accepts even the rosalias without doing
much to mitigate them.   Nor is the treatment of the tonic-and-
dominant portion of the theme, with its closely telescoped canons at
the octave, of any special significance.   But there may be a reason for
this reticence, and that is to give greater effect to what is to follow,
after a close that leaves the music curiously suspended in mid-air.

VARIATION XX: *Andante*.   What comes now is the most baffling
and haunting music in the whole work, a modification of the theme
that seems to have arisen from nothing but the dropping fourth, C–G,
which Diabelli was clumsy enough to double between tune and bass
in the first bar of his country dance.   Beethoven here retains a regular
periodicity: there are still thirty-two bars (without repeats, however);
but he is for the moment interested in almost nothing but harmony,
and harmony that is still the strangest imaginable in any music which
retains the major-minor system of tonality.   There is an atmosphere
at once solemn and sinister about this Variation that somehow makes
one think of it as an apt introduction to the witches' scene in the
fourth act of *Macbeth*.   Nothing less than Shakespearian drama can
come to mind, for one cannot think of weirdness without beauty here,
and beauty of an unearthly and unfathomable kind predominates.
There is no traceable melody and only the barest suggestion of rhythmic pattern; yet the whole piece shapes itself inevitably from beginning
to end, so that, although the hearer is puzzled by it, he cannot imagine
a single change that could possibly make it more convincing.

VARIATION XXI: *Allegro con brio—meno allegro*.   Suddenly there
is a vigorous outburst of brilliant shakes followed by octave drops,
falling down through four octaves, first in the tonic and then in the
dominant.   This takes the hearer who is unfamiliar with the work
completely by surprise, for it seems to open a Variation as purely
virtuosic as a keyboard transcription of a Paganini capriccio.   But it

represents the first eight bars of the theme only, and the listener's astonishment does not lessen when he finds that the 'rosalia' part is treated entirely differently, with a change from common time to 3–4, from rhythmic energy to an interlacing of soft and sustained melodic parts, and from a brisk pace to a slower tempo. It is as though Beethoven had at first written two different variations and then, with some humorous intention the explanation of which has been lost, discarded half of each and patched together what remained.

VARIATION XXII: *Molto allegro.* That he was certainly in a humorously impatient mood when he arrived at this part of the work is shown by the present Variation, which is in the nature of an interlude. In addition to the tempo indication Beethoven marked it 'Alla "Notte e giorno faticar" di Mozart.' Those who do not recognize the title may still know what the allusion means the moment they hear this motif:

Ex. 22

which is obviously derived from Diabelli's bass, and they will hardly be put off by the fact that it is transposed from Mozart's F major into Diabelli's C major. It is, of course, Leporello's complaint at the opening of *Don Giovanni* that he has to slave day and night for his master and is getting little reward and no pleasure in return for his pains. It seems that Diabelli was impatient to bring out the Variations and that Beethoven, urged by his publisher 'day and night' to finish them, cast himself for the part of Leporello hard at work for an exacting taskmaster. But as he was offered an exceptionally good fee for the work, we may be sure that he did not take the quotation seriously. It is simply a characteristic manifestation of his humour. Nor need we suspect that he failed to derive pleasure from the composition of the Variations. They are themselves the best witness to the contrary.

VARIATION XXIII: *Assai allegro.* The work proceeds with unabating vigour of inventiveness. The theme is once more closely adhered to in this Variation, which is cut into separate portions by emphatic chords at the beginning of its periods. The first part of each section of the theme is treated in smoothly running semiquaver phrases in contrary motion, the second in detached chords broken up by rapid syncopation.

VARIATION XXIV: FUGHETTA—*Andante.* We are once more a long way from the theme, although there is no feeling of irrelevance and its two main sections are clearly differentiated, the second bringing the principle of thematic inversion into the composer's scheme. The four-part fugal texture is remarkable for not following the laws of either 'real' or 'tonal' fugue-writing, but adjusting itself to both tonic and dominant positions by a compromise between the two:

Ex. 23

Andante

una corda

The change from the descending fourth to a fifth is distinctly 'tonal,' but the fact that the next note restores the original interval of a minor sixth and that the succeeding intervals retain their first relationship approximates more to the procedure of a 'real' fugue. The episodic passages remain closely related to the subject and the four-part texture is conscientiously respected throughout: where one part happens to be silent for a moment, it is still accounted for by rests.

VARIATION XXV: *Allegro.* On a moving bass rather resembling gently rolling waves the right hand plays a simple broken rhythm in chords. A fascinating feature is the attempt of the first section to establish A minor definitely and its immediate frustration by the intervention of other keys—C major at first for the repeat and then F major for the continuation. Other harmonic deflections leading as far away as Db major, and then sharply back to C major, occur in the second section.

VARIATION XXVI: No tempo indication is given here, but from the nature of the music as well as the direction that the expression is to be *piacevole* (pleasant) it is clear enough that the motion should be moderate. The figuration looks as though it were devised in pairs of triplets, but the time-signature of 3–8 shows that there are two semi-quavers to each beat and that the grouping in threes is merely a matter of phrasing, six notes being slurred together against the beat and across the bar-lines throughout:

Ex. 24   (R.H.)   (L.H.)   (R.H.)   (L.H.)

p piacevole

VARIATION XXVII: *Vivace.* Now, however, while the time remains 3–8, there are three triplets to the bar, and the music is much more lively and energetic, though technically not unlike the preceding variation.   Descending groups of figures divided between the two hands and runs in contrary motion which occupy the space of the rosalia incident closely resemble the composer's procedure in Variation XXVI.

VARIATION XXVIII: *Allegro.*   The feeling of contrast is now all the greater for having been left indeterminate between the last two Variations.   There is a new time-signature, too:

Ex.25 Allegro

The *staccato* delivery persists from beginning to end, and the regular *sforzandi* on each beat never cease during the whole of the first section and only rarely in the second, though then with an all the more surprising effect.

VARIATION XXIX: *Adagio, ma non troppo.*   This is only the third really slow Variation (and only the second bearing a tempo indication slower than *andante*).   C minor returns, and while it had previously been established for the duration of one variation only (Var. IX), it now persists for the next three.   As these are all more or less slow, the minor key has plenty of time to establish itself thoroughly, as it is indeed made to do for a very definite reason that will show itself presently.

We have seen in Variation XIV that Beethoven, to compensate for the greater amount of time occupied by the music, halved the number of bars of the theme.   Here he condenses even more drastically, covering the whole ground in a mere twelve bars and thus, for the first time, departing from Diabelli's regular metrical scheme more than incidentally, though even here it is still perceptible.

VARIATION XXX: *Andante, sempre cantabile.*   The original shape becomes even more indeterminate: the first section occupies twelve bars, without repeat, while the second contains only four, repeated, the proportion being thus 12 to 8, at any rate in appearance.   Actually the place corresponding to the opening of the original second section comes at the ninth bar of the present first, so that, counting the repeat, there are eight bars plus twelve, the double bar standing in the middle of the second section instead of at its beginning.   Each single bar of the Variation corresponds to two of the theme.   The following diagram will make the relationship clearer:

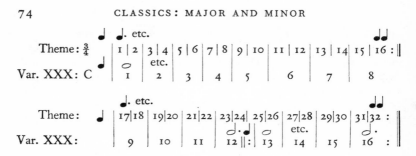

This is an extraordinarily beautiful and profound movement with softly and smoothly interlaced parts beginning in free imitation:

The music is richly chromatic and, winding through a series of modulatory changes on the flat side of the circle of keys, arrives at A♭ major where Diabelli, at the end of his first section, had merely got to the dominant. The dotted figures (*a*) are now turned upwards instead of down, so that the musical progress appears to be effected by inversion; but Beethoven is not content to let the music simply reflect itself, as in a pool: he continually makes it undergo new developments. It should be noted what has become of Diabelli's rosalia: an exchange of two different figures between the two hands while they move a whole tone upwards:

VARIATION XXXI: *Lento, molto espressivo.* The time now is 9–8, so slow as to accommodate note-values that can become as small as $\frac{1}{128}$ of a semibreve. The figuration is thus extremely rapid at times, although the basic tempo is very deliberate, as is often the case in

Mozart's slow variations.   But Beethoven, unlike Mozart, who as a rule made his slow variations inordinately long by adhering to the metrical divisions of his theme, condenses his music as he had already done in another slow movement (Var. XIV), only much less systematically.   There is, in fact, a very baffling feature about the present Variation.   It is plain enough that the first two bars of 9–8 time cover the same ground as Diabelli's first eight.   The tonic-and-dominant pair is still present, and the effect is now that of a transformation of each half occupying three groups of triple rhythm, thus:

The rest of the first section, up to the repeat, consisting of four bars, corresponds to Diabelli's bars 9–16.

It is after the repetition, when there is an alternative bar to conclude the first section, that we come upon a very striking oddity; for that alternative bar contains not nine quavers, as it should according to the time-signature, but twelve, and yet the time-signature has not been altered by the composer.   No metrical explanation can be found for this anomaly—at any rate not immediately, since, taking three of Beethoven's quavers (a third of his 9–8 bars) as a unit, we do not arrive at Diabelli's sixteen bars at the end of the first section, but at eighteen with the first ending and at the very odd number of nineteen with the alternative one.   But we now discover that the second

section is shorter by one 9–8 bar (or three units) than the first, so that
with five normal bars it would arrive at the figure 15 to correspond
with Diabelli's second group of sixteen bars.   Beethoven, however,
has again extended his last bar by three beats and thus given it twelve
quavers (or four units), so that now he does arrive at an exact equivalent of Diabelli's number of bars and thus ends normally after all
what he had begun as a movement built up of very abnormal periods.
The only things that remain difficult to explain, therefore, are the
apparently redundant bar in the first section and the fact that he did
not mark any change of time-signature when he passed from 9–8 to
12–8.

VARIATION XXXII: FUGA—*Allegro*.   The preceding Variation
had no full close, but remained arrested on a dominant seventh chord
of Eb major.   We now see the reason for the long stretch of C minor,
covering the last three variations—all of them slow ones: it was to
prepare us for the establishment of its nearest relative among the major
keys, from which C major would have been too far distant to justify
a movement in Eb major which is in the nature of a final summing-up.
For this fugue now definitely abandons the metrical plan of the theme
and develops at considerable length.

But why, it may be asked, must it be in Eb at all?   We have had
C major and minor for so long a time that we might have endured it
to the end, more especially as we expect a certain monotony of key in
a variation work.   There is an explanation, though, which on reflection will, I think, seem perfectly convincing.   The fugue is so
large and so important that, had it been in the principal key of the
work, it would inevitably have made the effect of a crowning feat of
composition, a finale to which any afterthought would have been an
irremediable anticlimax.   But Beethoven did have an afterthought
and so had at all costs to see to it that the fugue did not make an
impression of finality.   The only way to do this was obviously to let
it appear in a key foreign to the work as a whole, yet not so unrelated
as to make this large movement seem irrelevant.   Hence Eb major and
the long preparation for that key by its relative minor.

The last Variation but one is a double fugue, developing two
subjects simultaneously:

Ex. 29

There is no necessity to try to connect these two themes with anything
in Diabelli's tune or even to make the obvious point that Beethoven's

repeated notes come from the repeated chords in the theme; but there is about the whole fugue a subtle suggestion of relationship to the work as a whole rather than to the tune on which it is based, because it is a climax that would not have grown into just what it is if it had not been that the composer's inspiration had been fired by the effort of carrying out a great task; and this is true even if one remembers that among Beethoven's sketches for Op. 120 those for the present fugue were made quite early, long before some of the variations now standing in front of it were written.   Sketching is not composing, and there is no question that this fugue is a crowning feat of composition which cannot be imagined to have been just the same had it been written as a separate piece.

With the two subjects quoted in Ex. 29 before his eyes the reader will not find it difficult to follow the convolutions they undergo, either in performance or on paper.   A curious fact is that, although a fugue is supposed to be much more strictly written than a fughetta, Beethoven here does not mark all the rests to indicate a four-part texture, as in Variation XXIV, but allows the fugue to appear sometimes in three parts and sometimes in four.   Contrapuntal devices such as inversion (turning a subject upside down) and stretto (overlapping of the entries of a subject) abound, but not augmentation or diminution, which in this case would merely have obscured the contrast between the shorter and longer note-values of the two subjects.   On the other hand, about two-thirds of the way through, Beethoven introduces a contrast in motion by adding a new quaver pattern to a slightly transformed presentation of the crotchet subject. Here the second subject remains absent for some time, but it comes in with an effect of heightened tension towards the end.

Suddenly, on the dominant of A♭ major, the music breaks off and halts on a chord of the diminished seventh that stands discordantly over the dominant note (E♭), which remains obstinately fixed.   This is followed by an extended arpeggio on the same chord, with the bass E♮ still sustained by the pedal, and to this succeeds one of Beethoven's most astonishing and magical transitions, leading directly to the final Variation:

VARIATION XXXIII: *Tempo di minuetto, moderato*:

p grazioso e dolce

This finale, which is marked 'but not dragging' in addition to *moderato*, keeps quite closely to Diabelli's theme in its general conduct, so to speak, though it is immeasurably more beautiful—a kind of limpid sunset illumination of it. The two pairs of sixteen bars of the theme are reduced to two pairs of twelve, which however does not mean that the tune has been shortened. On the contrary, it has been extended: Beethoven makes one of his bars correspond to two of Diabelli's, so that he has four left over, which he fills by adding a sort of cadential, non-thematic, purely decorative appendix to the theme, as though he could not leave the topic after all this time without an extra comment. This happens at the end of each section and quite astonishingly well suggests a feeling of peroration.

Still, mere rhetorical flourishes are not enough to conclude so vast a discourse, and when Beethoven has actually done with the theme, he adds a coda exactly as long as the last variant of the theme itself, not counting the repeats of the former, or exactly half as long if they are counted. This is one of the most wonderful and poetical final pages of his last period. He had written magnificent codas long before 1823, codas which summed up a movement or a work inimitably; but here is not so much a summing-up as a dispersal, a manner of saying farewell to a work entirely characteristic of his fullest maturity. The material seems to be gradually broken up and scattered into dust by being dissolved into ornamental figures of gossamer lightness. Nothing could have been less conventional or more unexpected than this leave-taking of an overwhelmingly great work, and it is quite conceivable that at a first hearing it may merely perplex, perhaps even disappoint the listener who expects some stately proclamation or some positive affirmation at the close of the long examination to which a theme has been subjected. But once it is realized that Beethoven wrote these Variations to give an outlet to his inexhaustible fantasy and poetry, not for the sake of demonstrating that Diabelli's country dance was worth so much attention, which in any case he did not believe, it will also be admitted that a more fitting close to such a work could not possibly be imagined.

Schubert's Favourite Device

(*Music & Letters*, October 1928)

THE signs of strong personality in an artist's work, though they may be but vaguely apprehended by the bulk of his admirers, appear rarely quite impenetrable to the observer versed in the chemistry of art, for they may as a rule be traced ultimately to purely technical procedures. They may be so recondite as to be inexplicable to the artist himself and only with difficulty accessible to the analytical mind projected upon them subsequently to the procedure of creation. But Schubert is the most transparent of composers. His style bears a hall-mark that is plain to all. Anyone with even a superficial knowledge of his work, combined with the most elementary musicianship, who was asked to name the chief outward distinction of his writing would surely, without hesitation, refer to his free and frequent interchange of the major and minor modes. It is a device as conspicuous and familiar as Rembrandt's chiaroscuro, though no such convenient tag has as yet been found for it. If such a descriptive label were really needed for what must be called a mannerism, but a mannerism used again and again in its primeval innocence to serve the ends of genius, there could be no objection to our talking about Schubert's chiaroscuro.

The trick of distributing harmonic light and shade in this way is not a subtle one: it verges upon the commonplace in its obviousness. It was not even a new one in Schubert's time; but it is this very simplicity that lies in the inmost kernel of Schubert's art which makes him of all the great masters the most accessible. He, less than any of them, causes the untutored music-lover to shy at the forbidding classicality which is unfortunately thrust posthumously upon those most qualified to give universal delight. He lightly accepted the handiest and most ancient means of producing a commonly understood musical effect: his reward for not being over-fastidious is a measure of freedom from the unhappy exclusiveness of the great that is enjoyed by no other musical classic—perhaps by no classic of any sort.

The wonder is that, for all his simple way of helping himself to what came but too readily to his hand, he does not offend any musician who keeps his mind reasonably free from prejudice. That his casualness did not prevent him from producing superb art with surprising frequency is due to an extraordinary fund of instinctive good sense which he had to set against it.   Though the practice of making major and minor alternate is nearly as old as any music using these scales, his way of carrying it out is as startlingly and unaccountably different as his music altogether was from that of his predecessors.   In fact, it brings us as near as anything may to discovering the secret of the newness of Schubert's music.   The novelty of his use of transitions from major to minor, and more especially from minor to major, is in part technical, as may be judged from the decisive steps and short cuts they enabled him to make in modulation ; but it is a literary—and often literal—employment that gives the device the character of a new departure, of a heading at full tilt towards romanticism, with its striving to convert what had once served purely musical ends into a kind of hyper-flexible vocabulary for the expression of poetical ideas in a way that was at once more vague and more clearly illuminating than mere words.

Schubert, of all the great masters, is seen least clearly as a link in musical evolution.   He appears even to a fairly close scrutiny as a curiously detached phenomenon, the characteristics of whose idiom are singularly little apparent in his precursors and become all but lost again after his disappearance.   It is true that he retained form exactly as composers before him had used it ; but that connects him only superficially with the chain of events, for he was utterly unenterprising in this direction and would have adopted and somehow filled any musical form that might have enjoyed currency in his days in place of the prevalent moulds of the sonata, the scherzo and trio, the rondo and the varied theme.   If anywhere, it is in his handling of major and minor that his connection with what came before and after is to be seen.   The fact that he uses the procedure at all, and so readily, shows his indebtedness to the past : but his individual manner of using it points to the future.   There we have the significance of this favourite device of his, not only as the chief symptom of his style, but as a clue to his place in musical history seen as a continuous sequence of events rather than a series of separate occurrences.   It can be traced as far back into medieval history as the moment at which the tierce de Picardie made the finality of the major triad triumph decisively over the comparatively inconclusive minor [1]; and there is no limit to what it may be considered to have engendered.   Before he was twenty, Schubert made a setting of a short poem by Hölty, 'Klage,' where he was induced by the poetic antithesis of a happy past and an unhappy present to commit the formal trespass of starting the song in F major and ending it in D minor, a thing quite inexcusable then on musical grounds and only thought permissible by a very daring youngster on

---

[1] Johannes de Muris, in the fourteenth century, still considered both the major and minor triads as discords.

a literary plea. We need but telescope the procedure a little—the song is not thirty bars long—and we have the modern trick of adding the sixth to the final chord which amounts to nothing more than the production of a clash between the relative major and minor triads. The habit of going into the relative major for the last movement or the final pages of a work cast in a minor key, which has grown exasperating with some composers, especially the Frenchmen and Belgians of the César Franck school, is also to be traced to Schubert. It is a singularity of his petrified into a convention and then undeservedly exalted into a principle. Again, Schubert brings unrelated keys into such perilous proximity at times by his steep modulations that modern polytonality is none the less closely related to his harmonic approximations because it took musicians another century to make the decisive final contraction. That he did not share his contemporaries' rigid adherence to a key centre is shown by the frequent estrangement in tonality of his sonata movements as well as by his modulations and his capricious drawing upon major and minor.

But what attaches Schubert immediately to those who followed him is his discovery of the literary implications of major and minor. It makes him the first to wed poetry and song with a genius unknown since the days of the madrigalists and lutenists and in a way that differed from theirs, the first conspicuous modern figure among the passionate matchmakers between music and words. Nevertheless, his ideas as to the fitness of such unions are profoundly influenced by tradition. His view of major and minor as vehicles of expression is not markedly different from that of Josquin des Prés and the rest of the 'Picardesque' composers of the fifteenth and sixteenth centuries. Like them, he felt that relatively to the major triad that of the minor is discordant. But if to them it was so lacking in finality that they had to sharpen the third degree of any mode containing the minor third in the concluding chord or to omit it altogether rather than risk the ambiguous impression left by the minor triad, he welcomed that impression as a means of creating poetic inferences more varied and suggestive than any composer before him had done. In the main he firmly held to the notion, still common to-day, that minor spells the mood of the departure platform, while the major is proper to the arrival platform. Only the modern cynic who has lost his respect for key altogether would remind us that there may be circumstances in which departure means joy and arrival vexation. Schubert and his time did not quibble about individual cases; he and his poets were content to generalize about broad human verities. They did it badly at times, no doubt, with neither taste nor insight; but on the whole they were right.

In his uses of major and minor Schubert was almost infallibly right

To him the former meant happiness, confidence, strength, consolation, all that life enters on the credit side of human fate; the latter was for him sadness, discouragement, grief, trouble. Trouble, indeed, it is in all the incontrovertible literalness of technicalities. A fundamental tonic note sounds the major seventeenth, which is the major third in the third octave above, as its fourth harmonic, and the introduction of the minor third produces, to an ear sensitive enough to perceive the overtone, a clash comparable to the confusion of waves in a pond into which two pebbles have been cast at the same moment. The chord that meant trouble and agitation to Josquin still meant it to Schubert, and had in fact meant it to every composer between them. More than that: it was for some of them a chord distinctly subordinate on purely theoretical grounds to the major triad, whose freedom from inharmonious disarray it did not possess. Rameau, for instance, called the major mode 'the sovereign of harmony' and regarded the minor as its satellite, emanating from it by inversion.

There is no reason to think that Schubert knew this scholastic distinction or remembered it if Salieri or whosoever had told him of it. One must not without clear proof regard the great composers as having been theorists otherwise than by instinct. But Schubert was somehow right about his preference of the major mode, at any rate in so far as his own purposes were concerned. And now that the word has slipped out, let it be admitted that preference is what it comes to with him. He is fully aware, it must be repeated, that the minor mode paints every form of human misery far more poignantly than the major: it becomes more prominent as the cycle of *Die schöne Müllerin* proceeds to its tragic end, and two-thirds of the songs in the gloomy *Winterreise* are in minor keys. But then, Schubert did not face misery gladly, much less wallow in it: he welcomed any excuse to be relieved of it, as he welcomed the major mode on the slightest provocation. The fact that the minor was tragic for him did not prevent the major from being the more emotional, since he clearly deemed joy a keener emotion than sorrow. It meant more to him, perhaps because he had so much less of it and perhaps only because he evaded life's greater troubles by embracing jollity as a substitute for joy. He had the easy and incurable, or as he would prefer it, incorruptible optimism that was the only possible outlook for so naïve and instinctive a genius.

A glance at the songs will throw much light on Schubert's attitude towards the major and minor modes and on his peculiar manipulation of them. To begin with the most obvious cases, a simple poetic antithesis is often seen to be matched by an equally simple juxtaposition of major and minor. In *Lachen und Weinen* the very title gives the game away. This kind of thing seemed to him so manifestly called for that one need not be surprised to find it in many of the very earliest songs. Examples can be taken almost anywhere from the songs of Schubert's boyhood to the *Schwanengesang*. In 'Der Müller und der Bach' (*Schöne Müllerin*, No. 19) the despairing miller speaks in minor and is answered by the consolatory brook in major until he himself falls into that mode at the end. It is worth noting that here for once the melancholy is intensified by the Neapolitan sixth which makes a kind of redoubled minor effect that is very sparingly used melodically [2] by a composer so ready to dispel trouble. The setting of Werner's *Morgenlied* has a similar dialogue between the poet and the birds. 'Rückblick' (*Winterreise*, No. 8) has a major section for a reminiscence of summer. In *Die Rose* the antithesis is between heat and cold, in *Der Jüngling auf dem Hügel* between grief and consolation, and in *Am Grabe Anselmos* between sorrow and happy recollection. The storm that rages in the first part of *Die junge Nonne* is in F minor and the ensuing calm rings out in the tonic major, an admirable contrast being thus obtained without any violent breaking away from the original musical idea. In the wonderful *Totengräberweise* the opposition between the ideas of death and resurrection is quite simply enforced by that between F♯ minor and major, in spite of the surrounding modulations which border on an extravagance that might well have driven the righteous Franz Schubert of Dresden to another indignant request not to be confused with his Viennese namesake.

An amusing thing happens in the first verse of *Lebenslied*, where the poet—it is Matthisson—hammers away so fast at his antithetical imagery that the composer cannot possibly ring the changes with the same frequency; but Schubert flutters from minor to major and back as rapidly as he dare. The idea has been set going in his mind and he cannot renounce it, even if it works in badly with his text. It is in such songs as 'Mut' (*Winterreise*, No. 22) and 'Ihr Bild' (*Schwanengesang*, No. 9) that the matching of the modes—or moods—of poetry and music may be seen several degrees more subtly effected. A verbal contrast is still there and has to be dealt with in the peculiar way that has by this time become almost a matter of course with Schubert; but there is no suspicion of interference with the spontaneous shaping of a perfect artistic pattern by an exaggerated deference to the poet. The poise between the two arts is perfect and music knows its worth. In the three cycles alone, if we leave aside the other five hundred odd songs for the moment, there are numberless instances of changes between minor and major which reinforce the poetic idea and often add to it a beautiful significance of their own. In 'Der Neugierige'

---

[2] Harmonically, of course, Neapolitan inflections are uncommonly prevalent in Schubert's music.

—to begin with *Die schöne Müllerin*—there is the apprehensive clouding of B major by a momentary depression of the D♯ to D when the miller reproaches the brook, first with being silent and afterwards with being capricious. 'Tränenregen,' though in A major, ends in the tonic minor, and a similar close is given to 'Die böse Farbe,' which wavers throughout in tonality like a soul in trouble. In 'Trockne Blumen' there is a great major section for the idea of a springtide which the singer is never to see, but just before the end Schubert remembers the true situation and returns to the minor.

The *Winterreise* has changes to the minor for the painful resolve in 'Der Lindenbaum,' the absence of a letter in 'Die Post,' the disillusion at the end of 'Frühlingstraum.' Conversely, 'Auf dem Flusse' goes into the major at the episode of the lover's carving the loved one's name into the ice, and to enforce the point Schubert cunningly poses the voice-part on the major third at the very point of the change. This lovely passage with its tremulous figuration and its stealthily creeping basses one feels to be carried along by a flood of emotion that is due mainly to Schubert's decision to use his pet device just at this juncture, and thus only indirectly to the stimulus of the poetry. It all works so naturally that he often thinks of changing the key signature before he has hit upon a new idea to place behind the double bar. Then something stupendous happens: he quite calmly puts down the old idea and produces an effect so disproportionate to the means employed that he must himself have gasped with astonishment at the priceless treasures he could at times uncover by the simple removal of three flats or addition of three sharps. The very first song of the *Winterreise* springs this surprise, which has the faculty of always renewing itself that is the secret of all great artistic conceits. Even more than to the major section in 'Gute Nacht' this applies perhaps to that in 'Der Wegweiser.' The perennial thrill of this passage is as inescapable as it is unaccountable. One can at best grope after the explanation of the redoubled force of the device in this instance by pointing to the ingenious way in which the tune, after a beginning identical with the minor version, is given a new turn that is both harmonically and poetically ideal, and by suggesting that the tinge of unpleasant self-pity at this point of Wilhelm Müller's poem is effaced by a lucky hit of instinctive taste.

Schubert is so fond of this opening of the sluice-gates of emotion by a sudden release of the major mode that he often delays it deliberately or goes out of his way into the minor for no other purpose than that of indulging his predilection. In *An die Nachtigall* he has the excuse of the word 'ach ' for the intrusion of G minor, but it is not felt to be nearly so strong as his musical intention, which is to give the utmost point to an entrancing G major cadence. For *Auf dem*

Wasser zu singen he uses the key signature of A♭ major and then goes and sets the bulk of the song to A♭ minor for the sheer joy of resolving the key and so letting loose all his feeling in the middle of that sustained E♭ at the end of each verse.

Enough has been said to show that Schubert's peculiar manner of interchanging major and minor is due to a literary mental process. We know, moreover, that he would read through a poem attentively several times to allow his invention to bend to it and then write the music down as fast as his pen could move. The instrumental works, of course, are harmonically coloured in this way no less frequently than the vocal music, but we are so filled with reminiscences of characteristic passages of the kind heard in the songs that we involuntarily think of similar poetic situations whenever we come across one in a symphony, a quartet, a sonata or a piano piece. That Schubert, all unconsciously, had similar flashes of poetical inspiration at such moments can hardly be doubted. The famous description of him as the greatest poet among musicians who ever lived reposes surely in the last analysis upon Liszt's recognition of this obsession with lyrical imagery.

Original as he was and unlike as his music is to anything that came before him, at any rate along the high road of art pursued by his equals, Schubert would have no claim to the distinction of having taken a decisive new departure except for his adaptation of technical resources to a literary purpose. It is by no means exclusively a matter of his treatment of major and minor, but may be seen most clearly in his manipulation of that particular expedient. None of his predecessors, though many of them used it freely enough, did so in anything but a purely musical way. Bach is fond of the tierce de Picardie, which occurs at the close of all but one fugue (XVIII) out of the twenty-four pieces in minor keys in the first book of *The Well-tempered Clavier*, and the long-deferred key of B major in his *French Overture* in B minor for clavier has a ravishing effect. In the Sonatas of Domenico Scarlatti, who appears to a superficial scrutiny to be the true forerunner of Schubert in this particular, there is, of course, no question of anything but an absolutely musical contrivance. In Gluck's *Orfeo* the sudden burst into C major in the duet between the reunited Orpheus and Eurydice, which is the emotional peak of the opera, is still only a musical effect, for it does not occur at a textual point where it is more appropriate than it might have been at several others. *Don Giovanni* has no more striking instance of an unexpected major chord than in the overture [3] and other examples from Mozart that come to mind are also in instrumental works: the slow movement of the piano

[3] The tierces de Picardie at the close of the statue's utterances in the churchyard scene are deliberate archaisms.

G

Sonata in F major (K.332), the first movement of the 'Prague' Symphony (second subject), the G minor Quintet (conversion of the minor cadence in the minuet into the major subject of its trio) or the D minor piano Concerto (coda of finale). Weber, it is true, shows an understanding of the musical colouring of words that looks suspiciously like influence; but Vienna knew Weber too late for the suspicion to grow into an accusation.

Doubt grows stronger in the case of Beethoven. He was not as close a contemporary as Weber, but he was a co-citizen, and Schubert could not have withstood the magnetic influence diffused throughout Vienna by so compelling a genius even if he had not admired him as he did. So far as there is any indebtedness to be traced in the singularly independent Schubert, Beethoven is the only one among the great masters who left a noticeable mark upon him. No other composer, certainly, used the interchange of minor and major so much before the one whose very finger-print it was to become. But it is still, even with Beethoven, a purely musical objective, as indeed it must needs be in the case of a composer so much more at his ease with instrumental than vocal music. Even *Fidelio*, in which Schubert must have soaked himself at his most impressionable age, contains no mutations between major and minor which seem to have been irresistibly dictated by the text. The two outstanding passages of the kind are the major portion of the arias of Marcellina and Pizarro in the first act, and they would impose a hard strain on anyone anxious to credit Beethoven with the creation of an important precedent in the use of a procedure that is more than any other in music Schubert's own. It may occur elsewhere in Beethoven's vocal works, as it certainly occurs in those of many pre-Schubertian composers; but its appearance there is either a casual musical turn or a momentary matter of euphony. Even if, in isolated cases, it throws light on the composer's text, the expedient remains only one of many possible ways of turning the phrase musically. But with Schubert one feels in a hundred instances that for the first time no other way was possible. His illumination of literary images by a striking opposition of major and minor is a singularity of style held within bounds of art by a great instinct of fitness. It is not only the very essence of his idiom because it grew into an almost excessive mannerism, but a clear indication of his significance for the music that was to come; because he was the first to make it into a vehicle for the expression of things outside music which was to be the distinction—or the bane, if you will—of the century he ushered in. His changing cloud and sunlight effects, his hoverings between fair and rainy weather, make him in a sense the John Constable of music, a more fitting comparison when all is said than that which brought up the name of Rembrandt at the beginning of this article.   What Constable was for the Impressionists—a pioneer who came into the world too soon—Schubert is in a way for later musicians.   In him we see the April weather of romanticism, a romanticism still in its coy springtide and free as yet from the sultriness that was to make it scarcely bearable at times in the height of its season.

The Prophecies of Dussek

(*Musical Opinion*, December 1927–August 1928)

It is one of the most common fallacies in musical criticism to accept unchallenged a good many petrified views of minor composers of the past. Unfortunately, it is fatally easy for the critical mind to form a fairly accurate idea of a vast deal of music of secondary importance without ever having heard or seen it. The expert, directly he knows a small composer's place in history, the influences that were at work in forming him, and the social environment in which he lived, can as a rule be so sure of his man that he may confidently rush a few generalities into print without the least fear of going so far wrong as to risk censure. He need not be acquainted with a bar of music by Muffat, or Jommelli, or Hasse, or Isouard, to have a more or less precise notion of their work. It is in fact startling to find how again and again one discovers, on reading through the score of a previously unknown work by an unfamiliar composer, that it is as like the idea one had formed of it as one pea is to another.

Even critics who study every phase of music with intelligent curiosity are in danger of arriving sooner or later at a stage where they will feel so secure in purely deductive valuations that they will no longer think it worth while to verify them by actual perusal. But it is the critic's business to have first-hand knowledge, not only of what he discusses in detail, but even of what he touches upon in a casual reference. If he persists in trusting to that historical instinct which can certainly be cultivated to a remarkable degree of safety, he will one day be found to have recklessly exposed a vulnerable spot in his critical armour.

This brings me to my case in point—Dussek. Here is a composer whose sonatinas we have all practised in those far-off days when we and the piano were on terms of reciprocal coolness, and of whose work most of us have steered assiduously clear ever since. We have vague recollections of a neatly tinkling music, of something dapper and debonair and quite devoid of any characteristic flavour save a faded odour of the period to which it belongs. Dussek is usually looked upon as a sort of musical Jane Austen, a mixture of provincial orderliness, primness and small gossip, and few take the trouble in the musician's case, as people happily still do in the novelist's, to ascertain by personal investigation what depth of character and force of style lies behind the apparently tame and humdrum surface. Dussek, directly his Sonatinas are safely behind us, is usually pigeon-holed for the rest of our lives with Clementi, Hummel, Steibelt, Cramer, Himmel, Kalkbrenner, Pleyel, *e tutti quanti*, a host of once fashionable pianist-composers whom we discard with one sweeping gesture as if they were all of exactly the same significance—in other words, of none whatever.   Unfortunately, this summary condemnation will not do, as we shall soon find on examining the case of Dussek in a more judicial spirit; and directly we have found how easy it was to go hopelessly astray in judging him on next to no evidence, we are bound to reflect that it is equally possible for us to have done an injustice to any of the others.   No student of Clementi's sonatas, for instance, fails to revise his opinion of that other bugbear of his youth, and I should not be surprised to find something worth the modern pianist's attention even among the unknown works of Diabelli, while in Czerny's Preludes and Fugues there is some very remarkable music.

Dussek will certainly astonish all those who think themselves safe in their third-hand estimation of him, according to which he can only be dismissed as a composer without originality, more or less exactly like a good many others.   There is no denying that in a sense this view is correct: Dussek really is full of other people's music.   But, one may ask, whose music?   Well, among his contemporaries, he is at least as much like Beethoven as he is like the small fry of virtuosi to which he belongs; and since he was Beethoven's senior by nine years and developed more rapidly than the latter, it is at least questionable whether he was at all influenced by the infinitely greater master. When it comes to the question of innovation—which is, after all, not a question of greatness, but one of resourcefulness—Dussek keeps always a little ahead of Beethoven.   It was only after the former was no longer in the running that the latter shot ahead.

But let us see who the other composers are whom Dussek 'imitates.' It is true that we find traces of Haydn, and more rarely of Mozart in his work; but they are negligible, because they appropriate common currencies rather than personal properties.   What strikes us on playing through his most representative work is one passage after another evocative of composers who were all his juniors.   It is all very well to condemn a creative musician for incessantly reminding one of others: but what if he reminds one of those whom he himself cannot possibly have known?   What if Dussek should prove to have sown the seeds from which were to spring many of the characteristic features in Weber, Schumann, Chopin, Liszt, in the minor romantic piano composers, and even in a musician so late as Brahms?   Are we to interpose a Napoleonic 'la recherche de la paternité est interdite,' lest we rob the great ones in order to pay one of music's smallholders his due?

On the contrary, let us administer justice so impartially that the rich and the poor benefit alike.   Let us see what we can trace that stands to Dussek's credit for being prophetic of the future as well as significant on its own merits.   The examination may be limited to his piano Sonatas, the most interesting branch of his output as well as the most readily accessible to the modern student.[1]

Although to play through the sonatas for the first time is in itself a pleasurably surprising experience, their chief interest lies in the particular aspect they assume next to the music with which they are contemporary, and still more in the curious impression of daring progressiveness they yield when examined in the light of what came after them—in some cases not until long after.   Regarded as an isolated figure detached from the enormous development of keyboard music in the early nineteenth century, Dussek is scarcely an eminent personality; but placed in the rank and file of all the composers who completed the transition from the harpsichord and clavichord style to that of the *fortepiano*, he stands out as a pioneer whom it is difficult to picture as being in truth nothing more, in point of time, than a unit in that regiment of keyboard recruits.   Since his chief attraction for the modern musician is the conspicuous anachronistic position he occupies in history, it is important to fix his career definitely in one's mind in relation to such simultaneous events as are relevant to the present inquiry.

A few biographical details may be of use to peg down the chief events of Dussek's career in the reader's memory.   Born at Čáslav in Bohemia on 9 February 1761, Jan Ladislav Dussek (or Dušek or Dusík) began to learn the piano at the age of five, and the organ at nine.   About 1773 he was sent to Jihlava to be educated at the Jesuit College, and to become a choirboy at the Minorite Church.   Two years later he went on to Kutná Hora and by the time he was sixteen received an appointment as organist there.   He seems to have finished his education with some sort of academic degree in Prague.   His varied cosmopolitan career began when he went to Flanders about 1780, settling down at Malines as organist and teacher of the piano. From there he went to Berg-op-Zoom in a similar capacity, and about 1782 gave up the organ, removing first to Amsterdam and afterwards to The Hague.   The commercial and the political Dutch capitals both esteemed him as a remarkable pianist, and it was here that he began to

---

[1] There is in the Litolff Edition a collection of the Sonatas in two volumes, which is practically complete and to which the present discussion adheres.   The Sonatinas are included in the first volume, but not dealt with here.

make his name as a composer with the early concertos, trios and sonatas for two instruments.² In 1783 he went to Hamburg and studied for a time under Carl Philipp Emanuel Bach who, nearly at the close of his life, no doubt taught him much in the way of handling the modern sonata form. Dussek cannot have enjoyed Bach's instruction for long, however, for the same year finds him in St Petersburg, where he seems to have opened a period of travel, chiefly in Germany, as pianist and exponent of the glass harmonica. After this artist-showman's expedition, he took his ease for a year or so on Prince Radziwill's estate in Lithuania. Somewhere about the autumn of 1786 he arrived in Paris and was offered an appointment by Marie Antoinette; but he was anxious to visit Italy, where he made a brilliant if superficial success, more with the harmonica than at the piano. In 1788 he returned to Paris and stayed there until the Revolution drove him to England with the multitudes that scurried off the sinking ship of the *ancien régime*. He remained in London nearly eleven years as a popular virtuoso, a fashionable teacher and, like Clementi, Cramer and other composers of the time, established himself as music dealer and publisher. The business flourished at first, but in 1800 Dussek saw himself threatened with ruin. Once more abandoning a leaking vessel—this time his own—he fled to Hamburg. There is a vague story of a princess who at this juncture is said to have detained him somewhere in North Germany near the Danish frontier, but this tale is probably as mythical as that of Ulysses and Calypso which it resembles; at any rate, Dussek appeared in German cities and visited his native country during these legendary years. In 1803 he met Prince Louis Ferdinand of Prussia, himself a composer, with whom he remained until the prince's death in the battle of Saalfeld in October 1806. After a year with a certain Prince of Isenburg, Dussek once more went to Paris and entered the service of the Prince of Benevento (Talleyrand). Dussek died on 20 March 1812 at Saint-Germain-en-Laye, whither he had retired some time previously, suffering from chronic gout.

The first thing that strikes one on making a comparative study of Dussek's work with that of the great keyboard composers of whom traces are found in his work is that we are so often forcibly reminded of those younger than himself, and that where we come across Haydnesque and Mozartian features, they are scarcely decisive enough to attract our attention as anything more than such fashionable commonplaces as might be attributed to any composer of the period. The

² According to the fashion of the time, Dussek composed many sonatas for piano with violin or flute accompaniment. Two sonatas among the sets thus published (Op. 18 No. 2 and Op. 25 No. 2) are for piano solo, but do not appear in the Litolff Edition. There is a considerable confusion among the opus numbers. Op. 10, for instance, also exists in a version with violin.

1786. *Weber* born.

1796. *Beethoven*, first 3 Sonatas (Op. 2); 3 Sonatas (Op. 10).
1797. *Schubert* born.
1798. *Beethoven*, Op. 10 published.
1799. *Beethoven*, Sonate Pathétique (Op. 13), and 2 Sonatas (Op. 14) published.
1800. *Beethoven*, Sonata (Op. 22).
      Weber, 6 Variations (Op. 2).
1801. *Beethoven*, Sonata (Op. 26), 2 Sonatas (quasi una fantasia: Op. 27), Sonata (Op. 28).
1802. *Beethoven*, Opp. 22, 26, 27 published, 2 Sonatas (Op. 31 Nos. 1 and 2).
1804. *Beethoven*, Waldstein Sonata (Op. 53), Sonata Op. 31 No. 3 published.
      Weber, Variations on a Theme by Vogler (Op. 5).
1805. *Beethoven*, Sonata (Op. 54).
1806. *Beethoven*, Sonata Appassionata (Op. 57).
1807. *Beethoven*, Op. 57 published.
      Weber, Variations on 'Vien quà, Dorina bella' (Op. 7).

1809. *Beethoven*, Sonata (Op. 78).
      Chopin born.
      Mendelssohn born.
1810. *Beethoven*, Sonata (Op. 81a), Op. 78 published.
      Schumann born
      Weber, First Concerto.
1811. *Beethoven*, Op. 81a published.
      Liszt born.
1812. *Chopin*, aged 3.
      Liszt, aged 1.
      Mendelssohn, aged 3.
      Schubert, aged 15.
      Schumann, aged 2.
      Weber (aged 26), First Piano Sonata (Op. 24).
      Dussek dies, 20 March

DUSSEK, PIANO SONATAS

(Numbered as in the Litolff Edition)

Nos. 1–3, Op. 9⎫ Before 1790.
Nos. 4–6, Op. 10⎭

(Nos. 7–12 are Sonatinas)

No. 13, Op. 23 ⎫
Nos. 14–16, Op. 35
Nos. 17–19, Op. 39   Between
No. 20, Op. 43   1790
No. 32 (no *opus* number, 1 January 1797)   and
No. 21, Op. 44 (? 1797–8)   1800
Nos. 22–24, Op. 45
Nos. 25–26, Op. 47 ⎭

No. 27, Op. 61⎫   1806
No. 28, Op. 69⎭
No. 29, Op. 70.   *c.* 1807
No. 30, Op. 75⎫

            ⎬1808–11

No. 31, Op. 77⎭

features pointing to later piano writers, on the other hand, are so pronounced that they immediately impress us as unmistakable predictions of strongly personal traits.   Anyone with only a vague idea of the dates involved would certainly denounce Dussek, not perhaps as a wholesale plagiarist, for there is scarcely ever a note-for-note identity, but as a musical weakling whose ready imitativeness has to do duty for an absent gift of invention.   It is important, therefore, to make quite sure, before I deal with the sonatas in detail, that the reader should know how they fit in chronologically with the music of which they are often so strikingly suggestive.   The assertion that Dussek is one of the unacknowledged explorers in music will be accepted when it is found that what he prognosticates must have been completely unknown territory for him, for the simple reason that the men who were to settle down on it had not yet so much as set foot in the vessel that was to take them there.   His claims to be regarded as a miraculously endowed seer may best be gathered from a tabular sketch of the chief events coincident with the sonatas, given on pages 92 and 93.

It is difficult to fix down the dates of the sonatas definitely.[3]   I was careful to compute the above table in such a way as to place each sonata as late as possible, in order not to be accused of unduly strengthening the claim made on behalf of Dussek that he is entitled to be regarded as one of the prophetic personalities in music.   At the same time, I have not endeavoured to establish any evidence from *dates of composition*.   It is true that the early editions scarcely ever give the year of publication, which however can sometimes be guessed from the publishers' names.   Op. 39, for instance, was published by Longman, Clementi & Co., and can therefore not have appeared in print before 1799, if the edition I have seen is the first.   It must certainly have been written considerably earlier.   Again, the fact that Dussek himself *printed* such and such a sonata during a period when, as a publisher, he had unique opportunities for doing so, does not prove that he must have *composed* it at that time.   He not improbably had old manuscripts in hand to which he imparted an air of novelty by giving them opus numbers in the order of publication.   From internal evidence it would seem highly probable that the sonatas are not numbered strictly according to the sequence of their composition.   One's experience with the confused order in which Beethoven's works appeared serves as a warning not to rely on the publishers of that time to the length of assigning a work to a certain period in the composer's career on the mere testimony of an opus number or a date of publication.   The dates of Dussek's sonatas, then, are here conjectured

---

[3] I have failed to trace any similar attempt to date Dussek's sonatas: if it has been made before, I do not regret my labour, since comparisons of several independent inquiries into matters of this kind often lead to the establishment of the truth.

independently of the early printed editions; except, I repeat, that they are, of course, not given as later. My conclusions, although by no means drawn haphazard, require perhaps some justification, and I will endeavour to defend them briefly.

The first sonata that can be definitely attributed to the English period, i.e. the last decade of the eighteenth century, and in fact dated with any approximate certainty, is Op. 23.[4] Its dedication to Mrs Chinnery[5] is sufficiently conclusive. True, it may be objected that Dussek could easily have discharged a friendly obligation of this sort by fishing out an old manuscript of his; but it is significant that, while all the earlier sonatas are grouped in sets of three under one opus number, this one stands alone: it was therefore almost certainly actually written with the object of inscribing it to a friend. Since a good many sonatas seem to fall within the English sojourn, we may confidently place Op. 23 fairly early, and deduce that the distant Opp. 9 and 10 were written some time before the composer's arrival in London, though not, judging from the considerably greater maturity of the latter set, as closely together as the numeration would imply. Numbers 2 and 3 of Op. 10 especially show a great advance on the rather shallow and characterless Op. 9. My next conclusion to be defended is that all the sonatas up to Op. 47 were written in England.[6] Op. 44, dedicated to Clementi, is also known under the title of 'The Farewell.' Clementi did not leave England during Dussek's London period, except for a visit to Vienna in 1799, which was no occasion for such a valedictory tribute. The first supposition would therefore be that the latter wrote this sonata on his own departure in 1800. But is it likely that a man, worried by impending bankruptcy and beating a precipitate retreat, should, in hot haste, create one of his best works? Moreover, even Op. 47 is by no means the last English work (apart from the sonatas), for we find under Op. 52 a set of six Canzone with Italian and English words, obviously designed for the English market. The balance of probability is certainly in favour of the view that the sonatas up to Op. 47 were written in London, even if we do not believe in the strict chronology of the opus numbers. The 'farewell' to Clementi seems to fit in best with that artist's retirement from public appearances in 1797, or possibly with his loss to the musical profession on going into business with Longman & Hyde[7] the following year; on this hypothesis, there is an ample space of time left for the five sonatas,

---

[4] Wrongly numbered Op. 24 in the early English edition.
[5] Doubtless the wife of George Chinnery, the painter. Dussek seems to have been well connected with pictorial artists; another sonata, Op. 43, is dedicated to Mrs Barto-lozzi, wife of the engraver.
[6] I still disregard publication. Even the last works of Dussek, which he cannot possibly have composed in England, were brought out in London.
[7] The firm was not called Longman, Clementi & Co. until 1799.

Opp. 45 and 47, to have been written before the catastrophe of 1800. The considerable gap of six years, so sparsely filled by Opp. 48 to 60 (which include no solo sonata), may be accounted for as satisfactorily by a busy concert life and a visit to the old home as by the possibility of that Odyssean retirement on the Danish frontier. The chamber music, which occupies some of the opus numbers 53 to 60, is explained by the association with Prince Louis Ferdinand, to whom Op. 53 is actually dedicated. The date of Op. 61 is determined by the death of the prince, on which it is an elegy[8], and the subtitle of Op. 70, *Le Retour à Paris*, fixes that work down with almost equal certainty to the end of 1807.

The first three of Dussek's sonatas, Op. 9, although of little intrinsic interest, may well serve as an introduction to some characteristic outward features of his music, unencumbered as yet with the more striking aspects of the later works. Almost entirely free from personal feelings or even moods, they are brilliant, modish music of the *concert sans orchestre* type. Of the

SONATA NO. 1, B♮ MAJOR, OP. 9 NO. 1

(*Allegro non tanto—Allegretto graʒioso*)

it is difficult to convey a descriptive impression other than that of a pleasantly vivacious and superficially garrulous music, expressing only whatever glib commonplaces may have been current in its time, but expressing them with a good measure of worldly accomplishment. One or two of its attributes may be noticed at once as acquainting us with some of the peculiarities which remain apparent with greater or less obtrusiveness throughout Dussek's work. We perceive immediately, from the two main subjects of the first movement, and from the blandly fatuous rondo theme, that Dussek is a poor melodist. His tunes have no firmness of curve, no balance of rise and fall, no decision in coming to a clean termination. The uncomfortable feeling that a melody is thrust upon the world by a creator who cannot make due provision for its well-being again and again assails the hearer of these sonatas. On the other hand, a certain independence and elasticity of form is already apparent in the initial movement of the first sonata. After a working-out with a dramatic breaking loose from the subject-matter and a Schubertian general pause followed by a still more Schubertian entry in a remote key, we come to a recapitulation where the second strain of the main theme is boldly cut out and held over until the close of the movement.

The true pompous concerto style marks the

[8] Already in Op. 62 we reach 'La Consolation.'

SONATA NO. 2, C MAJOR, OP. 9 NO. 2

(Allegro con spirito—Larghetto con espressione—Presto assai)

from the start, and the writing is correspondingly brilliant. Right and left hand snatch showy passages from each other and revel in their execution. The rather vapid second subject is interrupted by a vigorous and flashy episode and again, after a more extensive appearance, by triplet runs in thirds. In the working-out there are traces of originality, contributed by a minor tune that is first cousin to the second subject and by a remarkable modulation just when we prepare ourselves for the conventionally grandiloquent announcement of a cadenza, which is happily averted. The music, always hovering on the confines of the concerto style, is thus saved from a real trespass and led to meditate upon its adventures in the recapitulation. This only outlines the chief events quite briefly, and one begins to see that Dussek's condensation of the reprise, a persistent feature of his sonata form, amounts to more than a wise admission that his material as a rule does not bear repeating at full length. After all, if a summing-up of plain facts is necessary for the sake of clearness and balance after their thorough discussion, it is surely logical that the restatement should be reduced to essentials, very much as the main points only of a speech are finally driven into the hearer's memory by a practised orator. Even as a pure formal abstraction, the usual shape of a Dussek sonata, which may be reduced to the following diagram:

Exposition
Working-out
Recapitulation and Coda

is quite as satisfying as the more common form with its tendency to inflate the subject-matter towards the end:

Exposition
Working-out
Recapitulation and Coda

It is simply a question of transferring the formal (as distinct from the dynamic) climax from the close to the centre.

The slow movement speaks the language of Haydn, but its accent is curiously akin to that of Beethoven, whose sonatas Op. 2 still lay in the womb of time when this piece was written. Can it be that the true mediator between these two masters who had much more in common between them than Mozart had with either[9] was Dussek? I

[9] I can never resist an opportunity to repudiate the critical tag that the early Beethoven is simply Mozartian.

am not attempting to magnify Dussek's importance as a creator, but it is quite possible for a small artist to perform such an office between two dominating figures, especially a small artist who, like Dussek, was by no means so considered by his contemporaries.   What this *Larghetto* presages is a Beethoven who has somehow mislaid his intellectual grasp, but it certainly utters the sentiments of his younger days.   The jolly finale, in sonatina form, is for the most part strangely unpianistic.   It looks rather like the arrangement of some comic opera overture; and sure enough, as soon as we try to discover of whose overtures it particularly makes us think, we are compelled to look into the future.   The stealthy entry of a sprightly theme that swings from tonic to dominant and back again, its lusty repetition, as it were by the *tutti*, and the slender but neat and swift development of the whole, irresistibly conjures up Rossini.

As will be seen by comparing the tempo indications of the

SONATA NO. 3, D MAJOR, OP. 9 NO. 3

(*Allegro maestoso con espressione—Prestissimo*)

with those of the two preceding works, Dussek from the start achieves considerable variety between his movements.   Although these sonatas resemble concertos in character, he is not always content with the usual *allegro* pace for his first movements.   There is for him no such thing as an understood *tempo ordinario*, to be applied on all occasions 'unless otherwise mentioned.'   The player who starts the third sonata too quickly will soon discover that everywhere the music is tightly packed with difficulties to the capacity of a quite moderate speed.   The octave scales, runs in thirds and widely spread sextolet passages are all calculated to fill the frame of the *maestoso*, though otherwise they hardly do justice to the implications of the term.   In its actual vocabulary this movement is scarcely indicative of the future; even the rather startling augmented octaves in the second and tenth bars are softened by the fact that the bass D against which the upper D♯ clashes is in the nature of a pedal.   At the opening of the working-out, we come upon a phrase turned as Mozart in his most classical detachment might have turned it, a resemblance that is rare in Dussek, who seldom looks behind him.   The recapitulation is again shorn of several features of the exposition.

The finale once more sets a thought of Rossini going in one's mind, this time by an actual thematic prediction.   We have only to embellish this phrase:

and its recurrence a degree of the scale higher to be at once in the midst of the *Barber*. Altogether the whole brilliant piece suggests footlights thrown on a curtain that is soon to rise on some bustling *opera buffa* scene.

There is a noticeable advance between Op. 9 and Op. 10. The first number of the latter,

SONATA No. 4, A MAJOR, OP. 10 No. 1

(*Allegro moderato—Adagio cantabile—Allegro assai*)

though the least interesting of the set, already shows a good deal more character. But, for the moment, progress in that direction is gained at the expense of formal clarity. The first movement is discursive and hesitant; its second subject affords a pathetic example of Dussek's often pitifully shambling tunes; the working-out gropes about rather aimlessly until it breaks down altogether, not knowing how to broach the first subject again for the recapitulation, which stumbles in from nowhere and is summarily dispatched. The tiny coda, however, is surprisingly good.

The form of the other two movements, probably from an increasing consciousness of uncertainty, is artificially consolidated by a rigid use of the formula A B A C A. In the *Adagio* we still have the classical slow movement of the Haydn type, which is almost purely design. There is an impression, nevertheless, not of an advance so much as of a coming decay, a mellowing into romanticism, an almost imperceptible sign that presently music is going to concern itself more with the colour of the composer's mood than with abstract beauty of line. The final rondo is Haydnesque, both in shape and character: a lively piece that presages nothing.

Very different is the

SONATA No. 5, G MINOR, OP. 10 No. 2

(*Grave—Vivace con spirito*)

Here we suddenly feel ourselves heading full tilt towards romanticism. That the *Vivace* has a greater resemblance to Mozart's G minor Symphony than merely that of tonality does not impair the argument in the least, for that work is itself a distinctly romantic utterance of

personal emotions.   It is time that someone wrote a serious study of
Mozart in his aspect of first German romantic as distinct from his
phase of Italian classicism.[10]   But this remark is by the way, as is also
the observation that the present sonata is probably contemporary with
if not actually earlier than the symphony in question, which Mozart
wrote in July 1788.   Can Dussek, who was in Paris at that time, have
known it so soon after its completion, or can it be that even here he
was first in the field with a comparatively unimportant composition
that seems quite palpably inspired by a great one?   The *Grave* which
precedes this impassioned outburst of pent-up individuality is also
laden with a smouldering romanticism that is well ahead of its time.
Its elegiac note supplies not only an effective contrast, but an appropriate mood for the dramatic quick movement to spring from.

Sonata No. 6, E major, Op. 10 No. 3

(Allegro maestoso e moderato—Presto con fuoco)

In the first movement of this sonata, Dussek seems to say a lingering
farewell to his early concerto style by cramming the music full of
technical difficulties that arouse no commensurate amount of feeling.
Once again the initial subject has to be started with a spiritless modera-
tion of tempo in order to set a manageable pace for the later passages
of display.   The theme itself is not without a good working quality,
but the music very soon runs to seed.   Presently a tune is reached
which is surely the worst example of Dussek's helpless, divagating
melodies.   Being in the key of the dominant, it is naturally taken for
the second subject; but by the time the recapitulation is reached one
discovers that a later passage, which has the character of a mere
ornamental episode, serves in that capacity.   The meandering theme
in the exposition, not being put to any further use, becomes thus even
more pointless.   It is like a fragment of dialogue in a play which
delays the action with a digressive argument that does nothing to
carry the plot forward.   From these shallow waters it is refreshing to
plunge unexpectedly into a movement where Dussek washes off his
early style.   The music, all at once and quite inexplicably, is decidedly
Beethovenian:

Ex. 2   Presto con fuoco

&c.

[10] Dyneley Hussey has since done this in his book on Mozart.

not only in thematic invention, but also in the manner of presentation. There are signs of that curious bluntness of utterance that is so characteristic of Beethoven, an impatience with mere formal phraseology, an insistence on making each passage perform the twofold function of saying something decisive and providing a link in the structure. This *Presto*, in the tonic minor, is the first of Dussek's sonata movements which does not content itself with occasional glimpses into the future, but from beginning to end lives in it. In this two-movement sonata as a whole, by the way, it is perhaps not too far-fetched to see another, more superficial anticipation of Beethoven, whose key-scheme in the two-movement Op. 90 (E minor–E major) it reverses.

And now, Dussek having gained his start ahead of the great composer to whom he stands nearest in point of age, sets about outdistancing others who are farther off. There is something of Schubert's manner of contrivance in the

SONATA No. 13, B♭ MAJOR, OP. 23

(Allegro con spirito—Allegretto moderato con espressione)

The first thing that strikes one here is that Dussek evidently took immediate advantage of the superiority of the English pianos of the time.[11] In the first movement there is much revelling in the fine tone obtainable all over the wide range of these instruments. The little group of four semiquavers in the principal subject is deliberately transferred here and there to the extreme octaves, and the working-out is in fact nothing but an excuse for scattering this figure up and down the keyboard, with the result that invention is here rather noticeably sacrificed to mere laying-out. But the rest of the movement is richly expressive and the harmonic turn in the second subject into A♭ major, when it is only expected to change from F major to F minor, is definitely Schubertian in its original grasp of modulation. The way in which the periodical returns of the affably pastoral rondo subject are conducted, especially one appearing in a foreign key, is also vividly evocative of that master, who was not yet born when this sonata was written. There is a romantic feeling of pastures and woodland borders, haunted by vague sounds of far-off horns, about this second movement, suggested, it is true, in terms of the drawing-room. An increasing attention to detail may also be discerned here: see for

---

[11] I had already come independently to this conclusion, which indeed jumps to the eye, when I discovered to my great satisfaction that the original title-page bears the inscription 'for the grand and small pianoforte with additional keys.'

H

instance the nice differentiation in the treatment of the bass in the first two appearances of the subject.

In the

SONATA No. 14, B♭ MAJOR, OP. 35 No. 1

(Allegro moderato e maestoso—Allegro non troppo, ma con spirito)

there is no longer a trace of that conversational detachment that characterizes the polite musical entertainment of the late eighteenth century.   For Dussek the sonata form becomes more and more the carrier of intimate feelings.   Needless to say, he is not yet—and for that matter never will be—a musical poet concerned only with personal impressions and not caring in what terms he conveys them to his hearers.   A good deal of ostentation still clings to his musical language, but a darker colouring, a brooding introspection, now begin to temper his effective rhetoric.   Eloquence, no longer an end in itself, becomes a means of intellectual and emotional expression.   Romanticism is foreshadowed quite unmistakably now; not the German romanticism of fantastic fairy lore, still less the idealized licence of the French romantics, nor the ironic self-analysis and self-torture of Byron, Heine and Lermontov, and least of all the grisly horrors of the 'Symphonie fantastique' or the wolves' glen in *Freischütz*.   It is the romanticism that tends to leave the princely palace for field and forest and the courts for the habitations of the common people.   Dussek, being before his time, can never get more than half way, however: on emerging from the state apartment he is held up in the citizen's drawing-room, and in forsaking exalted circles for the populace he only reaches the bourgeoisie, of which his music ever retains some of the orderly complacency.   He will not go out, like Weber, into a stormy night when the oak creaks, the owl hoots and ragged clouds flit across a pale moon, but he does at least care for the sunny landscapes among which Weber's muse loves to roam sufficiently well to lock himself up in his studio and paint them with a none too tractable brush.   This passage in the fourteenth sonata is pure Weber of the more artificial sort:

Ex. 3   Allegro moderato

If that master did not actually write this very phrase, which is hard to believe, he certainly ought to have done so. One is almost sure of having heard it played on the clarinet somewhere in his work. Curiously enough the whole first movement of this sonata has a kind of clarinet quality, something deep and tranquil and shadowy, something laden with one knows not what tremulous wavering on the brink of a confidential revelation. If on looking at this movement we think of the clarinet, we find that it would make, with a minimum of arrangement, an ideal little concerto for what is surely the most romantic of instruments. (Or does it only seem so because it was first exploited to the full by that most romantic of romantics—Weber?) The bold modulations here and there and the scales which at the end of each section shoot over into the minor ninth, only a pretty daring composer could have written before the close of the eighteenth century.

The finale has a vivacity and nimble wit that again makes one think of Rossini at his jolliest, indeed almost of Offenbach at his best. But there is no longer the impression that one is playing the transcription of an orchestral movement: the piano writing now is supremely good, and the brilliant polish which this piece can be given with comparatively little technical effort is astonishing. A feature of Dussek's music which here emerges decisively for the first time is syncopation, and in the working-out there is a passage of fugal writing truly Mendelssohnian in its spruceness of thinking and handling. Indeed this page, in its pungent originality, is even very much more modern: with a little imagination one may see in it a sort of potted epitome of the rhythms and the harmony in Borodin's *Prince Igor* overture.

A temporary return to purely external brilliance is marked by the first movement of the

Sonata No. 15, G major, Op. 35 No. 2

(Allegro—Molto allegro e con espressione)

which opens with a tense little phrase that is afterwards elaborated by a good deal of flashily effective embroidery. But although a momentary set-back in some ways, this piece shows an immense advance in pianistic aptitude. For sheer sound the whole movement is miraculously contrived, even when the subject-matter, such as the floundering second theme, is poor. Dussek, it seems, was unable to progress steadily in the direction of matter and that of manner at once, and it is only towards the end of his career that the two merge together quite naturally. But there are at least a couple of happily invented things in this first movement: the Beethovenish pounce upon the shake on an unexpected note and an auxiliary subject of the most winsome grace which serves to round off both sections of the movement and smiles for a moment into the working-out.

Beethoven is again uppermost in the rondo, as will be seen from the opening bars:

Ex. 4 Molto allegro

The bad clash of false relation and open octave progression in the third bar even points to that master's late period, when in his deafness he sometimes passed such clumsy passages. Only pedantry, of course, would condemn harshnesses of this kind on theoretical grounds if they happen to be satisfying in their effect or to express something vitally necessary to the character of the music. But Dussek himself evidently felt that this bar did neither, for he studiously avoided its repetition in the same form later in the movement. There is fertile inventiveness in the use of episodes, great variety of pianistic device, and not only are the periodical recurrences of the main subject well managed, but everything is logically connected with it. The Beethoven-like idea quoted above becomes even more so in a sort of last-minute reflection that throws a new light on it at the very end.

But what is one to say to a work which in key and technique, in instrumental writing and in feeling might be passed off for an authentic Beethoven on the most knowing expert, provided he could be made to believe that one of that master's works, and a good one at that, had eluded his notice? If the unavoidable label of *Sonate Pathétique* had not fitted one of Beethoven's works more or less well, it would surely have fallen quite naturally upon Dussek's

SONATA NO. 16, C MINOR, OP. 35 NO. 3

*(Allegro assai agitato—Adagio patetico ed espressivo—Presto—
Allegro molto)*

In either case, 'Sonate Dramatique' would have suited the first move-ment better.[12]   Without resorting to Beethoven's slow introduction, Dussek plunges straight into the febrile turmoil of his *Allegro*.   Once again, even in a work where the likeness is so continually striking, let it be remembered that it would be futile to expect any passage that can be actually retraced in Beethoven.   Dussek has enough originality to invent his own details, in fact a surprising variety of them; the re-semblance lies in the spirit of the music, in that indefinable mental process which blends imagination and realization together into a distinctive flavour, the ingredients of which can be analysed, but whose sum-total is beyond description.   Incidentally, Dussek may be held up as a warning example to those who look upon original ideas in an artist as a sure hall-mark of greatness.   It is perfectly possible to produce ideas which are quite individual in the raw, but become clothed in a standard fashion in the act of presentation.

In respect of piano writing, if in no other, this sonata is superior to the *Pathétique*.   There is nothing in it like the lifeless accompaniment to the second subject in the latter work.   The likeness to Beethoven, though no longer to one particular work, continues in the *Adagio*; and although it does not penetrate beyond his first period, it is still ahead of him, as my calendar shows clearly enough.   Apart from a modulatory seam that shows badly in the middle, this slow movement is rich in long stretches of sombre beauty.   The short intermezzo, *Presto*, with a broad half-close, foreshadows the main theme of the finale, where it appears transformed and in the major.   The whole conceit has something of Mendelssohn's practice of binding his move-ments lightly together; indeed, if one will strain the point a little, it has more than a hint in it of the *Leitmotiv*.   The last movement has the peevish humour of Beethoven's late bagatelles and the boisterous energy of *The Rage over the Lost Groat*.   It flows on unremittingly and the theme does not merely recur temporarily, but is threaded across the warp and woof of the episodic material with great dexterity.

The set numbered Op. 39, dedicated to Mrs Apreece[13], may be dealt with more briefly.   It is altogether less important than several of the works which precede it, and one is tempted to cite it in support of the view that the sonatas were not published strictly in the order of their composition.   The first movement of the

Sonata No. 17, Op. 39 No. 1

(Allegro—Andantino ma moderato e con espressione: Allegro ma non troppo)

[12] It is generally the initial movement alone which invests a sonata or symphony with a badge of this kind; but note the *patetico* superscription of Dussek's slow movement.

[13] An improbable name, whoever the lady was; I suspect an English transformation of the Welsh Ap Rhys.

has the graceful fluency of a Mozartian work turned out glibly in response to an urgent commission.   It is neatly fitted into a standardized form and plays delightfully, but leaves no impression worth recording.   In the second movement, where the *Andantino* and *Andante* are interlinked, we find, however, a glimpse of genuine Schumann, not only in the character and the song-like shape of the initial theme:

Ex. 5   Andantino

but also in a certain formal shiftlessness which substitutes repetition of alternative sections for development.   Some displaced accents in the *Allegro* portion are the only striking features in its pallidly charming countenance.

Still less satisfactory is the

SONATA No. 18, C MAJOR, OP. 39 No. 2

(*Allegro moderato—Andantino quasi larghetto—Allegretto*)

where even the keyboard writing is careless.   Evidently the inscription to Mrs Apreece was dictated by nothing more than politeness, and the task carried out with the polished indifference of the prudent man of the world.

SONATA No. 19, Bb MAJOR, OP. 39 No. 3

(*Allegro con spirito—Andante espressivo, ma con moto*)

A study of the first movement is almost profitless, but in the rondo there is at least some writing *con amore*, and we are once more in the presence of Dussek's various harbingers of the future.   To look at this characteristic passage:

Ex. 6   Andantino

is to exclaim: 'How delightfully this smacks of the period!' But the period, we must remember, is still the eighteenth century and what this little *tyrolienne* does suggest is a time well ahead into the nine-teenth, when a sentimental public delighted in Swiss and Tyrolese yodelling, in William Tell's chapels and in the descent of decorous waterfalls, musically reproduced in a lilting tonic-and-dominant prettiness and issued in covers adorned with romantic landscapes in dainty steel engravings. The whole of the rondo is replete with this sort of vicarious enjoyment of a nature that could only be appreciated in comfort through the music page, much as it is nowadays appreciated by staying at an up-to-date hotel. But technically this movement is by no means tame. It contains keyboard effects almost Lisztian in boldness of handling and luminosity of effect, and at least one *fioritura* that points straight to Chopin.

Liszt again, a Liszt with a Schubert complex, peeps out of the first part of the

Sonata No. 20, A major, Op. 43
(*Allegro moderato e con espressione—Allegro*)

one of the most outwardly effective of Dussek's sonata movements. It is frankly virtuoso music, full of digital problems and ingenious exploitation of the keyboard. Surely all that the early piano was capable of yielding in dynamic effect and variety of colour must be turned to account in this piece, and probably a good deal more which Dussek vaguely foresaw as possible and desirable in the ideal piano of the future. Had Liszt been born half a century earlier, this is how he would have treated the instrument of the time and triumphantly over-ridden its limitations. In the rondo we have Schubert pure and simple, not at his very best, but as good as he is in any of his last move-ments of a pleasantly ambling and rather uneventful type. The sudden gasp in the middle of a phrase towards the end is especially like Schubert, who at a pinch might also have perpetrated in one of his weak moments the bad modulatory patch that follows it.

But it would not do for Dussek only to forestall a composer who at that time was in his mother's womb. In the

SONATA No. 21, E♭ MAJOR, OP. 44

(Grave: Allegro moderato—Molto adagio e sostenuto—Tempo di minuetto piuttosto allegro—Allegro moderato ed espressivo)

we find him therefore outranging all those within whose reach he had previously come and anticipating a composer who was not to be born until twenty-one years after his death. That composer is no other than Brahms. In this 'Farewell' Sonata, dedicated to Clementi, Dussek reaches full maturity and gives of his best. In a magnificent slow introduction in E♭ minor he adumbrates the main theme of the first movement proper with a close and gorgeous musical texture; and the *Allegro moderato*, although going into the tonic major, retains a seriousness and intellectual depth that immediately makes one think of Brahms, although the keyboard treatment is much more lucid and apposite. Once again it is the spirit rather than the letter of the music that is predictive; yet, rewrite the rhythmic grouping of a certain passage thus:

Ex. 7 Allegro moderato

and you have a Brahms that seems authentic enough. The whole movement is rich in fanciful turns of invention and presentation; and the thematic development is, if anything, too tightly packed. The same fault must be found with the *Adagio*, where the working-out (the movement is in sonata form) makes too much of a subsidiary theme that is only apparently developed by mere restatement with a dazzling variety of treatment. The first and last sections of this slow movement, however, have not only outward splendour, but a deep emotional glow and daring harmonic colour. Note this specimen of a quite modern use of two parts which obstinately pursue their own way without heeding a momentary jar:

Ex. 8   Molto adagio e sostenuto

The third movement reaches forward, for a change, to the scherzo manner of Chopin, where he is impatient, acrid and ironic; while in the trio section we encounter the elegant Chopin of the waltzes as he would have been had he followed Weber's *Invitation to the Dance* rather more closely than he did.   Before acquainting himself with the final rondo, the reader should refresh his memory of the finale of Brahms's B♭ major Sextet.   He will be amazed to find that, although there is perhaps not a single similar sequence of two notes in Dussek's rondo, the two movements are absolutely identical in mood, invention, manner and everything else.   The central idea itself is of exactly the same type in either case: it is a theme, not a tune—that is to say, a fine idea stated in order to be expounded, not a phrase given out in sheer pleasure of melody-making for its own sake.   Incidentally, syncopation seems to grow upon Dussek as he develops.

The three Sonatas, Op. 45, are again much less important.   By this time one almost begins to be conscious of a dual musical personality in Dussek.   Without any exterior interest he seems able to turn out only pretty, shapely and well laid-out music such as the

Sonata No. 22, B♭ major, Op. 45 No. 1

(Allegro cantabile—Adagio patetico—Allegro di ballo)

the first movement of which especially is devoid of feeling or character. He seems to require some sort of emotional experience to bring out the best in him—a farewell, a bereavement, a reunion with old friends. What else need be adduced to prove that he is a romantic in full bloom, though he blossomed before the time appointed for romanticism? He was at heart a subjective composer, sensitive to influences and responsive to feelings outside his art; and if the study of psychology as revealed in music could be reduced to any scientific precision, it might be possible to show that the magnificent Op. 23 was inspired by a warmth of feeling for Mrs Chinnery such as Dussek did not harbour in his breast for Mrs Apreece, Mrs Bartolozzi or Mrs Rose Marshall.[14]

The *Adagio* does not strike the modern hearer as in the least pathetic in the sense intended, but it has a harmonic richness which may once have touched more responsive chords in the human heart. Somehow or other one has a notion that a Richard Strauss born a century too soon would have written music of this kind for the first act of *Rosenkavalier*. The Marschallin, no doubt, would have indulged in coloratura such as that which occurs in this movement, but essentially she would have been a no less touching figure in Dussek's harmonic dress. So perhaps the *patetico* is right after all. The final rondo-scherzo is surely one of the most bubbling movements in all music. Don Giovanni's 'Finch' han dal vino' is not more effervescent than this, and Offenbach himself has not a more sparkling vintage in his abundant store of mirth.

SONATA No. 23, G MAJOR, Op. 45 No. 2

(*Larghetto sostenuto: Allegro di molto—Andantino con moto*)

The first movement is almost as lively as the final rondo-scherzo of the Sonata in B♭ (No. 22). After a slow and too elaborate introduction, a variation without a theme, it bursts into an exhilarating *Allegro*, written with an economy of means worthy of Scarlatti. Much of the music is restricted to two parts and there are rarely more than three, yet the effect is rich and full and the whole thing flashes by with the lightness of a well-told jest. The amiable rondo is not altogether dull, but quite undistinguished. In the opening movement of the

SONATA No. 24, D MAJOR, Op. 45 No. 3

(*Allegro moderato—Larghetto con moto—Allegretto moderato*)

the thought of Strauss—surely remote enough to make one wonder at its obstinacy—again obtrudes itself in a passage that might come unaltered out of the music for *Le Bourgeois gentilhomme*:

Ex. 9   Allegro moderato

p con espressione

---

[14] To whom Opp. 29, 43 and 47 are respectively dedicated.

But that is not all. See how in the working-out the main theme entangles itself with the kind of nervous excitement that is exactly what happens to Strauss's thematic material in a more modern sort of way.[15] In other respects this movement has a counterfeit Mozart character. This unexpected meeting of the two vastly different personalities through the good offices of Dussek recalls that Strauss honestly thought he had written a Mozartian opera in *Rosenkavalier*. One reflects, not without dismay, that perhaps he only succeeded in being like Dussek.

The shapely *Larghetto* is conventional in its sum-total, but abounds in original detail. The finale reminds us that music is approaching a time when the polka, most sedate and square-toed exponent of a decorous gaiety, is about to become the rage all over Europe.

Even less significant are the next two works, which may be dismissed quite briefly. The first of these two, the

SONATA NO. 25, G MAJOR, OP. 47 NO. 1

(Allegro con spirito—Adagio—Allegretto moderato)

is remarkable only for the finale, a mildly amusing 'Rondo à la Militaire,' which recalls 'The Dashing White Sergeant' and all the tin-soldiering and round-pond sailing in which the Napoleonic age delighted.[16]

SONATA NO. 26, G MAJOR, OP. 47 NO. 2

(Allegro moderato ed espressivo—Andantino con moto)

Of this work it is difficult to speak except as an example of Dussek's music such as it presents itself to the imagination of those who only

[15] Even Strauss's realism finds its parallel in Dussek. In *The Sufferings of the Queen of France: a Musical Composition expressing the Feelings of the Unfortunate Marie Antoinette during her Imprisonment, Trial, etc.* the execution is depicted in much the same terms as the hanging of Till Eulenspiegel is suggested by Strauss.

[16] To show that Dussek was not above writing the immensely popular descriptive pieces of *The Battle of Prague* variety, the following title-page may be copied here: 'The / Naval Battle and Total Defeat / of the / Grand Dutch Fleet / by / Admiral Duncan / on the 11th of October, 1797 / A Characteristic Sonata for the Piano Forte / Composed and Dedicated to / Viscount Duncan / By J. L. Dussek.' The piece is full of naval signals, cannons, hoistings of sails, distress, shouts of victory, 'Rule Britannia,' general rejoicing, and what not.

know the sonatinas or the 'favourite rondo, "Les Adieux."' To look at this feeble specimen alone is to relegate the composer to the things one has done with for good and all.

We now come upon the *Élégie harmonique* on the death of Prince Louis Ferdinand of Prussia, the

SONATA NO. 27, F♯ MINOR, OP. 61

(Senza ornamente: Tempo agitato—Tempo vivace e con fuoco, quasi presto)

which might be described as a *sonata quasi una fantasia*. One is vaguely conscious here that the composer strikes the dramatic attitude of grief rather than uttering quite spontaneously what he feels. His somewhat theatrical manner of delivering his funeral oration again savours strongly of Liszt, and so does—more than ever before—his bold encompassing of the keyboard and taking advantage of every resource that two hands and the pedals can command. But for all the ostentation of this music, it does not strike us as insincere; it is rather an effort to hide the poignancy of personal emotions by restricting them to such outward show as the public at large is likely to appreciate. After all, in 1806 music had not yet learnt to bear the creator's most intimate thoughts to the listener; and even what Dussek actually does in this respect is a good way ahead of his contemporaries. The odd direction, *senza ornamente*, at the head of what is obviously a slow introduction, would appear to mark a decisive stage in music, a final breaking with the licence formerly allowed to the performer in the way of embellishment—such as mordents, shakes and cadenzas. Henceforth the composer is to dictate exclusively in such matters.

The second movement should make the jazz bands blush: it is the very apotheosis of syncopation. Dussek syncopates every single bar from start to finish, except the last five. The movement being a very long one, we begin to feel somewhere near the end that we shall shriek if it goes on much longer. There is no denying the stunning audacity of this movement, but it wears too palpably the air of a preconceived idea kept up at all costs.

The next number,

SONATA NO. 28, D MAJOR, OP. 69 NO. 3

(Allegro maestoso brillante—Larghetto espressivo—Allegro)

is the last of a set of three sonatas the other two of which have an accompanying violin part. It is quite negligible and probably an

early work renumbered for publication. The hunting piece at the
end is mildly amusing as an indication to the taste of the period.[17]
Dussek is at his best again in the

SONATA No. 29, A♭ MAJOR, OP. 70

*(Allegro non troppo ed espressivo—Molto adagio, con anima ed espressione
—Tempo di minuetto, scherzo quasi allegro—Allegro con spirito)*

Le Retour à Paris doubtless meant a good deal to him in many ways,
for the range of emotional expression covered by this work is extensive
and its sincerity unmistakable. The first subject is akin to Schubert
in the harmonic restlessness that cannot restrain a blossoming into
modulation already at the fourth bar:

but there is also much of Chopin's manner in the extraordinarily
crowded writing that weaves the music into a rich fabric of an infinity
of detail. A certain indefinable *morbidezza* about the music—a hectic
flush rather than a pale sickliness—is also very like the Polish master,
however the popular conception of him may seem to oppose this view.
The magnificently treated second subject again has that curious
momentary sideslip of the harmony:

[17] In Op. 25, Three Sonatas for piano with violin or flute accompaniment, Dussek uses
'The Fife Hunt' and 'Rule, Britannia' as rondo themes.

Incisive subsidiary themes, such as a restless syncopated idea and the vigorous thrusts of a figure ingeniously worked in imitation, are admirably turned to account in the development.   The slow movement is overwrought to the verge of turgidity, but under its elaborate dress is grave beauty.   It might be said, without being unduly paradoxical, that Dussek here came so near Chopin that the difference between the two composers can be more clearly seen than their resemblance.   It is plain that Dussek bequeathed his pianistic wealth to Chopin, who might easily have gone straight along the older composer's path had not his strong idiosyncrasies turned him aside.   The irascible Chopin of the Scherzi is again uppermost in the fascinating and quite modern third movement of the present sonata, and the trio is the stuff of which a whole school of small lyrical composers—such as Heller, Gade, Jensen and Kirchner—are made of; but it is carried a step or two farther than these minor figures, or at any rate the earlier ones among them, ever advanced.   The finale is a delightful Victorian polka, which shoots past the time of the crinoline to that of the bustle.   The movement is splendid in its pianism, the kind of thing to which the early Chopin might easily have turned, and the music sometimes approaches the carnavalesque moods of Schumann.

Sonata No. 30, E♭ major, Op. 75

(Allegro ma non troppo—Andante moderato—Allegro moderato grazioso)

This sonata is not so uniformly good as No. 29 in A♭ major. The first movement is especially uneven in quality, much of it being mere showy passage work.   The *scherzando* phrase of the second subject, however, is a sudden shaft of brightness, and there is a particularly long stretch of genuine Weber in the passage beginning with the following cadence and running into figures which again suggest the gurgling sound of the clarinet:

Lest the general drift of this essay should tend to give the impression that Dussek has no inventive originality of his own, let the slow movement of this sonata, and especially its minor section, be cited as proof to the contrary; also the delicious finale, which is Schubertian only in the fertility of an invention that is in itself very individual.

The last of Dussek's works in sonata form, the

SONATA NO. 31, F MINOR, OP. 77

(Allegro moderato, ma energico—Tempo di minuetto, con moto—Adagio non troppo, ma solenne—Allegro moderato)

also known under the title of *L'Invocation*, makes a fitting conclusion. It is throughout steeped in a profound seriousness that sounds like a premonition of death, and the workmanship is a final triumph of not merely technical but intellectual attainments. The first movement is grand, sombre, and so copiously worked as to become perhaps a little diffuse. The second is minuet-like only in tempo, for any suspicion of frivolity is anxiously averted by a particular application to scholarly writing. The whole of the first part is an elaborate canon first in the *seconda grave* and then in the *seconda acuta* —in other words, in sevenths and ninths—possibly rather dry, but impressive for that very reason after the luxuriant initial movement. The trio is undiluted Brahms, not only in the main theme:

Ex. 13 **Tempo di minuetto**

but still more in what follows:

After a big shadowy slow movement with a sort of purple velvet quality, even the final rondo remains almost gloomy. The feeling of oppression, and occasionally of agitation, is only relieved by a glimpse of sunshine in the very Schumannesque major section:

Very little need be said of the

SONATA No. 32, F MAJOR
(*Adagio—Allegro*)

entitled *La Chasse*, and known to have been published on 1 January 1797, in No. 1 of Pleyel, Corri[18] & Dussek's *Musical Journal.* It is

---

[18] Corri was Dussek's father-in-law as well as his publisher and business partner.

a conventional hunting piece with horn calls, barking hounds and galloping horses complete, and the excitement of the chase suggested by the usual Italian *stretto*. The *Allegro* that follows the slow introduction is certainly in sonata form, but this is hardly a sufficient reason for the inclusion of this work in the Litolff collection or for its discussion here. However, since I have blown Dussek's trumpet with some vigour in this essay, it may fittingly close with his own fanfares.

I

John Field

(*The Chesterian*, June–August 1930)

MUSICIANS know vaguely that John Field influenced Chopin and that he invented the nocturne; they may even have heard or played the particular pieces with which the Irish composer anticipated the Polish master. There, as a rule, the acquaintance ends, unless perchance they have heard the epithet 'the Russian Field' applied to the Irishman to distinguish him from Henry Field 'of Bath'—quite superfluously, since the latter would be completely unknown but for this distinction.

It is the parrot-cry that Field foreran Chopin that is responsible for his neglect. He is mechanically accepted, and dismissed, as a composer who did primitively a certain thing in which another excelled. This fate he shares with many others, such as some of the organ masters who came before Bach, and taught him a great deal. His is the tragedy, in short, of all minor precursors who, having done their piloting for the captains of the art, are forgotten by the public and consigned to the dull society of historians.

Yet it is nearly always worth while to cultivate such a pilot's acquaintance, for he will generally be found to have had unsuspected high-sea adventures of his own. This is certainly true of Field. In getting to know him at first hand we find, in fact, that his task of steering Chopin into the nocturnal harbour was only that of a man who gave the benefit of his experience to another. It did not amount to all that is habitually made of it. He simply showed a much younger confederate where a certain land lay, but did not teach him a great deal about the secrets of his craft. That Field's influence on Chopin has been exaggerated anyone may see who looks even casually, not only at these two composers, but at the other piano writers of a generation or so before the latter. The whole trend of the pianistic writing of that period reappears in the Polish master, greatly modified by his immense originality, but plainly discernible all the same.

Field is part of this evolution: that is all. For he too has his own artistic physiognomy. He is far more interesting as an independent personality than for his contribution to the making of Chopin. It will therefore not do to set him aside as one of those numerous figures in music who did their share in bringing about certain developments, but whose work is no longer of any account. The composers of the Mannheim school, for example, are really superseded by Haydn, who did very much what they did and improved upon it. But Chopin, though much the greater and more versatile genius of the two, cannot displace Field for anyone who has once cultivated an affection for the elder composer. And this affection, it cannot be too emphatically maintained, is worth cultivating.

To call an exclusively pianistic composer like Chopin—to dispose of him here and now—versatile may appear odd; but he is not only far more resourceful than Field in his choice of various types of pieces, but much more adroit in modifying his invention and style according to each type. Field too is purely a pianist-composer (even his Quintet is simply a concerto movement with string accompaniment, so printed that the string parts can be omitted altogether), and one considerably limited within the range of the piano itself. The truth is that in the nocturne alone he achieved that originality which cannot fail to endear him to those who study his work, and it is noteworthy that he was thirty-two by the time he wrote the first three pieces of that kind. His sonatas and concertos, his rondos, variations and other smaller works all conform to the conventions of the day. There must, of course, be a reason for this late emancipation, and another for the fact that he made so little of his freedom once he had won it. Both these reasons, it is not difficult to see, are biographical, and a short outline of his life will therefore be to the purpose here.

John Field was born on 26 July 1782, only twelve years later than Beethoven and nearly ten before the death of Mozart. He was the son of Robert Field, a violinist at the Theatre Royal in Dublin. At an early age he showed marked preference for the piano and was taught by his grandfather and namesake, who kept a kind of private musical academy with his son Robert. Two things spurred the child on to a rapid development: his enthusiasm and his grandfather's rod, but no doubt the latter was also the first cause of his taking so abnormally long to gain independence.

By the time he was nine, he was ready to take finishing lessons from Tommaso Giordani, who had long lived in Dublin and was a power in the city's musical life. Whether Field really did become a finished pianist then and there may be questioned, for no doubt Giordani, who was then near sixty, had been brought up in the harpsichord tradition. However that may be, he was ready at the age of ten to appear as one of the 'musical children' at a concert given for the benefit of Tom Cooke, who was his exact contemporary and evidently another youthful prodigy. Soon afterwards Field played at one of Giordani's 'Spiritual Concerts,' a venture that seems to have been copied from a

famous Parisian enterprise. His success was so great for 'a youth of
eight years of age' (as he was described) that he reappeared a second
and third time that year, in which his first compositions saw the light:
two rondos for piano based on songs by his Italian master. His fame
as a wonder-child now rapidly increased.

The summer of 1793 was spent at Bath, where Rauzzini had engaged
Robert Field as leader of the orchestra. The boy's first sight of the
quality and fashion of England may well have done something to
develop that inferiority complex from which one gathers he suffered
all through the early part of his life. In December of the same year
he saw London for the first time, his father having obtained an appointment as leader of the orchestra in the Haymarket Theatre. About
this time he wrote a set of variations on an Irish air, 'Go to the devil
and shake yourself.'

Let us glance at the state of music in London in 1794. The prevalent taste was for light entertainment. Vauxhall, the resort of the
ballad, was in its heyday. Farces and sentimental plays with incidental music were all the rage and the new Drury Lane Theatre,
opened in April, was forthwith devoted to that kind of fare. Arnold
produced one such piece that year and Shield no less than three, while
Stephen Storace not only brought forward a ballet, a comic opera and
an occasional piece, but also an operatic adaptation from Cherubini
and Kreutzer. Even more popular were Dibdin's famous Table
Entertainments at the Sans Souci Rooms in the Strand, where the
'Tyrtaeus of the British Navy,' who had six years before given up a
voyage to India because he found the sea too rough in Torbay, made a
sensation with his nautical songs. The Catch Club and the Glee
Club flourished, and Callcott, John Stafford Smith and many others
wrote their choral fancies and musical conundrums. Among the
purveyors of light stage music Linley was the veteran, and he was to
die the following year, as did the French composer and chess player
Philidor, who was now blind but could still play three games simultaneously. Attwood, Braham, Hook and Kelly were also men of
fame, or rising to fame, in the theatre.

Field, though he remained in London, was in no position to take
part in frivolous musical pursuits. Early in 1794, before he was
twelve, he was apprenticed to Clementi, whom he was to assist in his
music warehouse in return for lessons. Moreover, his father had to
pay Clementi a hundred guineas for the privilege of having his son
taught music and the music trade, which in those days often went
hand in hand. Dussek as well as Clementi had a music shop in
London at that time. That Field was influenced by both these
eminent pianist-composers cannot be doubted, for there is as much of
Dussek's sweet abundance and pianistic richness in his music as of

Clementi's spirited invention and lean, springy and lucid writing. Both masters, each in his own way, found a style that definitely showed the piano to be a new instrument, not merely an improved harpsichord.

The chief event of the year was Haydn's second visit to England. Field must have been present at his triumphal appearances at the Salomon concerts, for although Haydn eclipsed Clementi, who had shortly before played there, the latter felt no resentment and cannot have failed to draw his pupil's attention to the great visitor. No doubt Field heard much of what went on in the way of good concerts, nor can he have escaped the fascination of the great singers of the day, such as Mara or Mrs Billington, to say nothing of that universal charmer, Mrs Bland, the ballad singer. This is no unimportant point, as we shall see. It was not long before he himself appeared in public, not at Salomon's concerts, but at one of those given by Barthélemon, where he played one of his master's sonatas in May 1794. This is the more remarkable because Clementi had at least two highly gifted pupils older than Field in Cramer and Bertini.

For several years Field now drudged in Clementi's shops while the firm repeatedly changed its name and trembled on the brink of bankruptcy. He remained faithful to his master even when the business actually went into liquidation in 1800, and had the satisfaction of seeing Clementi soon on his feet again. Meanwhile he had also begun to take violin lessons from Pinto, at one of whose concerts he played a piano concerto of his own in February 1799. His success was almost as great as that of Steibelt had been the year before with a concerto that contained the famous 'Storm Rondo,' one of those fashionable descriptive pieces which the steady improvements of the piano called forth along with much that was new in a more purely musical way. For with its fuller tone the instrument could now thunder as well as sing.

Among the best of the new pianos, the Broadwoods, the Stodarts and others, were those of Longman, Clementi & Co. They contributed to the development, not only of the instrument as such, but of the music written for it. But scarcely less than composition it was improvisation, an accomplishment the early pianists took for granted, which at once profited from the new improvements and encouraged them. Clementi gave up appearing in public in 1797, but he continued to show off instruments in his shops, more particularly after he had set up his own manufacture in 1799. As he had establishments in the Haymarket and Tottenham Court Road as well as in Cheapside, he could well do with an assistant as talented as himself, and Field was constantly at work extemporizing to clients at one of the shops, and perhaps at all of them in turn. That he helped to impose a new style upon his contemporaries as much in this way as by composition, and more than by his occasional public appearances, is certain.

Clementi, a conscientious teacher, was also an exacting taskmaster, intent on giving his pupil experience as well as tuition. Field could hardly have been more fortunate in his musical training; but social advantages he had none, and the repressed existence in a music shop was the worst possible preparation for a shy, awkward youth to taste freedom when he gained it at last. True, his talent procured him unusual opportunities once in a while. In 1801, for instance, he was engaged to play one of his concertos at the 'Grand Oratorio Concerts' at Covent Garden between Handel's *L'Allegro ed il Penseroso* and Mozart's Requiem, and the same year Clementi & Co., as the fickle firm was then called for a change, published some of his music, including the three Sonatas dedicated to his master and labelled Op. 1, according to the old custom of numbering works in the order of publication, not of composition. But one fancies that such advantages, exceptional for a music dealer's assistant of nineteen, were entirely due to the patronage of Clementi. There may have been a sting in the casual benevolence of a master who had kept him hard at work for seven years on a basis of mutual advantage, but certainly at the cost of the pupil's independence. However, Clementi was clearly fond of him, and at length he decided that the time had come to put an end to an arrangement that had become one-sided. In July 1802 he took Field to Paris with him.

Clementi and Field stayed for a time at Pleyel's house, and although Clementi's chief aim was that Field should exhibit the merits of his pianos, he allowed him enough leisure to appear in public. The young pianist's success in Paris was almost sensational, and it was repeated in Vienna about a month later. There Clementi and Field stayed with the publisher Domenico Artaria. Of Beethoven they saw nothing, for he was out of town. About that time Clementi prepared to go on to Russia. He proposed to leave Field behind, recommending him to take lessons in counterpoint from Albrechtsberger; but the young musician recoiled from the prospect of submitting to the rules of an ageing pedant. The new liberty was sweet, and art would have to make the best of what life was now asking the more urgently for the past restraint. So he persuaded Clementi to take him to St Petersburg.

The music of the polite Russian society, but for Bortniansky's efforts in the Imperial Chapel, was still entirely under foreign sway. The Italian Cavos and the Spaniard Martín y Soler held the Opera, which Sarti had left only the preceding spring. The drawing-rooms everywhere resounded with amiable balladry and sparkling pianism of the most insipid sort. The new pianos from the west were much in

demand. Clementi opened a temporary showroom for his instruments, and once again Field was at work applying his gifts to his
master's profit.   Spohr found him there at the end of 1802, as clumsy
and diffident as ever, knowing no language but English and clad in an
Eton suit—without so much as the liberty to grow up.

By the following July Clementi, having established the reputation
of his pianos, left Russia; but Field, seeing some prospects of freedom
and of independent success at last, decided to remain behind.   Having
won acclamation at more than one concert, he quickly emerged from
his obscurity and became a fashionable piano teacher.   He made
money and was petted by people of rank, and this unaccustomed good
fortune had a heady effect upon him.   When Clementi revisited the
Russian capital in 1806, he was glad to see his pupil well established
there.   He acquired a Concerto, the piano Quintet and several other
works from him for publication, the payment being a new piano.
Not that there was very much to be bought from Field.   His output
remained astonishingly small, though the reason was no longer hard
work, but excessive leisure.   In so weak a character as his the reaction
could hardly be otherwise: he made poor use of the time he had on his
hands, became wasteful and indolent, and frittered himself away in a
series of love affairs.   His marriage in 1808 to a young French actress,
Mlle Percheron, failed to steady him for any length of time.   The
match grew more and more unhappy and, whatever his wife's character
may have been, it was doubtless mainly his fault that by 1813 a
separation was found to be inevitable.   Meanwhile he had produced
nothing but a few piano pieces, including a 'Grande Marche Triom-
phale' in honour of General Witgenstein and the Russian victory of
1812, which came out in a patriotic collection that included all manner
of topical inanities, vocal and pianistic.

He was now frequently in Moscow and by 1814 had risen to the
height of his fame as performer and teacher; but, at any rate as far as
posterity is concerned, he only now began to make his name as a
composer of real distinction.   For it was in that year that he composed and published his first three Nocturnes.   They were not
followed by the fourth and fifth until 1817, when a characteristic
Concerto, *L'Incendie par l'Orage* (more thunder), also appeared.   The
following year or thereabouts Glinka, aged fifteen or so, became his
pupil for the piano for a short time.

In the spring of 1822 Field went to live in Moscow for good.
There he plunged deeper and deeper into dissipations; he was not only
an amorist, but he had taken to drink.   He began to neglect his
lessons and engagements, with the result that the handsome fortune
he had made quickly declined.   His health too showed signs of giving
way, yet he grew more and more recklessly intemperate.   Before he

was fifty, he had so far withdrawn from the public that within three years his death was twice falsely reported and he was obliged to contradict the rumours in the press.

A brief triumph was yet in store for him.   In 1832, as he approached his fiftieth birthday, he revisited London, where he had not been for thirty years.   In February he played his E♭ major Concerto with immense success at a Philharmonic concert and on 29 March he was the chief mourner at the funeral of Clementi in Westminster Abbey. Two days later he played at a Haydn centenary concert with Cramer and Moscheles.   Everything wore the saddening air of change.   An unknown young generation was ready to step into the places of their elders.

In June Field went to Paris, in response to many invitations. There again all was changed, and for the better as far as the piano was concerned, thanks to Liszt and Chopin, to name no others.   Chopin he heard soon after his arrival, but can have had no inkling of his own reputed influence upon him, for he thought him 'a sick-room talent,' thus making himself directly responsible for an ill-founded critical generalization.   He did not meet Chopin until the following December.   Another interesting acquaintance was that of his countrywoman, Harriet Smithson, and it can hardly be doubted that he also met Berlioz, who was then engaged to the Irish actress.

After a triumphal stay in Paris, he went on a prolonged tour which took him to Brussels in February 1833, then through the French provinces in the spring and summer, later to Switzerland and, in November, to Italy.   He had enormous successes everywhere.   But in May 1834 he was taken gravely ill at Naples.   His health, undermined by his excesses, had given way under the strain of his continuous travels.   He underwent an operation at a Neapolitan hospital and remained there for many months, spending all the money he had made on his tour.   He was too proud to write to his wealthy Moscow friends for assistance and left the hospital in great poverty early in 1835.   In June, by a fortunate chance, he came across a Russian family whom he knew well, and they took him to Ischia for a cure. A few weeks later he went to Venice and then to Vienna, where he stayed with Czerny.   Having given three concerts in the Austrian capital, he returned to Moscow with his friends at the end of August. By November 1836 he was once more dangerously ill.   There was no lack of friends this time, but none of their efforts availed to restore him.   On 11 January 1837 he died.

This biographical recapitulation has perhaps spread itself unduly; but it has at least served to place John Field in a chapter of musical history from which he is usually all but excluded.   Seen from his own angle, that chapter is one 'in which the piano grows up and engages in sundry adventures,' as a picaresque writer might entitle it. With Clementi and Dussek, Field forms the triumvirate of the first composers of real piano music whose work still has life in it, if we take the trouble to revive it. Haydn and Mozart, though they used the piano, still retained much of the harpsichord style; moreover, they were not primarily keyboard composers. Beethoven's sonatas, though they are pianistic enough, are so in a prophetic way rather than in a manner congenial to the instrument of his time. They forced its development by exacting from it things that were not then essentially adapted to its nature and in a measure never became so, whereas the music of the triumvirate tactfully went with the évolution step by step, now offering a suggestion, now taking a hint. The relations of these composers to their medium are never anything but amicable: their music thus strikes us as all too bland to-day, but the mild pleasure of its unfailing fitness remains undiminished.

Each of the three composers took advantage of all the qualities he found in the new instrument, but they differed in their special predilections for this or that particular quality. Clementi was most fond, perhaps, of the new possibilities of achieving extreme rapidity and lightness combined with a full and yet transparent tone; Dussek found that the sustaining-power which the harpsichord had lacked gave immense scope to a saturated harmony which, however thickly spread, gave a clear ring to every note and thus made bold modulations possible without danger of ambiguity; chief among Field's specialities is unquestionably the striking use he made of the singing tone that was the greatest and most unexpected feature of the new pianos of his time. It is not, indeed, until he comes to exploit this *cantabile* of the keyboard to the fullest in the Nocturnes that he grows into a truly individual composer. He begins by being little more than a clever disciple of Clementi, and, to a lesser extent, an imitator of Dussek. The three Sonatas, Op. 1, look as if Clementi had written the first movements and Dussek the finales.[1] These works are surprisingly mature and interesting, and the third, in C minor, has a passionate impetuosity tempered by wonderfully lucid writing that would be worthy of Clementi at his best, and a long and close working-out that holds the highest promise; but of individuality they have none and there are, significantly enough, no slow movements where a sustained tone could display itself.

It is not until we reach his Sonata in B major, with a very original rondo that begins surprisingly on the dominant seventh, a work of the Russian period, that we come upon anything like the same grasp of

[1] Especially the Scherzo in A major, to be found in the *Popular Pieces* edited by E. Pauer (Augener), which also contain the finale of the first Sonata, here called 'Rondo scherzando.'

structure. Such formal beauties as the concertos show are over-
grown by a luxury of brilliant passage work, ingenious, varied and
ideally pianistic, but rather empty of meaning. The rondos, polonaises and similar pieces are as a rule in the conventional bouncing
manner of the time; the variations and 'Fantaisies élégantes' on airs
from this or that opera are for the most part ornate vanities. There
are even lapses from his habitual good taste to be found, as in the
Quadrille on rhythmically distorted melodies from Weber's operas,
where each piece is named after a character in *Oberon*, Titania adopting
a new changeling in the shape, or rather a mangled likeness of the
shape, of Max's aria in *Der Freischütz*.

In the Nocturnes, however, Field is unique. If we neglect them,
as too many pianists do, there is nothing else to take their place, not
even Chopin's similarly named pieces. Here he sings his heart out,
and it is because he has learnt to sing that he becomes so entirely himself. Not that he is a great melodist in the sense that his tunes are
original, for they rarely have a personal distinction. Field transferred
to the piano the kind of thing he heard from the great singers of the day
just as Chopin later did with the limpid operatic tunes of Bellini.[2]
The most striking of the Nocturnes in this respect is No. 14, in C
major. This is simply a dramatic vocal scena—orchestral introduction, arioso, recitative, coloratura and all. Again, No. 16, with its
thirds and sixths, is like a vocal duet, anticipating Bellini, in whose
work this kind of tune is very familiar:

Ex. 1   Molto moderato

etc.

In No. 8 we seem to hear Mrs Bland embroidering charming affecta-
tions upon some Irish ditty at Vauxhall:

[2] On this point, now disputed, see 'Verdi as Musician,' p. 138.

In his songfulness, then, John Field remains something of a tradi-
tionalist: he does little more than make instrumental novelties out of
certain vocal conventions.   But his instrumental command is astonishing, and there is at least one great discovery—among many minor
ones—that must be credited to him: the device of spreading the
accompanying harmony into far-flung undulating figures, of which
his fluid and velvety basses are the direct result.   The two most
popular Nocturnes, No. 1 and No. 5, both contain striking examples,
and others abound elsewhere; the most arresting are perhaps the
creeping figures in the charming No. 3:

and the very original left-hand treatment in No. 11:

which is endlessly varied.   This last I would undertake to play to any
musician who did not know it as a piece by no earlier a composer than
Nicolas Medtner.   The deception would be sure to work.   Thus
long has Field's influence lasted in Russia, where practically every
composer who specialized in the piano, from Henselt through Balakirev
and Arensky down to Skriabin and Medtner, owes something to him.

Field is never maudlin or hysterical, which is curious in a composer of intemperate habits.   His sensibility has an unusual poise and,
allowance being made for the fashions of his time, his taste is almost
unexceptionable.   The only weakness in some of the Nocturnes
which is not to be excused, or converted into a quaint attraction by the
consideration of their date, is a certain shapelessness.   They sprawl,
some of them, or can find no end.   The lovely E major piece, No. 17,
is spoilt by two redundant pages after a passage (with the tune in the
bass) that would have made an ideal close:

Ex. 5   Lento

No. 7, on the other hand, is but artificially held together by the con-
tinuance of the same figure which goes on so long that the very
ingenuity of the trick grows wearisome.

His range of mood within the species of the Nocturne is extraordinary—far greater than Chopin's.   This is not a question of genius:

the reason is probably that night held more varied experiences for an artist of his stamp.   The last piece of the collection, with the stroke of twelve o'clock at the close, is in his swaggering rondo style and suggests clearly enough some merry midnight bout.   But he can also enjoy the calm of night out of doors, languishing under a moonlit sky: No. 10 is a kind of effeminate 'Moonlight Sonata' movement.   Beethoven's influence amounts to almost nothing in Field, but there is a little of it here and in No. 13, as also in the whimsical No. 15, which again is quite different from any other and has something of Beethoven's splenetic 'Bagatelle' mood beside being closely enough modelled upon the *Andante* of the Sonata Op. 14 No. 2 to let one suspect a tribute.

To continue characterizing each Nocturne would be to continue for some time a record of delighted surprise.   Let us make an end to words and advise all who play the piano to make better discoveries for themselves by procuring a copy of the little masterpieces whereby John Field gave something to the world of music without which it would be as the world of flowers without the daisy: no worse for those who do not know what they miss, but not free from wistful regret for those who had once beheld the modest blossom.

Verdi as Musician

(*Music & Letters,* October 1931)

MORE than one earnest musician may ask whether Verdi is worth attention as a musical craftsman, whether indeed there is anything in him to engage the critical mind outside a theatre. One can but try to convince the sceptics. Most of them will concede that inside the opera-house Verdi is a satisfactory artist; but their tendency as musicians is to attribute his success to his being, as they will condescendingly allow, a magnificent dramatist, a composer endowed with unfailing stagecraft. They never seem to ask themselves whether it can be possible for an opera composer to be a magnificent dramatist without being also a magnificent musician. Is there a single instance of a theatre composer who kept his work alive for many years—to say nothing of a rebirth of his half-forgotten operas—on the strength of dramatic power alone? Indeed, what is dramatic power in opera if it is not musicianship pure and simple, properly applied to a particular purpose? [1]

What operas of any fame are there in which dramatic interest predominates over musical? Marschner's? They are dead. Meyerbeer's? They make but ghostly appearances in the haunts of a stale repertory. Those of scores of Italians like Ponchielli, Giordano, Montemezzi, Zandonai? They are moribund. In their dead-alive company Verdi would be by this time, had he been a dramatic manipulator only, however eminent. As it is, he not only lives but flourishes more than ever to-day, and that because he was a great musician. I do not say a faultless musician; but I hope to show that he is in the company of those absolute masters of their art whose faults one accepts willingly as part of the individual make-up of a sturdy creative personality.

With what cubbish superiority soever one may have sneered at Verdi in younger years (I plead guilty), one learns to look forward to the prospect of hearing one of his operas with a thrill. It is, one knows, going to be a meeting with genius in its apt environment, an experience such as only two other masters of music can always be

---

[1] There are rare cases of superior musicianship concerned with opera, yet not ideally applied: to wit, Beethoven's *Fidelio* and the operas of Cherubini. They are due to a casual preoccupation with an uncongenial medium.

counted on to offer in the theatre—Mozart and Wagner.   After them, who is to be encountered there so unquestioningly?   Without them, it comes to choosing this or that man's outstanding masterpiece: Purcell's *Dido and Aeneas*, Gluck's *Orfeo*, Weber's *Freischütz*, Mussorgsky's *Boris Godunov*, Bizet's *Carmen* or Strauss's *Rosenkavalier*, let us say.   These given their due, we descend to preferences accounted for not by any consensus of opinion, but only by individual taste.   Monteverdi, Handel, Cimarosa, Bellini, Rossini, Borodin, Berlioz, Smetana, Gounod, Puccini, Debussy, all give pleasure to different people in different places.   Verdi, like Mozart and Wagner, is universal.

And when it comes to that, who would not rather listen to an early opera by Verdi, say *I Lombardi* or *Ernani*, than to Wagner's *Rienzi*? Again, comparing the two masters' actually completed first works for the stage, there can be little doubt that *Oberto, Conte di San Bonifacio* would make some sort of a live entertainment, while *Die Feen* can be no more than a study of absorbing interest to a handful of historians.

No disparagement of Wagner is implied here, even if we agree that he matured more slowly than Verdi.   It must be borne in mind that the Italian settled down without protest to an accepted convention, whereas the German from the first began to grope towards a new manner.   Still, the fact remains that Verdi is not only comparable to Wagner, but may be regarded from certain viewpoints as actually superior to him.   It is simply a matter of creeds.   The choice between the two is not determined by any radical difference of eminence, but by the question whether, as musicians, we accept the Reformation or prefer to remain Romans.

Verdi, though not a reformer, is a liberal-minded catholic.[2]   If he was not for thoroughgoing changes, he was amenable to gradual evolution along rational lines of his own.   His life-work is one of steady progress.   That is why, as Ferruccio Bonavia pointed out long ago, it is wrong in his case (if indeed it can be right in anybody's) to speak of three styles.

As for the current theory that Verdi was indebted to Wagner in his later years, it is not worth refuting nowadays.   Verdi is the opposite pole to Wagner.   Much of the disparagement to which serious musicians have subjected him is due to their failure to recognize this fact.   They dislike him because he is not like Wagner instead of admiring his independence, and where they can no longer withhold admiration, they must needs seek an approach to Wagner in his work.

Their great objection to Verdi is that he is theatrical—a terrible indictment indeed to level at a man who writes for the theatre.   If they

[2] I continue to write metaphorically in a purely artistic sense, although, as it happens, Verdi's religion was by no means orthodox.

intend the term to designate quite literally something written for the stage, they may well use it, so long as they agree to imply that it is suitably written; but if they are thinking of something aesthetically inferior to music of absolute worth, then the answer is emphatically that they are arguing on a false postulate.

Well, the word 'theatrical' does convey some sort of obloquy, and this will not do for Verdi. Let us say, then, that his operas are not theatrical but dramatic. So is the Requiem in a smaller and, from the composer's own point of view, quite permissible degree. It is worth observing here that a purely superficial stage device which occurs regularly in the operas is entirely absent from the Requiem. This is the long protraction of closing chords in rhythmically broken patterns at the end of a scene or act, which is simply the dramatist's 'curtain' converted into music. Verdi knows this to be a necessary evil and never makes the mistake of the inferior musician, who will use a convention without knowing what it stands for.

We must now try to draw a distinction between what is theatrical and what dramatic. Two well-known examples may do it for us. Mascagni's *Cavalleria rusticana* is a piece of sheer theatricality; Verdi's *Rigoletto*[3] is pure musical drama. The heroines of these two operas are in much the same plight, and we sympathize with both; but we cannot possibly, unless we be utterly devoid of taste, shed tears over Santuzza, whereas it is quite difficult, at any reasonably good performance and in any but an entirely unfavourable mood, not to cry over Gilda. Now what is it that makes Santuzza a hard creature who flaunts her woes shamelessly and Gilda a sensitive and lovable girl whose tragedy touches every heart? Not any difference in the librettos, which is not appreciable. It is that Mascagni's music is actually flaunting and Verdi's touching. But why so? Because the former exploits every cheap effect within his reach (which is distressingly short), the latter makes every point by purely musical and musicianly means, again only so far as his own not all-embracing resources and ideas go, but thus far wholly satisfactorily. In other words, Mascagni imposes on us by theatrical means of no specifically musical merits, while Verdi's music is artistic according to its own aesthetic code and hence not theatrical but, since it also fits the scenic situation, ideally dramatic.

[3] Only about half of Verdi's operas (and the Requiem) are referred to in this article, so chosen that works of every period are included in more or less equal numbers. The selection has been made in order to render reference not too troublesome and expensive for those who wish to consult the scores. The following abbreviations are used throughout this article: Aid. *Aida*; B.M. *Un Ballo in maschera*; D.C. *Don Carlos*; Ern. *Ernani*; Fal. *Falstaff*; F.D. *La forza del dsstino*; L.M. *Luisa Miller*; Lom. *I Lombardi*; Mac. *Macbeth*; Mas. *I Masnadieri*; Oth. *Othello*; Req. Requiem; Rig. *Rigoletto*; S.B. *Simon Boccanegra*. The pagination referred to is that of Ricordi's vocal scores.

Let us look at Gilda's 'Caro nome' (Rig. I. ii. 110). It is as shapely and economical as a Scarlatti sonata.   You can do with it what you cannot conceivably do with any passage from Mascagni—play it on the piano and find that it makes a faultless piece of music quite apart from the stage situation which it fits so miraculously.   There is a principal theme which is not only the very picture of an innocent young girl very much in love and repeating with a tremulous heart the name of her lover she has just heard for the first time, but a symphonic thesis developed with the strictest musical logic and deliciously varied in a coda that presents it again in a refined form, letting it linger as if reluctant to die away in that 'last sigh' in which Gilda declares she will still breathe the 'dear name.'   The second theme is no less beautifully treated, in spite of the fact that the composer keeps the requirements of a coloratura singer constantly in mind, and the episodes that follow it drive irresistibly towards the coda by way of a climax and that lovely staccato dying fall (see Ex. 1 below).   Even the cadenza, though an unwelcome excrescence, is rightly placed, which cannot be said of the majority of Verdi's vocal flourishes. They are, in fact, a serious blemish on his art.   Coming at the very end of a song, as they generally do, without an instrumental peroration to balance them, they produce the uncomfortable feeling of a violent wrench.   There are two particularly bad examples in this very opera: the Duke's 'Parmi veder le lagrime' and Rigoletto's 'Miei signori' (Rig. II. 138 and 173).

I have just referred to an incident in 'Caro nome' as a dying fall. The description may be too fanciful to serve to identify the passage, so here it is:

It will do at the same time to demonstrate the distinction of Verdi's musical notions.   We have here one of those ideas that are perennial surprises.   No amount of hearing can wear off its ingratiating charm.

To try to account for the fine quality of a particular fragment of musical invention is to come up against the very boundary-line of knowledge, on the hither side of which lie the vague regions of intuition and taste; but at the risk of being caught in a bog, one must

K

try to get to the bottom of this ultimate aesthetic question. It is matter for a bóok on the whole of music, but here Verdi may help us to a sample.

One of the tests of quality, I think, is memorability, and Verdi, of course, stands that test magnificently. An opera by, let us say, Giordano, acts on the memory like water on a duck's back; one by Verdi remains indelibly engraved on it after a first hearing. You may not be able to visualize all its features in musical notation, just as you cannot always see the face of a beloved person with your mind's eye, but you carry it in your heart ready for instant recognition.

Through another test, that of lasting surprise, Verdi comes equally well. It is highly characteristic of much of his music that it often lingers in one's memory in a slightly different form from that which it actually takes. And what is significant is that it is invariably more distinguished than one had thought. A case in point is the Aida theme (at the opening of the overture and elsewhere), which few people, I fancy, keep in their heads just as it is, nor in so refined a form.

But let us keep to my dying fall. For a long time, even after several casual hearings of the opera and the song, I persisted in thinking that the passage quoted above went something like this:

Ex. 2

One expects, I suppose, a continuous pattern of melodic movement up a third and down a fifth, and the surprise lies in the change to the downward movement of a fourth in the middle. Perhaps it may be assumed that Verdi himself at first had the more regular pattern in his mind. If so, he made an astonishing improvement by avoiding those repeated middle E's towards the end and by making that interesting chromatic approach to the bass dominant through the flat submediant instead of setting down the conventional subdominant-dominant-tonic cadence.

Verdi's music is full of such subtleties. Often they are gained by the quite simple expedient of inverting his chords and placing their bass notes in an unexpected position. Simple—yes; but like all divine simplicities, it took a genius to use this at precisely the right moment. A striking example of this discriminating removal of the bass out of the root position is to be found in so early an opera as *I Lombardi* (1843), in this Bellini-ish passage:

and another in *La forza del destino* (Leonora's aria):

In the space of an article it is necessary to limit oneself to isolated specimens of Verdi's ingenuity in this or that particular. It is not even possible to touch upon every aspect of his musicianship. One might, for instance, argue from his management of basses that he was an excellent contrapuntist and go on to prove the assertion with such things as the handling of double counterpoint in the *Aida* march (Aid. II. ii. 117–18), a place where from the dramatic point of view such a musical effort was superfluous, and the original *stretto* (with entries on A♮, F♯, E♮, D♭) in the second Requiem fugue (Req. 202).

An interesting case of the inversion of chords in the most effective way possible is this extraordinarily modern passage in Iago's false account of Cassio's dream:

This points forward as far as Delius, but one may imagine a smaller composer hot on the scent of such an innovation letting his harmony progress in a more rigid formation, thus:

All was grist to Verdi's mill, but the miller was intent on doing his job honestly.   Whatever the occasion demanded, that he would furnish, not caring whether it be ever so conventional or ever so daring.   He was quite capable when it suited him of stringing together a series of chords in one single position after the manner of Ex. 6. The following passage from *Falstaff*, which is as astonishing to-day as ever, will bear witness:

The descent of common chords at the close of the second act of *Othello* is another case in point (Oth. II. 201).

While we are on the subject of modernities, it is perhaps worth while pointing out that one of Strauss's favourite chords seems to be a Verdian heirloom.[4]   It is the first inversion of the subdominant triad with the root sharpened (*Don Quixote*, A♭ major interlude in *Le Bourgeois gentilhomme* music, etc.), and we find it in the final scene

[4] Carl Moor's song, 'O mio castel paterno' (Mas. I. 8), by the way, looks suspiciously like Strauss's model for the tenor's aria in the first act of *Der Rosenkavalier*.

of *Aida* as the last of those pangs of beauty with which that opera so sweetly afflicts our hearts:

Verdi can write pungent dissonances, which have the greater effect for coming rarely, as in the tremendous moment where Othello has forced Desdemona to her knees:

Again he can make the boldest use of a device such as consecutive fifths, which were still a shocking trespass upon musical propriety in 1887. In Iago's *Credo* he writes them thus:

Verdi's main pursuit is that of beauty. Even when he has ugly situations to deal with he contrives to give us music that holds the ear spellbound. But, finding at the same time the musical expression that exactly fits the situation, he achieves a quite extraordinary individuality at such junctures. I do not say originality, for he is not precisely an original composer. For that he too often took things as he found them, from Bellini, from Rossini, from Donizetti, from Meyerbeer. Sometimes he was content to let the music of such people simply run over into his without doing a great deal to colour it to his own dye. The overture to *Luisa Miller* is a charming piece of Rossini; Bellini's shallow brilliance we find in Amalia's 'Lassù risplendere' (Mas. III. 137), his march tunes in *I Masnadieri* (III. 144) and in *Macbeth* (I. 19–20), and his type of *cantabile* in a duet between Ernani and Elvira (Ern. II. 154–7), with accompanying figures pointing directly to Bellini's influence on Chopin. This has been vigorously denied by Arthur Hedley on the ground that Chopin had already evolved this type of melody before any Bellini opera was heard in Poland; but it was fashionable everywhere in those days to play music from new Italian operas on the piano, as lessons, in selections and in the form of fantasies. As for Verdi, it would be quite possible to make a pianistic disguise of the cabaletta in *I Lombardi* (II. 155 et seq.) that would pass for one of Chopin's mazurkas, polonaises or nocturnes, according to the treatment.

There are traces, too, of composers farther afield. The handling of a recitative (Mas. II. 113–14), the line of an aria (Mac. II. 113–15), is occasionally astonishingly Weberish, and the drop into a remote key without modulation in the chorus of nuns in *I Lombardi* seems to come straight from Schubert:

With the latter he also shares a love of unexpected exchanges between major and minor.[5] Even Berlioz appears in the incantation scene in *Macbeth*, perhaps not unnaturally, since that also develops the Mephisto Waltz eruption that marked the romantic music of the mid-nineteenth century.[6]

Still, one has to look hard enough to collect a few examples of obvious influence in Verdi's whole output, and even where they are found they are seen to have become individualized in passing through his mind. This individuality of his is as much harmonic as melodic; for all that people will allow him to be little more, from a purely musical point of view, than a great melodist. It is significant that the musical examples so far given, though not designedly chosen for that purpose, show a predominantly harmonic interest. Verdi not only finds endless new combinations, but new blends arrived at by apt chordal distribution, which is a much more musicianly procedure than that of merely concocting unheard-of mixtures. The striking of twelve o'clock in the last scene of *Falstaff* is striking in another sense quite as much owing to the wonderful spacing and inverting of the chords as to their actual constitution (Fal. III. ii. 347). One feels, too, that if the Windsor clock had chimed midnight according to

[5] See 'Schubert's Favourite Device,' p. 79.
[6] Francis Toye, in a lecture, mentioned Beethoven and instanced the motif running through *La forza del destino*, which first appears at the opening of the prelude. No doubt he was thinking of the *Egmont* overture.

the modern continental time-tables, he could have found another twelve combinations without straining his resources so far as to destroy the unity of this passage, which is kept with an unfailing instinct, for all its manifold diversity.

Falstaff is the last of the operas; but harmonic nicety is to be found quite early in Verdi. It matures and widens its scope as he gathers experience, but it is a fundamental, not an acquired artistic possession. In the *Lombardi* of 1843, for instance, we find this arresting turn:

and Giselda's prayer in the same opera contains phrases which point straight to the Requiem of 1874 and would do no discredit to Desdemona's 'Ave Maria' in *Othello*.   Here is one:

Sometimes a harmonic turn makes all the difference to the melodic line, as in the 'Oro supplex,' which is one of the most poignantly beautiful tunes of the Requiem (Req. 80).   Elsewhere it is possible to feel that such a turn would have made a difference for the better, and one misses it, however fine the melody may be in itself.   A good case in point is the surging, impassioned love duet in the first act of *La forza del destino*, which begins thus:

The exact repetition of the first four bars before the music turns the
corner into a new stretch of fascinating melody is felt to be a flaw.
One expects at least a slightly different harmonic shading the second
time to give the song continuity; or better still, a small deviation in
the melodic line which the harmony is bound to follow.   Something
like this seems to be called for at the repeat of the third and fourth
bars:

Ex. 15

I do not pretend to correct Verdi.   Had he chosen to write such a
variant, he would have done it much better than I can.   I am merely
putting down approximately the kind of thing one would normally
expect of him at this stage of a tune.   There are plenty of instances to
be found in his work where he does introduce melodic and harmonic
deflections with the most consummate skill.   The latter occur particularly in cadences.   He cannot forbear to use the full close in
moments of emotional stress, but in his hands it rarely annoys the
hearer as a conventional expedient.   It can, on the contrary, become a
most moving culmination of a melody or of a whole scene.   One need
only think of Desdemona's outburst 'Ah! Emilia, addio ' (Oth. IV.
337), which on the face of it is an ordinary Italian cadence, but being

justly placed in the context and set down with an infallible instinct for the right line and spacing and colour, never fails to bring the listener to the verge of tears.

A few specimens of characteristic Verdian cadences may be given from his less familiar works. The reader's memories of the well-known operas and of the Requiem, which is worth special attention in this connection, will easily supplement them. (In all but one of these examples the voice parts are omitted.)

Ex. 18 Allegretto   B.M.II (146)

Ex. 19 Andante sostenuto   dim. e rall.

p No   a - mor per me   non ha!   A - mor. per me non

D.C. III, i (193)

ha!

Andante mosso

Ex. 20

ff   dim.

Mas. I (64)

p

In Ex. 16 we have a very interesting early indication of how Verdi likes to throw the weight of interest into the cadence. The episode from which this is torn is one of those rather superficially fiery tunes which abound in *Ernani*—C major with a curve to A minor on one side and a more interesting one through C minor to E♭ major on the other. But in the cadence modulations suddenly coil themselves closely together. Not only do we pass through three keys in as many bars, but our ear receives two shocks of pleasant surprise, first when the dominant of F major leads unexpectedly to A major and then when E major, apparently a dominant preparing for A minor, changes to that of C major.

Next, in Ex. 17, a quite ordinary cadential progression is made interesting and extremely beautiful by chromatic inner parts, while Ex. 18 shows that diminished sevenths, which Verdi once explicitly deprecated as too easy a subterfuge, could be used by him with charm and distinction. They serve here definitely as dissonances demanding resolution, not as first-aids to modulation, and once again his art of inverting a chord in just the right way and the proper place (last quaver of bar 1) is made manifest.

The harmonic attraction of Ex. 19, apparently a commonplace effusion of Italian musical emotionalism, yet a very subtly devised feat of composition, centres in the third beat of the second bar quoted, where there are two simultaneous semitonal clashes—the suspension of B♭ against the A in the bass and the F♯ in the voice against the G in the tremolo chord. Moreover, this passage has the additional thrill of revealing itself in the next bar as an interrupted cadence. It may be said that this is rather piling it up. The answer is that the piling-up comes exactly at the proper moment, as a glance at the whole context will show.

The last two examples (20 and 21) show Verdi's pet trick of suddenly plunging into a remote key at the very turn of a cadence. The first exhibits the device in its crudest form: the D♭ bar could be omitted without any change in the rest of the music. True, its surprise would be gone; but it looks as if it had been plastered on as an

afterthought to give some colour to a very plain formula.   Not so
with Ex. 21, which is all of a piece.

The placing of ordinary chords next to each other in distant keys
without modulatory transition came readily to Verdi's hand, especially
in his cadences (Req. 20–1, 105; Aid. 207; B.M. 58, 175–6; Mac. 113).
It is always convincing in his music, and this argues more than ordinary
taste and discernment, for we find it to be almost invariably jarring
and far-fetched in the work of other composers, even composers of
eminence like Strauss and Reger.

A cadence is for Verdi the natural crest of a melodic line, which
proceeds towards it by way of a statement, often an amplification or
variant of that statement, and a contrast.   The cadential climax can
itself take the form of a variant and so become particularly satisfying
as a rounding-off of the melodic curve.   Let us look, for instance,
at the love duet in *La forza del destino* already quoted from in Ex. 14
(F.D. I. 36–40), where the tune culminates thus:

This, with its characteristic chromatic sideslips which reinforce the
main point of interest, is in itself enchanting and would be wholly
admirable in the context, were it not for the defect of repetition earlier
in the tune.   The ideal melodic conduct is that of the duet 'Si,
fuggiam,' between Aida and Radamès (Aid. III. 240–2), where we
have a statement, a restatement with a modulatory change, a contrast
leading to an expectant pause and then a second modification of the
original strain touching a higher note than has been reached before
and marking a third stage of climax.   It is by this cunning third-
degree method that Verdi succeeds best in forcing a confession of
allegiance from his hearers.

One might go on drawing distinctions until one caught Verdi doing some definitely inferior things—a meandering tune with a shifty harmony (D.C. III. i. 236–7), an orchestral or choral inanity (Ern. II. 131; L.M. I. ii. 85–92; Mac. II. 128; Mas. II. 108) or whole stretches of indifferent dance music, as in the first act of *Rigoletto* or the last of *Un ballo in maschera.* (The shallow ballroom music in *Traviata* is justified because it characterizes the people in the opera and outlines their environment.) But when all is said, it is astonishing how little can be singled out from his total output for which the excuse of dramatic aptness at least cannot be made. However, purely musical considerations alone surprisingly often exonerate him, and when they fail, his unreckoning enthusiasm, his almost passionate desire to be popular, not from vanity, but from a sincere affection for his public, do the rest. It is all very well to say that *Trovatore* and *Traviata* are mere repositories of barrel-organ tunes; but if Verdi is responsible for every barrel organ in Italy and every Italian organ-grinder elsewhere who daily sings with the minstrel and errs with the courtesan, it is his merit rather than his fault. The most vulgar of his melodies began by being so in the proper sense of the word. A dozen or two have strayed into the gutter, but he wrote a dozen hundred that have kept their self-respect, as with a little more luck and less fatal attraction any might have done.

What is remarkable about Verdi's best melodies is that they are not only good in themselves, but always curiously appropriate to the situation in hand, even when at first sight they may appear almost ludicrously incongruous. (At first sight, I say, not at first hearing.) The secret of this appropriateness is doubtless that they fit in with the drama without being sacrificed to it musically. They remain fully developed tunes, whatever may happen on the stage. Such a dramatic cutting short of a melodic line as in Maximiliam Moor's lament (Mas. III. 163–4), which is only too obviously effective, occurs rarely. The true Verdian procedure is not to fly off at a tangent in a highly dramatic moment, but to keep to his melodic idea and to increase the tension less by insistence on accent than by a greater amplitude of melody. Rigoletto's despairing duet with the love-distracted Gilda (Rig. II. 189–94) is a familiar instance, and another of interest may be found in *Luisa Miller* (II. ii. 189–200).

An admirable and especially musical device of the same order may be instanced from the former opera (Rig. I. ii. 84–90). It is that of first stating a melody plain and then, when the situation requires it, adding something else: in this case Rigoletto's solicitude for his daughter's safety and her tender response to it.

Verdi's workmanship on such occasions is impeccable: hence the impression of a limpid beauty even where he studies the dramatic exigencies, as in the agitated duet between Amneris and Radamès (Aid. I. i. 14–17), which becomes a trio after the entry of Aida, who superimposes her own slow melody upon the rapid conversation—a perfect specimen of a dramatic aside converted into its musical equivalent.   On a larger scale, we may find an example of the splendid craftsmanship that lets drama and music flow on simultaneously and intermingling to perfection at the opening of *Un ballo in maschera*, where the material of the overture (with fugal treatment) is drawn into the first scene for page after page with an almost symphonic effect.

The most convincing mark of the musician who will not subordinate his art to the librettist's, though he is intent on co-ordinating the two, is probably the gradual subtilizing of the recitative in Verdi's operas. His recitative is often interesting from the very beginning, but there are too many arid patches of it in the early works.   In *Aida* recitative has all but disappeared, and what there is of it is not a conventional filling of a chasm between one set piece and the next, but a transition of musical significance.   True, it is kept on a low level of invention, but that is done on purpose.   Verdi, in fact, is past master in the art of distributing degrees of intensity throughout a scene or an act in such a way as to grip and relax the hearer's interest just as he sees fit.   We are in his hands: he sways us by his unfailing instinct for doing the right thing at the right moment.

One of the most interesting passages combining a new treatment of recitative with a subdued instrumental accompaniment is the conversation of Violetta and Alfredo in the first act of *La Traviata*, a rapid interchange of phrases which are almost speech, with frivolous dance music played off-stage.   Attention should be given also to the opening scenes of *Rigoletto, Simon Boccanegra, La forza del destino* and *Aida*, where we drop into the middle of a lightly sung conversation and, for music, are forced to listen to the orchestra.   Verdi, for all his magnificent vocal writing, is by no means always intent on bringing the singer to the fore.   There are countless passages in his works where the voice is kept to one note while the orchestra carries on the music.   Again, he is fond of giving the voice a secondary place in a duologue with an instrumental strain (D.C. IV. 273), or of assigning it the lower part in a passage in thirds and sixths, a device to which he seems almost as much attached as Schubert.

Verdi's mastery of distributing the musico-dramatic weight over a whole act may be studied by his handling of situations where suspense is followed by excitement, e.g. the last acts of *Rigoletto, La Traviata* and *Othello*.   But this is touching upon the aspect of his genius which I have agreed to take for granted.   Verdi as a musician is subject enough for an article: indeed it could grow into a volume before one had done with praise.   There would be occasion for blame too, and more than there is room for in the pages given up to this study; but for the moment my aim was to help in readjusting the balance of judgment.   Though this essay is itself admittedly ill-balanced, I hope that it may add a fraction to the weight of favourable criticism which has largely been accumulating against those who have too thoughtlessly discredited a great master of music with all sorts of prejudices and partisanships.

Vincent d'Indy's 'Enigma'

(*Musical Opinion*, September–October 1942)

IF IN these days of a ready spread of mass information a musical paper should aim at amusing and perplexing its readers with 'Do you know?' columns and 'quizzes,' it might make a good deal of mystery of an unfamiliar and unjustly neglected work for the piano which offers a chance for no less than three 'quizzical' questions. It is Vincent d'Indy's cycle of thirteen pieces entitled *Tableaux de voyage* (Op. 33), and the three puzzles could be thus formulated:

(*a*) What work, apart from Elgar's Variations, contains an 'Enigma'?

(*b*) Which French composer wrote an extensive piano work that makes use of a motto theme or *idée fixe*?

(*c*) Who are the composers who made use of Bach's name by constructing a theme on the notes (in German nomenclature) of B A C H?

The last would doubtless be confidently answered by most musicians with the enumeration of the names of Bach himself, Schumann, Liszt, Reger and perhaps Karg-Elert; but I doubt whether more than one or two would mention d'Indy, one of those composers whom most people greatly respect without taking the trouble of knowing them. He seems to be regarded as having had something a little inhuman about him, and it may be that he had; but he was certainly human enough to desire that his work should be known, and even liked, if possible.

If possible! But is it? Or is he too austere, too scholastic, too forbiddingly what one does not expect a Frenchman to be? Well, it is true that we have to reckon with these things if we take him up. But why should we not? Certain characteristics do not become themselves objectionable merely by appearing unexpectedly in a Frenchman. After all, Boileau was austere, Descartes scholastic and Racine in his own frigid and humourless way is as French as the gay and mordant Molière. To disregard d'Indy for no better reason than the difficulty of thinking of a French musician as being without a trace of frivolity is to adopt an attitude that is itself flippant. An artist may be accepted or rejected by anyone with a vestige of critical judgment, but he must not be dismissed on the ground that he fails to be something he was never predisposed by his own nature to become. We may as well reproach Bach for not being brief and witty or Beethoven for not being elegant as d'Indy for having nothing of seductive charm about him—and the comparison is not invalidated because it involves setting the great side by side with the less great, for the argument holds for all art that is good of its kind.

It is quite true, of course, that d'Indy keeps us at arm's length and will not let us warm to him at all readily. There is a certain aridity about his invention, a certain bareness about his textures, a certain angularity about his themes and tunes. These are negative things, though: in criticizing him adversely one finds oneself accounting for what one misses in him, not singling out matters that repel. It is hard to think of anything that is positively displeasing in his music, and much more so to find anything obtrusively tasteless. One cannot, for instance, say 'Oh, but he is so sentimental!' or call his work pretentious, over-ripe, luxuriously spiced and scented, intemperate either in imagination or in display. He never has the heated sensuality we find, for example, in Wagner, Liszt, Strauss or Skriabin; like Berlioz, he is always admirably cool and fresh in expression, while unlike that master he is ever moderate in what he expresses. Indeed, in most respects he is very different from Berlioz; but the two are nevertheless readily brought into comparison because they are both Frenchmen utterly unlike what artists among that nation are conventionally thought to be and even expected to be—either fastidiously reticent or cloyingly perfumed. Yet neither could possibly be, if one comes to think of it, anything but French.[1]

If I have singled out the *Tableaux de voyage* from among d'Indy's works for discussion, it is not only because the set could be introduced as a possible 'quiz,' though from that point of view it is quite an interesting case. The chief reason is that it happens to be an easily accessible and easily performable work. Pianists predominate vastly among executive musicians, especially among amateurs, and there is no doubt that a great many among the latter would get much pleasure from this set of pieces, if only they knew it, not to mention the fact that it would make an admirable recital work for any enterprising pianist looking for an extended suite to take the place, if only for a change, of

[1] This has not always been recognized by d'Indy's compatriots, among whom it is almost a commonplace to call him the most Germanic of French composers. Some colour is lent to this by the predilection for German subjects shown in several of his works—e.g. the dramatic legend, *Le Chant de la cloche,* which is based on Schiller, as is, of course, the orchestral trilogy of *Wallenstein,* and the song, 'Plainte de Thécla,' taken from the same cyclic drama. There are also three pieces for the piano entitled *Schumanniana,* and d'Indy's critical writings include studies of Beethoven and of Wagner's *Parsifal.* That the *Tableaux de voyage* also point towards German regions will be seen presently. On the other hand, we should bear in mind such purely French works as the *Poème des montagnes* for piano, the symphonic poem *Jour d'été à la montagne* and the *Symphonie sur un chant montagnard français* for piano and orchestra, all inspired by the composer's ancestral country of the Vivarais, as well as his important collections of French folksongs.

L

Schumann's *Carnaval*, let us say.[2]   I can imagine a far worse concert-goer's fate than having to listen to it once or twice, though I think that most people would want something in the nature of a programme note in order to get the most out of it, since some of its ingenuities are technical features that might escape them at a first hearing.   What follows may possibly serve the purpose of such a note.   Let us, first of all, consider the *Tableaux de voyage* in the light of that hypothetical 'quiz':

(*a*) What is d'Indy's 'enigma'?   It is, like Elgar's, a theme, but it can hardly be supposed to go with another, unheard but familiar theme, since it frequently alters its rhythmic shape in the course of the pieces in which it appears.   That it is meant to mystify us is indicated by the title of the introductory piece which serves for its exposition, for that title is ' ? '.   Nor does its sequence of notes, which is the following:

Ex. 1

disclose anything.   It is shown in semibreves above, for neither its expository statement in ' ? ' nor any of its later transformations can be taken as a definitive form.   The notes themselves, not any of the shapes they may take on, are the repository of d'Indy's secret.   What these notes mean is unimaginable and has never, to my knowledge, been explained.   The names of the notes do not spell anything recognizable, either in French nomenclature or in our own, or even in the slightly more resourceful German, with its additional H (B♮) and S (Es = E♭).   It is possible, of course, that the notes may stand for a selection of the musical letters alone in some name or other, as those in *Carnaval* stand for S.C.H.A. in 'Schumann'; but if so it is beyond conjecture what they can possibly mean.   In any case A♭ is a snag, and another is the fact that the theme does not always appear in the same key.

(*b*) What is d'Indy's motto or *idée fixe*?   As the reader will already have gathered, it is the 'enigma' theme itself which serves in that capacity.

(*c*) How does d'Indy use the B A C H sequence of notes, and why?   The eleventh piece is a gravely gentle, rather organ-like fugue, during which it is quite natural to think of Bach.   The composer must almost inevitably have done so, and when he found that B A C H would fit in with his scheme as a counter-subject used three times, twice in the bass (the second time in augmentation and with octave doubling), he had every excuse for not resisting this flash of inspiration. The 'how?' and the 'why?' are thus quite plausibly answered at one and the same time.

All the thirteen pieces have titles, two of them being place-names which only very roughly indicate the itinerary of the composer's journey. The German sound of one, Lermoos, and the French look of the other, Beuron, seem to point to such a region as Alsace-Lorraine, or more likely (since some of the pieces suggest mountain country) Switzerland. A good gazetteer, however, reveals the fact that Lermoos is in the Tyrol, and that the name of Beuron is not French at all, the place being in South Germany on the banks of the Danube, some twenty miles east of its source at Donaueschingen and situated in that curious scrap of the Prussian state of Hohenzollern, flung off its main territory into the middle of Württemberg. The remaining titles are picturesque evocations of a variety of sights and sounds which the music not merely illustrates admirably but turns into true poetry.

Let us now look at each piece of the *Tableaux de voyage*. (The numbers marked * are those containing thematic references to the 'enigma'.)

*1. '?' *Assez lent*. After six introductory bars adumbrating the motto theme vaguely and very softly, it appears quietly, sustained and lingering, in slow 5–8 time. It is repeated by means of a kind of irregular rosalia, and then briefly developed in a groping chromatic manner that betrays the César Franck pupil, yet maintains a distinctive individuality. A final statement of the theme, newly and more sparely harmonized, lets it die away with a different cadence, made very originally of piled-up harmonic suspensions. The mood of the piece is one of subdued pain—a pain too deep and perhaps too remote to lend itself to dramatic expressions of yearning and self-pity. One thinks of some loved and lost travelling-companion, whose image is destined again and again to become intertwined with these recollections of a journey she may have shared, or during which she was never far from the traveller's thought. That her name may be concealed in some way in d'Indy's theme appears the more likely because its succession of notes seems to be too queer and irregular to be due solely to spontaneous invention.

*2. 'En marche.' *Joyeusement*. A brittle, light-stepping piece, rather laboured as to invention and spiky as to part-writing, but throughout in a free counterpoint that always remains delightfully transparent. In the middle is a section marked 'Causerie,' obviously a playful colloquy between a female and a male voice, which sometimes imitate each other's phrases, with the light walking pace continuing uninterruptedly. At least, an interruption does not occur until after the recapitulation of the first section, where the dialogue, just as it is about to be resumed, slackens and hesitates while the bass utters the first five notes of the 'enigma.' But the piece ends resolutely with two bars in the original brisk tempo. The 'walk' is resumed lest the 'talk' should yield to tenderness.

3. 'Pâturage.' *Modéré sans lenteur.* A lovely, idyllic piece, reminding one a little of Liszt's *Années de Pèlerinage* at their quietest and most lucid; but far more original—in fact, on the whole, unlike anything else in music that one can think of. It is very largely written in two parts only, but that, instead of resulting in a meagre sound-quality, only makes it beautifully limpid and serene; and the point of a third part's joining in for a moment at the ninth bar with the gentle friction of a major second is delicious. So, too, is the intermittent slightly discordant rubbing of the parts against each other throughout the piece. The rural atmosphere is beautifully maintained, and the suggestion of clear and pure air persuades one that d'Indy's pasture is on some alpine upland.

4. 'Lac vert.' *Tranquillement.* This piece, no less lovely than the last, is very distinctly Franckish. One thinks inevitably of the first movement of d'Indy's master's violin Sonata. The key (E♭ major) is far away from it, but the swaying motion is the same, and some procedures—notably the upward-striving rosalias in the middle, and much of the shifting harmony—are pure Franck. Still, even here one is conscious that d'Indy had a mind of his own.

*5. 'Le Glas.' *Lent.* For whom the knell sounds nobody knows: perhaps not even the traveller himself, who is probably witnessing a burial at some village churchyard where he does not know a soul. But the thought of his companion haunts him for a moment, as with some personal dread or sorrow, for the first four notes of the 'enigma' are heard arising inevitably out of an ominous harmonic passage. The classic funereal key of C minor is used, and hollow open fifths in the left hand are a frequent feature.

6. 'La Poste.' *Assez vite.* One of the most original pieces in a very original work. The fanfare of the post-horn is heard alone at first. Then the left hand sets going a semiquaver accompaniment— a curious figure stretching over an eleventh and remaining unchanged in 2–4 time almost to the end, while a crisp and cheerful tune blares lustily against it in the treble in 3–4 time. The horn-call returns towards the end, heard as from a distance and still over the same accompaniment, which then scatters itself in a final arpeggio.

*7. 'Fête de Village.' *Mouvement de valse très modéré.* A lumbering bucolic dance, which begins by so misplacing the accompanying chords that the ear is at first uncertain of where the rhythmic accent is supposed to lie. Later on there is a suggestion of merry fluting and fiddling that almost tempts one to think this music better suited than Schumann's to the ninth song in the *Dichterliebe* cycle. Suddenly this gives rise to an accompaniment of the 'enigma' in the bass, the longest fragment yet heard, consisting of all but the last two notes of the theme.   The uncouth waltz then goes on with renewed vigour, but towards the end it is for a moment wholly silenced by a second allusion to the ' ? ' theme, worked in at a curious angle, so to speak, with strangely oblique harmony, until it is arrested on the leading-note of C major (the key of the piece), and made to melt unexpectedly into a dominant-seventh chord that leads back to four concluding bars of dance music.

8. 'Halte au Soir.'   *Modéré*.   Another exquisitely idyllic piece, as fine in its way as Nos. 3 and 4, and once again remarkable for d'Indy's ascetic way of writing in two parts.   Only eleven of the forty-nine bars show more than two notes at a time, and even there we never find more than three parts, with the only exception of a single chord of four notes.   Yet the effect is more than sufficiently satisfying, and it is enhanced here and there by right-hand octaves, which need not be regarded as additional parts any more than octave couplings in the organ performance of a fugue would be.   There is just a suggestion of the quietly lyrical and gently descriptive Schumann of the *Waldscenen* in this piece; yet d'Indy, here as elsewhere, writes like no other composer.

*9. 'Départ matinal.'   *Gaîment et assez animé*.   This is one of the three most extended pieces of the set, a large-scale, fully developed composition of great interest as such, but also an exhilarating piece of music.   The springy energetic opening sets one tingling with pleasure, and it is harmonically interesting for being first poised awry on the subdominant of C♯ minor and plunging deceptively into E major before settling down to a cadence in the former key, which is the tonic one of the piece.   New matter arises buoyantly, and a roundabout enharmonic change brings with it the return of the opening theme, now set at a different harmonic angle.   A bass persistently repeats F♯-G♯, and over this *ostinato* the 'enigma' reappears, now not only at full length but with the extensions heard in the introductory piece, though in 3–4 time and differently treated with an accompaniment of broken chords.   At last the brisk opening theme returns in new keys, beginning with a canon followed by a series of interesting and highly effective variations—one with a new 2–4 cross-rhythm, another with a forcible left-hand pounding of the theme under running triplets, and one in right-hand octaves over triplet figurations led up to by a rushing upward scale.   In the end a reiterated muttering bass makes a background for a fervent yet subdued and hesitant final quotation of the 'enigma' to the full extent of its nine notes, closing with a tierce de Picardie of C♯ major.

*10. 'Lermoos.' *Modéré, plutôt lent.* This tranquil and appealing piece is written strictly in three parts, except where the 'enigma' turns up in fuller chords, followed by a strange echo for which the pitch is raised a semitone. The top part is a long-drawn, beautifully shaped tune, the middle one an accompaniment of smooth quavers with some chromatic displacements here and there, and the bass a syncopated pattern that hardly ever varies its rhythmic shape but lends its aid to a good deal of subtle modulation. During the quotations it suddenly becomes a rigid *ostinato*, with an effect as though the heart were being frozen by some numbing recollection. The close shows an extraordinary harmonic refinement, enhanced by basses which constantly side-slip a semitone too low and then immediately correct themselves. Even Fauré, that master of elusive subtlety, never wrote anything harmonically more cunning and fascinating than the last few bars of this piece.

11. 'Beuron.' *Calme et grave.* This is the fugue introducing the B A C H idea. Perhaps the traveller tried the organ in the monastery chapel during his visit to Beuron and thought of Bach—hence the B A C H cryptogram. The fugue is in three parts—again not counting octaves and making allowance for the licence of an extra note in the last bar. The intervals of the subject are unattractive but curious and very distinctive, so that its manipulations are clearly perceived throughout. An oddity is that although there are three parts, d'Indy lets them produce the regular four entries of a four-part fugue. The limpid tone of the whole short piece is so engaging that it lets one forget the rather unpromising nature of the subject and the composer's somewhat dry procedure.

12. 'La Pluie.' *Assez animé.* The *Tableaux de voyage* appeared a good three years before Debussy's *Estampes*, containing 'Jardins sous la pluie,' and one cannot help thinking that the younger composer must have been influenced by d'Indy's toccata-like piece in B minor, which exploits the keyboard quite as brilliantly and to much the same effect. Harmonically, there is a return to Franck here, however: the piece, or rather its opening section (for the rest is pure d'Indy again), might have been written by that master if he had been as sensitive to new pianoforte effects as Debussy was. 'La Pluie' is extremely brilliant without ever becoming insurmountably difficult, though it is certainly the hardest thing to play in this cycle. The rain here is not, as in Debussy's case, falling on gardens, but on mountain tops: for even through the showers we once again feel that clear rarefied air that had refreshed us in 'Pâturage' and is to some extent felt throughout this always cool open-air music. And indeed we find that the next section, marked 'beaucoup plus lent, estompé [a favourite word of Debussy's] et mystérieux,' bears the sub-heading of 'Sommets

dévastés.' It is written in a curious cross-rhythm of 12–8 for the right hand and 6–4 for the left, groups of three quavers being thus set against crotchets at the rate of one and a half of the latter. The whole of this lengthy section is deliberately kept monotonous in pattern and dynamics, as well as indeterminate in melody. As to that, however, one may suspect that the curious melodic formation of a kind often found in d'Indy's work is due to his preoccupation with harmonic processes to the comparative neglect of anything else. He will not exclude melody altogether, deeply absorbed though he may be in a certain harmonic scheme; but melody must take its chance and fit in as best it can, which it will sometimes not be able to do without all too tortuous feats of accommodation. There can be little doubt that it is this ruthlessness towards melody which makes d'Indy appear so forbidding to many music-lovers; or rather, since many have never taken the trouble of noticing him, to a number even of those who do study his work.

The toccata returns briefly in an even more dazzling version of sextolets, and then gives way to a slower coda in B major, entitled 'Au Gîte,' which transforms the B minor toccata theme into a deeply felt song of thankfulness for the shelter that has been found, perhaps in some lonely mountain-hut or under the spreading branches of a gigantic fir-tree. The music of the cross-rhythmed middle section then returns for a few bars of *pianissimo*, muted by the soft pedal, also in B major, whereas before it had been in the distant key of G minor. It is as though the rain were quietly ceasing to fall. The final cadence is an almost incredible feat of creating atmosphere with an infinitesimally small touch—the mere omission of two notes of a dominant-seventh chord and the substitution of one other anticipating the tonic followed by a beautifully spaced tonic chord:

This is one of those master-touches in music at which one never ceases to marvel: the real wonder being not so much its invention about the year 1900 as the fact that it seems to have occurred to nobody before, simple and inevitable as it is.

*13. 'Rêve.' *Très lent.* The final piece balances the introductory one, to which it reverts in part, and also rounds off the cycle as a whole by several thematic allusions to what has gone before. It contains, however, some gravely beautiful material of its own. After a few opening bars which, like those of ' ? ', seem to foreshadow the 'enigma' theme without actually mentioning it, comes a kind of serious dialogue, played by the right hand in the middle register of the keyboard over basses that present no salient feature. Here we really have very distinctive melodic material, which somehow manages to make itself memorable at once without falling into the commonplace or sacrificing the composer's strongly marked individuality. Presently a little quick figure intrudes and a moment later we find it turning into a vivacious presentation of what had previously been the slow and gloomy 'Knell' of No. 5. Dry and detached now, it has almost the effect of some sinister dance of death: the 'Dream' threatens to turn into a nightmare. But this vision vanishes and the main theme returns with a different counterpoint, only to give way to the lovely music of the 'Green Lake' (No. 4), now even more exquisitely lucid in tone and with even more Franckish harmonic turns. For the third time the principal theme comes back, but the dream has now become lighter and sweeter. An instant later we see what it leads to: a full statement of the 'enigma' music, in 5–8 as at the beginning of the cycle and, to end with, an unexpected contrapuntal combination of it with the dream music of this final piece itself—unexpected because d'Indy's themes seem gritty and unprofitable as material for polyphony. All the same, they work when it comes to the point. The final cadences again make ingenious play with multiple harmonic suspensions, as at the end of ' ? ', but are treated somewhat differently and freed from the touch of chromaticism which had troubled the earlier passage. A beautiful close to a beautiful work worth any pianist's attention, whether he plays it for himself or to an audience.

A Disgraceful Career

(*The Sackbut*, September 1926)

I AM not sure that it is fair to head this essay by a title so provocative of a curiosity that may be morbid, but is certainly universal, and thus to attract the reader's attention on what will probably be deemed to have been false pretences.   For there is no doubt that, though none of us is anxious to be involved in a scandal, we all dearly love to read about other people's.   And why not?   The delinquencies of others are balm to the virtuous and the erring alike, since it is as comforting to be conscious of being unlike the frail as it is reassuring to be aware of companionship in frailty.   Of course, we do not admit this little human weakness even to ourselves, but how many of us could deny, supposing we had to answer to a sterner tribunal than our inner self, that, although on Sunday mornings we all dutifully read one of the papers that make us think or claim to do so, we have no mind to resist the lure of one of their more sensational contemporaries that may happen to be lying about in the servants' hall—if there is such a thing in these days of involuntary labour-saving and enforced simplicity of existence?   It is true that we treat the thing as a joke—and this is where we are conscious of our difference from the domestics—but we pick up our dominical comic paper with a good deal more alacrity than we make for the workaday *Punch*, and savour its hotter spice with a keener relish.

But I digress from my point almost as far as De Quincey when he wanders from the mail-coach to the crocodile, in my anxiety to apologize for a delusive title, quite unnecessarily perhaps, at a time when the caption writer overrules the journalist and a heading that is as loose as it is flashy might have been taken for granted.   Briefly, my excuse is this: though I do not write, as the reader will have expected, about the adventures of human beings, I may perhaps succeed in showing that they are not alone in having exciting careers.   Any gold sovereign, if it chose to write its memoirs during its enforced exile in the vaults of the Bank of England, could tell as lurid a tale of sordid adventure as was ever read openly below stairs and by stealth above, and so could many other things in this world of unworthy objects.

Even those which go to the making of art are not immune from sliding into shameful ways, as I will show by the example of what is perhaps the basest hanger-on of music, the chord of the diminished seventh.

There is no doubt that chords have their distinctive characters which, although they can be modified by circumstances or position, remain fundamentally always the same. The common chord, for instance, is branded by its very name for what it is, though the term must in fairness be interpreted in the sense of ubiquity rather than in that of vulgarity. After all, one still sees its homely countenance gladly now and again, and on the whole prefers it when it does not deck itself out with added sixths and other newfangled trinkets, as if ashamed of its plainness. Again, the chord of the dominant major ninth is full of suppressed yearnings which do not easily find a direct outlet in immediate resolution. The augmented triad can only be designated as an upstart that does not know its place, being able neither to conform to the old diatonic order nor to the new atonal anarchy. The dominant seventh chord still remains in attendance upon the common chord, a humble drudge whose duty it is to clear the way for its plebeian master. But no other device of harmony is quite so sycophantically disposed to do any dirty work that may be required as the chord of the diminished seventh: an undersized, sneaking creature, always ready at any price to help a composer out of a modulatory embarrassment by the supply of a cheap line of least resistance.

As its surname implies, the diminished seventh is a family relation to the dominant seventh; in fact, it is a direct offspring of the latter. But it has ignobly disgraced the lineage with the many toadying offices it has performed. The dominant seventh, when it acts as intermediary between two keys, at any rate always acknowledges the same two as sender and recipient of its messages. It can be guilty, it is true, of taking them elsewhere, but if it does so, it is always in the manner of an interrupted cadence, a definite and frankly admitted temporary irregularity. But the diminished seventh will run errands anywhere with equal readiness. It is a slippery, venal, abjectly accommodating menial with an uncanny aptitude for disguising its appearance by enharmonically changing its three equal intervals, thus posing by turns as all sorts of outlandish chords while in reality always remaining the same. Having at least twice as many potential leading-notes as it has constituent sounds, since each can be written in at least two different ways, it is able to offer any key, close or remote, a helping hand in getting at a bound into a position that could otherwise only be gained either by circumlocution or by ellipsis. All that is lazy and shoddy and second-rate in music finds in the diminished-seventh chord a willing go-between. It is the friend of mediocrity, the pander to indolence, the procurer of the readiest effects obtainable at the least expense of thought and feeling. Its countenance is objectionable in the sight of the modern musician who is aware of its debased status. Those three minor thirds give its features a mean, pinched appearance. Its very sound has a quality of corruption about it, like milk that has turned in sultry weather. It may have been as mild and pleasant as fresh milk once, but all the stage thunder and lightning it has accompanied—and this is its second reprehensible function—has long staled and soured it past endurance.

First of all, let me exhibit a portrait of it, to be stared at in dismay by all and sundry, like that of a murderer outside a police station:

Ex.1

But this may fail to lead to its identification by anyone who meets its picture elsewhere, for it is here seen in comparative honesty for what it really is, a chord clad in the garments of a seventh, for its outer notes really are that in appearance, however sadly diminished. The trouble is that amateur detectives anxious to hand it over to justice may meet it in some disguise in which it is less recognizable for what it is, having tried to make its outside look like a sixth, brazenly augmented:

Ex.2   or, as it were, side-face: Ex.3   ; and other dis-

guises are equally possible.

Having now published this warning about its appearance, let us trace the career of the culprit and try to account for the degradation which has made it a byword to all musicians who care for the clean and decent behaviour of their art. It was an inoffensive enough newcomer when it made its first appearance as a harmonic entity, as distinct from a momentary convergence of contrapuntal lines, about the close of the seventeenth century, though the legitimacy of its origin is at least disputable. In the music of Corelli, of Stradella and other composers of the time, its progenitor, the minor seventh, was frequently found associated with the subdominant, though its legitimate alliance was with the dominant. Now, to keep its countenance, it compromised by shifting its position in the direction of the dominant by sharpening its subdominant bass note, thus giving itself the appearance of not having finally turned its back on the dominant, though its upper notes were as definitely as ever connected with the subdominant.   It was in this equivocal situation that the chord of the diminished seventh came to life, begotten in duplicity and destined to lead a baneful existence.

Yet in its youth the diminished-seventh chord was not an unpleasant creature, though always a little meek and anaemic.   Nor was it offensive in its adolescence during the time of Handel and Bach. The former could produce a fine effect by making an interrupted cadence pause upon it for an expectant moment, or treating its characteristic intervals of minor thirds fugally, as in the chorus, 'And to thy faith, illustrious youth' in *Susanna*.   Bach's immensely resourceful harmonic use of it in the *Chromatic Fantasia* shows that it had not as yet become a mere subterfuge for modulation; on the other hand, the way in which he turned it to account to convey anguish, notably in the St Matthew Passion, suggests that it began at an early age to grow into the romantic bogy that was to obsess the nineteenth century.   Here, in fact, we discern the first shooting-pains of romanticism, and although the chord falls in naturally enough with the texture of Bach's polyphony, one already suspects a kind of unconsciously stereotyped use of it.   There is no denying that Bach applies it as an expression of grief as mechanically almost as the uniform and scholastically formulated grimace of the weeping women we see in old Flemish and German pictures of the Crucifixion.

Bach was temporarily forgotten during the age that succeeded him and the romanticism he foreshadowed was for the moment repressed by courtly formality until etiquette was swept out of art's way by the French Revolution.   Yet the romantic eruption smouldered on before the upheaval that saw its definite outbreak.   Its travail is discernible in Rousseau's writings and in Mozart's music.   And in the latter's work it is again the diminished seventh that predicts all the supernatural phenomena and the personal plaints of which the art is presently to become the messenger in the wake of the new literary movement.   To Mozart's contemporaries the diminished seventh was doubtless still a harsh discord, to be used only in desperate situations, always sparingly and never without good reason.   But though Mozart did not let it get out of hand, he could not stay it on its way to becoming the sensation-monger-in-chief of music, who was soon afterwards to be always at hand to gloat over a distressed damsel, a dark deed or a spectral apparition, and to find its very breath of life in thunderstorms, shipwrecks and subterranean caverns.

With the approach of the nineteenth century, the diminished-seventh chord entered upon the most dismal stages of its downward path.   The romantic debauch into which it plunged headlong, though bad enough in all conscience, was not the worst, for now it began to demean itself (in the obsolete but picturesque sense of the term) to an ignoble harmonic servitude. It acquired the character of a kind of oily, mechanical pivot on which a greasy and slithering modulation could be made to turn with the utmost ease and to go to any remote key with a hitherto unheard-of directness by way of enharmonic change. The evil of the chord, of course, was not that it facilitated modulation, for that in itself would have been all to the good, but that by its too obsequious aid it ensnared the weaker composers into accepting it with fatal alacrity as a substitute for creative thought, and an excuse for all sorts of modulatory dissipations and indulgences which enervated and emasculated their music. The stronger men, of course, turned it to account without ever letting its servility lull them into lazy inaction. Beethoven knew well enough that this readiest of servants could turn into a harmful influence to restrict himself to its occasional use for modulations of a power previously unknown. Think, for instance, of the change from the dominant of F to that of E by way of the diminished seventh in the *Fidelio* overture (bars 28-9) or of the chain of these chords in the coda of the first movement of the Sonata in E♭, Op. 31 No. 3.

One is naturally curious to see how those two arch-romantics, Weber and Berlioz, reacted to this new device.   On the face of it, the Frenchman seems far more healthily scornful of it than the German, but it is highly probable that Berlioz avoided the snare by instinct rather than consciously.   He had a strong feeling for harmonic colour coupled to a weak sense of harmonic manipulation; he knew exactly what chord he wished to succeed another in any given situation without being clearly aware of the easiest ways and means of effecting the transition, and he would therefore force his way through the thorniest chordal thickets rather than avail himself of the convenient stiles continually used and considerably worn down by the ordinary pedestrians.   Hence not only the awkwardness of his music, but also its originality, which at the same time saved him from the abuse of the diminished seventh in highly dramatic or fantastic situations, for which he invented countless new harmonic combinations.   Not so Weber, whose work shows that in his days the diminished seventh was still used as a matter of course precisely in such situations.   A shudder of excitement or a shiver of horror was almost unthinkable without this conventional label.   It is characteristic of Weber's time that in his work the number of diminished-seventh chords is almost in mathematically corresponding proportion to the amount of dramatic tension or supernatural terror aimed at.   This may be observed in the *Freischütz*, where, to begin with, the wood-demon Samiel is afflicted with the curse of a diminished-seventh *Leitmotiv*.   The villain Caspar, too, is given a liberal share of the chord, and no wonder Agatha warns Max to keep away from the wolves' glen, where he is to receive the fright of his life from these stunted sevenths, which grimace at him incessantly under all sorts of disguises.[1]   But Weber has more to teach us.   We can actually trace in his work the petrifying of the diminished seventh into a cliché that inevitably saps the vitality of music.   The fact that *Euryanthe* is, as Beethoven pointed out to Schindler, 'an accumulation of diminished-seventh chords—all little back doors,' is certainly to be attributed to the want of interest taken by Weber in the egregious Helmine von Chézy's abysmally stupid libretto.   It is hardly an exaggeration to say that lack of interest, lack of inspiration, inferior musical mentality, may automatically be discovered in a composer from the frequency of his use of this greatest curse ever inflicted upon the art of music.

Opera was, naturally enough, the musical form most sorely stricken by this dire complaint.   Dramatic composers were now ready to sell their birthright for a mess of diminished sevenths on the slightest provocation.   These chords were found to be so easily swallowed by the public, and to give it so readily an illusion of satisfaction, that they were now ladled out wholesale by every dabbler in composition too resourceless to step gracefully from one key to another or too indolent to think of an original dramatic effect.   The evil had taken firm root, and it looked as if the formula for its exorcism had been definitely lost. It took a composer of the first magnitude to become at all conscious of the necessity of expelling it, and that composer was Wagner; but even he, saturated, no doubt, in all the fashionable operas he had to conduct at Würzburg, Magdeburg, Königsberg and Riga, began by taking the insidious snake to his bosom and nurturing it lavishly.   *Rienzi* of course, simply followed the example of Spontini and Meyerbeer, but the first operas where Wagner's personal genius begins to assert itself are still abundantly tainted with the universal operatic disease.   *The Flying Dutchman* is the opera of the diminished seventh as *Tristan* is the music-drama of the dominant major ninth.   It was not until Wagner came to write *Lohengrin* that he became aware how badly he had been bitten by the reptile he had cherished, and even then he was far from sure whether he would ever succeed in shaking it off.   In 1847 he wrote to Hanslick (with whom he was still on friendly terms) that he did not yet know whether music could adapt itself to every situation in a drama that transcended formality and embraced every human emotion.   The diminished seventh alone, so far as Wagner was aware, had hitherto been thought adaptable to certain dramatic

---

[1] It is interesting to study the various notations of the chord Weber attempts in this scene, without, of course, making the least difference to its character, and it should also be borne in mind that, since it is composed of three equidistant intervals, it remains entirely unaffected by inversion.   On the other hand, Weber often achieves variety of effect by spacing it in different ways: it is surprising how much less offensive it sounds when one of its notes is lifted out and placed in the bass at the distance of an octave or two.

aspects, and he was forced to survey his own resources for new and convincing means to express them.

That even composers of high standing who were fully conscious of the evil found it hard to rid themselves of it may be seen in the case of Verdi. 'It is the haven and refuge of us all, who cannot write a bar without smuggling in half a dozen of these sevenths,' he wrote to Florimo, and indeed even so late and otherwise gloriously independent a work as *Othello* still teems with this conventional means of suggesting dramatic stress. It must be said that in this respect, though in this only, *Othello* lags behind *Aida*, where intensely theatrical effects (no derogatory term in the sense in which it is applicable to Verdi) are often gained by more personal means.

It is in opera that the diminished seventh has survived longest, and in third-rate opera it still survives. This is perhaps the reason why it seems almost completely safe nowadays to measure the originality of post-romantic opera composers by the amount of diminished sevenths with which their music is sullied. Each diminished seventh, one might say, does something to diminish the composer's vitality and individual power. We may be reasonably sure that according to the statistics compiled by some assessor of diminished sevenths, we should come to the same conclusions about the relative value of various makers of opera as have already been formed by the consensus of critical opinion. We should find from this mathematical estimate, as we know from aesthetic valuations, that Mussorgsky is more original than Rimsky-Korsakov; Bizet more than Gounod; Puccini more than Leoncavallo; Debussy—but here we reach a period that scorns the use of the diminished seventh as too abjectly obliging a servant. This is not so much due, perhaps, to the fact that creative musicians have at last tired of its cringing manner of serving them, as to their having learnt to do without harmonic mediators at all. In this age of the emancipation of labour, the musician prefers to make short cuts where previously he would have expended a good deal of work to effect harmonic transitions. He no longer needs a pivotal chord for his harmony to revolve on from key to key; he simply gets from one point of the key-circle to another *per saltum*. Instead of travelling by train via Clapham Junction[2], he prefers to reach his desired destination by an aerial line that touches no intermediate point. Or, to put it differently, the diminished seventh was once convenient for modulation because it contained so many potential roots: to-day, music no longer lives radicivorously, but has become omnivorous in the matter of ways and means to subsistence.[3]

[2] 'Clapham Junction is like the diminished seventh—susceptible of such enharmonic change, that you can resolve it into all the possible termini of music.' Samuel Butler, *The Way of all Flesh*.

[3] The reader is asked to remember that this was written thirty-two years ago.

The chord of the diminished seventh, always a grovelling creature, at last lies broken in the dust.   Then, it may be asked, why raise this hue and cry over it?   Because, although it has now become harmless, it may serve as an example to other harmonic hangers-on that may lift their heads and try to find similar universal employment.   There is, to mention only one, the augmented triad, a parasite of the whole-tone scale, which has become so handy an expedient that even the shop ballad, of all musical species surely the one least open to novelty, eagerly welcomed it and hugged it with such persistent affection that one could only hope it would suffocate it in its ample and emotional bosom.   Its career threatened at one time to become no less disreputable than that of its elder cousin which I have tried to outline in the hope that perhaps the dubious adventures of a chord have proved to be not altogether devoid of a little sensational interest.

The Minuet-Trio

(*Music & Letters*, April 1941)

I T may have escaped the notice of musicians who have not had their attention drawn to the fact—though once that has been done they will hardly deny it—that there is a curious similarity about the contrasts aimed at by more than one classical composer between the minuet and the trio of important instrumental works in sonata form. The impression is not to be escaped that the only dance of the older suite which was somehow salvaged when the *sonata da camera* merged into the solo sonata and the symphony tries to make the most of two worlds. That the trio must as a matter of course provide a contrast to the main section of a minuet movement is obvious everywhere; but it is scarcely less plain that some classics aimed at a particular kind of contrast which recurs consistently enough to suggest the conscious or unconscious—far more likely unconscious—adherence to some tradition long taken for granted and now forgotten. Let us see whether we may be justified in suspecting such a tradition and, if so, where its foundation may be retraced.

For a rough description of the difference we so often find between classical minuets and their trios it will do to say that the former are urban and the latter countrified or, if we prefer, that the minuet seems to be aristocratic whereas the trio is rustic. It is so to the end of the eighteenth century, at any rate. After that, with the encroachment on aristocratic privileges by the middle classes, we find the courtly minuet losing its sway and changing into the scherzo in professional composition and into the waltz in popular music. But it is curious to find that in the scherzo of the nineteenth century and in what artificially survives of the minuet in professional music of that period the trio section very often remains rustic. Is the reason for this that the peasant class had suffered—or enjoyed, if one's sociological outlook tends that way—next to no change compared with the social upheaval among townspeople? It seems more than likely, since there is no reason to think that the trio maintained its older character by the composer's adherence to artistic precedent alone: for why, in that case, should not the minuet have done so too? True, the whole argument falls to the ground if the assertion that the trio so often shows the character of rusticity both in the eighteenth and the nineteenth century can be denied. But can it?

To begin with, the trio takes its name, as we all know, from the early custom of entrusting it to three instruments. Bach calls his alternative second minuets by that name only when he actually does write in three parts, though not necessarily for three instruments, as in the clavier Overture in F major and in the third French Suite. Now in Bach's time minuet-trios often approximate their musical character to that of the musette, which is to the gavotte what the trio is to the minuet—an alternative section—and as its name suggests and its drones show, the musette presupposed the bagpipe as its bass instrument. The bagpipe is the most countrified of instruments, quite unpresentable at courts or in drawing-rooms, and it was best represented in professional music by oboes and bassoons, which classical practice as well as the nature of their sound has associated in our minds with trio music as the most congenial solo instruments because they are the descendants of characteristically open-air instruments. Bach, in the second minuet of the B♭ major Partita, uses a flattened seventh, the classical expedient for suggesting the characteristic seventh of the bagpipe, half-way between the major and the minor seventh.

All the same, the 'rustic' alternative does not come conspicuously to the fore until the second half of the eighteenth century. We find hardly a trace of it in Rameau, who was only two years older than Bach and Handel, and neither the latter nor Purcell has any alternative minuets at all. Bach's pupil, J. L. Krebs, in a keyboard Partita, on the other hand, has not two minuets but three, the third being roughly a double-counterpoint interchange of the second; but there is no sign of contrast in mood, only in texture. Johann Schobert becomes more dynamic and dramatic, but still remains unaware that contrasts between whole sections as distinct from violent changes between phrase-groups are going to be irresistibly attractive to his immediate followers.

Attractive especially to Mozart, as we shall see in a moment. It is in his work that we find the most striking difference of ceremonious formality and something very like popularity between the minuets and their attendant trios. This is not unknown in Haydn, though such a bucolic trio as that in his G major Symphony, No. 88, with its augmented fourths and bassoon drone, is exceptional. No. 85, in B♭ major ('La Reine),' has a kind of peasant squareness in the trio, together with the ONE-two-three accompaniment the waltz inherited from the *Ländler*; but this is unusually like one of the characteristic Mozartian trios that will be discussed at greater length presently. The trio in the 'Oxford' Symphony begins in a folky manner, but gets away from it in the symphonically extended second part. The 'Surprise,' 'Clock,' and 'Military' Symphonies, as well as No. 99, in E♭ major, and No. 104, in D major, are familiar examples showing no trace of rusticity in their trios. A *Ländler*-like tone is distinctly present, on the other hand, in the alternatives of the Op. 33 string Quartets, 'Gli scherzi,' but they really are, as their nickname implies, early specimens of works containing the scherzo type of movement in place of minuets, and moreover there is no contrast of the kind we have in view between the main sections and the alternatives of these movements. In other Haydn quartets, too, both sections are sometimes countrified, but the composer's characteristic irregular phrase-grouping makes them metrically too subtle for anything more than a superficial feeling of folkiness to prevail. The sixth Quartet of Op. 64 for once shows a sharp contrast, but the trio might be Mozartian, in so far as it is not particularly Haydnish. The fourth work of the same opus has a trio with a yodelling theme that is distinctly unsophisticated, and it contains wide melodic skips of the kind Curt Sachs says are frequently found in the music of the Austrian *Ländler* of the older type (before 1800).[1] The trio in Op. 76 No. 1 comes near to the *Ländler* spirit in its theme, but its impish metrical extensions are purely personal, not folk-like in the least. In all Haydn's quartets, indeed, not only in Op. 33, where they do it avowedly, the minuets come near the scherzo manner and tend away from the folk-dance, even where they use material akin to it. In the piano Sonata in C♯ minor the trio, in the tonic major, is musette-like and pastoral, but in those works again Haydn is as a rule fancifully himself: he does not consciously archaize or unconsciously follow tradition, nor does he mimic folkiness, as Mozart sometimes humorously does in his orchestral dances.

Only about a quarter of Haydn's piano sonatas contain any minuets at all, and his rondo-finales in *tempo di minuetto* do not concern us here; in Mozart's works of the same category only two have minuets. That of the E♭ major Sonata, K.282, is wholly courtly, but the A major, K.331, has a pastoral trio of an idealized kind, with gentlefolk who have read Rousseau but followed him only as far as their comfort would allow masquerading as shepherds. But elsewhere, in the greater and maturer Mozart, we are often struck by a sort of deliberate lapsing from the perfect manners of the minuet into a freer and easier tone, not as an affectation, though sometimes by way of delicious parody, but from sheer pleasure in artless simplicity—if artless does not mean devoid of art, as Mozart never is, even where he may become shallow.

Is it necessary to remind the reader of such trios? Merely to talk about them is to recall a dozen examples in Mozart's familiar works. The minuet in the *Kleine Nachtmusik*, K.525, is stately, almost severe

---

[1] Curt Sachs, *World History of the Dance* (London, 1938). Sachs, who in this book rarely makes a point of specifically musical interest, says these skips often covered as much as two octaves. Mozart, in the fourth of his *Deutsche*, K.536, has leaps widening progressively up to fourteenths. Others are found, for example, in K.586 (No. 8) and K.600 (No. 4). See also Schubert's A major piano Sonata of 1828 (two and three octaves).

with its bare two-part openings of each section; the trio, on the other hand, is a simple, square-cut hurdy-gurdy tune with the barest accompaniment and bass.   That kind of primitive accompaniment, grinding out simple chord progressions in quaver arpeggios, is found in other trios of the rustic sort, including that of the great E♭ major Symphony, K.543, where the second clarinet gurgles out such figures while the lower strings thrum the ONE-two-three of the *Ländler* as though content with performing the meanest of services: and well they may be, for here in truth is humility exalted to the gates of Paradise.   So, too, with the trio in the G minor Symphony, K.550, the glorified transfiguration of the Austrian country dance—a *Ländler* of the Elysian Fields.   And perhaps the second trio in the clarinet Quintet is the Austrian mountaineers' dance, the *Schuhplattler*, etherealized and transported to the same heavenly regions, for what is it but a yodel with the barest waltzing accompaniment?   There is an immeasurable difference, it is true, but it is a spiritual, not a material difference.   The actual stuff of the music is that of common rusticity, as it still is in Bruckner and Mahler, where, however, commonness as such has come to be accounted a virtue.   The 'Haffner,' the 'Linz,' the 'Jupiter' Symphonies, all have festive, pompous minuets fit for burgomasters, counts and Olympians, and all are followed by trios singing country airs and wearing the most modest adornments.   The blithe milkmaid's song of the 'Haffner,' with its churning accompaniment, is perhaps the most characteristic.   But we meet similar things elsewhere.   The string Quintets in D major, K.593, and E♭ major, K.614, both show exceptionally striking contrasts between their minuets and trios.   The former are among Mozart's most sophisticated movements of the kind, and that of the D major is elaborately contrapuntal; both, again, have simple trios, that in K.593 being confined to wide arpeggios followed by plain cadences, that in K.614 having a barrel-organ tune in a waltzing motion, with the ancient hesitation between flat and sharp sevenths that recalls modal folksong. Yet the supreme virtue of Mozart's discernment unifies these movements: artfulness and artlessness are achieved with equal perfection.

Only two of the mature string quartets contain trios that are interesting from our present point of view.   Some—e.g. the G major Quartet, K.387, with its long and more than usually symphonic minuet—show no trace of these deliberately sought contrasts, which it is just as well to mention here, since it would be utterly wrong to convey the impression that all Mozart's minuet-trios fall into the plebeian manner—shall we say?—in order to stand out from the surroundings of the aristocratic dance.   But the D minor Quartet, K.421, is a conspicuous case in point, for its minuet in that key is in a tragic vein and very highly wrought, whereas the trio, in D major, has a very simple arpeggio theme over a thrumming accompaniment, with the wide skips and tonic-and-dominant yodels of a typical *Ländler*. The Quartet in E♭ major, K.428, is another, although the contrast is attenuated by the minuet's being itself a rather folky strain. It seems, indeed, to be more so than the trio when the latter begins in C minor, for Austrian dances are rarely in minor keys even in the form cultivated by the classics; but the trio too willy-nilly slips into the folk-dance manner, and it is actually not in a minor key, but in B♭ major.

The serenades, cassations and divertimenti may also be searched with advantage for relevant examples. There are fairly good ones, to go no farther, in the D major Divertimento for oboe, strings and horns, K.351, and in the magnificent B♭ major wind Serenade, K.361, and we may find an excellent one in the trio of the second minuet in the E♭ major wind Serenade, K.375, a straightforward dance piece with regular metres. But it is the 'Haffner' Serenade, K.250, not otherwise an outstandingly attractive work, as Mozart goes, to which special attention must now be given for a moment. It happens to throw out a suggestion of the reason for this rusticity so often found in the trio section of a classical minuet, particularly in Mozart—a suggestion it is hoped this attempt at accumulating further scraps of evidence may strengthen into a valid argument; or if not that, may at any rate prove of some interest in itself.

The 'Haffner' Serenade contains three minuets, a fact that distinguishes the serenade type very sharply from the earlier species of the suite, which may in some isolated instances have contained as many movements of the kind, but only as alternatives set side by side, never scattered through the work and interspersed with other movements. The first minuet is almost like an early version of that in the great G minor Symphony of 1788, of which we also find a later echo in the fourth of the *Deutsche*, K.600, where, so to speak, it comes down to earth. The 'Haffner' example is not only in the same key, but has similar poignant chromatic inflections in the main section and a pastoral simplicity, with a wind accompaniment reduced to the minimum, in the trio. What interests us more, however, is the difference between the second and third minuets in this work. The former, in D major, has a trio that is not in the least rustic, but was perhaps cast in D minor on purpose in order to keep up an attitude of aristocratic seriousness; and it is worth noting that Mozart went out of his way to call this a *Menuetto galante*, as though he wished to emphasize its courtly character, which is quite strikingly different from that of the third minuet, a very distinctly bucolic movement, not only in its trio, but as a whole. Did Mozart deliberately write his second minuet for the gentry who were present at the wedding of Burgomaster Haffner's daughter and reserve the third for the servants or for the country folk who may have been allowed to make merry on the fringe of the festivity at sociable, kindly Salzburg?

Let us come to the point which now insists on being made. It is only a step farther to the notion that Mozart very probably intended these minuets to be actually danced by the gentry and the country folk respectively. For he was not writing a concert work: he was writing a musical entertainment for a wedding. Is it likely that he, who always knew exactly how to fit music to its occasion as well as to its form, expected a crowd of lively wedding-guests to sit still listening to a work in eight movements taking up the time of two symphonies? No, a serenade for a wedding was evidently intended to be played piecemeal at intervals between refreshments and dances, and why should not the dances have taken toll of its music? Even if this is not what really happened at the Haffner wedding, we may be pretty sure that it was what originally determined the peculiar constitution of works of the serenade, cassation or divertimento type. Otherwise why three minuets in this case, when other dances might just as well have been borrowed from the older type of the suite for a purely musical entertainment? Well, other dances were no longer danced in the seventeen-seventies, while the minuet was fashionable. (Even in Bach's later years only the minuet and the *contredanse* were danced, the other dance forms in his suites being already archaic.)

Strictly speaking, it was one kind of minuet, a stately, ceremonious kind, that was fashionable, in the sense that it was the dance for people of fashion. But there was another kind of dance in triple time, similar in its leisurely motion, but different in character: a pastoral, rustic, bucolic kind. It was the *Ländler*, though that is its local Austrian name, more current in the nineteenth than in the eighteenth century. Collections of *Ländler*, from the time of Mozart to that of Schubert, were as often as not called *Deutsche Tänze*, or simply *Deutsche*, just as an artificialized Scottish dance became commonly known on the Continent not as *Danse écossaise*, but simply as *Écossaise*. *Ländler* and *Deutsche* are the same thing, a countrified sort of dance, as indeed the former name (literally 'land ones') indicated. Being cultivated mainly in Austria and in the mountainous south German region of Bavaria, their rusticity often assumed the primitive melodic arpeggio forms of the yodel. Here is an example of the yodelling type of melody as it got into one of Mozart's set of *Deutsche*:

K.536, No. 5 (Trio)
Ex. 1

We have here also the thrumming accompaniment that afterwards became the very foundation of the waltz, which of course in its Viennese form is the direct descendant of the *Ländler* through Schubert, Lanner and the elder Johann Strauss. Even in Johann Strauss junior, in whose hands the 'land dance' had become entirely urbanized, to the point of becoming the Austrian capital's monopoly, we occasionally find distinct echoes of this artless mountain-dweller's music, the classic instance being the *Geschichten aus dem Wiener Wald* waltz, particularly its introduction.

If we look at the numerous separate sets of Mozart's orchestral minuets and *Deutsche* [2], leaving aside the sets of country dances, which are in 2–4 time, and therefore irrelevant to this study, we shall be struck by the difference of character between them. The minuets are decidedly stately, courtly, aristocratic; the *Deutsche* as decidedly easy-going, countrified, plebeian. And if we suspect that the minuets in the 'Haffner' Serenade were actually danced, we know for a fact that these sets of separate orchestral dances were specially written for that very purpose, those dating from 1787 and after for the Austrian court. In December of that year, Gluck having died the previous month, Mozart was appointed to succeed him as chamber musician to the court of Joseph II, an honour that amounted to nothing more than an obligation to supply dance music for the court balls, held in the Redoutensäle during the Carnival. The emperor favoured these as an opportunity for bringing various classes of people together, and although he frequently appeared there in person with his retinue, anybody who could dress and behave decently was admitted, and enjoyed considerable liberty, as indeed did the upper classes, provided they were masked. Minuets and *Deutsche* were the chief dances, say Jahn-Abert [3], but only the lower orders took part in the latter, whereas the minuets were reserved for the gentry and the nobility, perhaps for the simple reason that by tradition they alone were ever taught the rather complicated figures of that dance. According to Sachs [4] the

[2] There are fifteen sets of minuets and ten of *Deutsche*, the last but one of which, K.606 (1791), is called *Sechs ländlerische Tänze* and thus proves the similarity of the dances going under the two names of *Deutsche* and *Ländler* (which may be called *Ländlerische Tänze* just as *Deutsche* may be called *Deutsche Tänze*). The list of Mozart's orchestral dances in triple time is as follows, according to the third edition of Köchel's catalogue, edited by Alfred Einstein, whose new numbering, where it differs from Köchel's, is followed by the latter's original numbers in brackets:

    Minuets: 61d (103), 61e (104), 61f (105), 61g, 61h, all 1769; 73t (122), 1770; 130a (164), 1772; 176, 1773; 363, 1780; 448a (461), 1784; 568, 1788; 585, 1789; 599, 601, 604, all 1791.

    Deutsche: 509, 1787; 536, 567, both 1788; 571, 586, both 1789; 600, 602, 605, 606, 611, all 1791.

[3] Hermann Abert, *W. A. Mozart: neubearbeitete und erweiterte Ausgabe von Otto Jahns Mozart*, 2 vols. (Leipzig, 1924).

[4] Op. cit.

minuet steps were made difficult by the complication of a kind of cross-rhythm between the three beats of the music and the left-right pairs of steps, thus:

Music	1 2 3	1 2 3	1 2 3	1 2 3
Dance	l. r. l.	r. l. r.	l. r. l.	r. l. r.

similar to a certain kind of Handelian cadence in triple time, the hemiolia, which may be thus formulated:

$$3\text{--}4 + 3\text{--}4 = 2\text{--}4 + 2\text{--}4 + 2\text{--}4 \text{ [5]}$$

It is quite clear, then, that these court occasions, for which Haydn, Eybler, Gyrowetz, Hummel and Beethoven also wrote, among others, made a strict class distinction, musically speaking, between the dancers and their dances, as socially they evidently did not while the freedom of the masquerade lasted among them; and Mozart made this distinction quite plain in his dance music.   That he was perfectly well aware of what he was doing, and why he did it, is proved by the ballroom scene in the first finale of *Don Giovanni.*   Every musician knows that the company at Don Juan's house dances to three little orchestras and that Mozart performs the incredible *tour de force* of making them play simultaneously the most famous of all minuets actually designed for dancing, a country dance in 2–4 time and a *Deutscher* in 3–8.   Now the minuet is danced by Don Juan's noble guests, and it is played by his little domestic orchestra with a complement of instruments, as Jahn-Abert points out [6], such as a grandee may be expected to possess.   The country dance and the German dance, on the other hand, are played by two little primitive village bands of violins and string basses, without violas, and they are danced, respectively, by Don Juan with Zerlina and by Leporello with Masetto, members of the lower orders joining in as the producer may appoint; but on no account must the nobles take part in these lowlier dances, the music of which is distinctly popular.

Popular, too, is Mozart's music of his *Deutsche* written for the Viennese court, whereas the orchestral minuets for his imperial patron, as well as those composed earlier, are courtly and ceremonial.   Also, the village-band element is preserved in the former, no set of which includes violas in the score, while freak instruments hardly any of which are found elsewhere in Mozart are often introduced, such as the

---

[5] See 'Handel's Two-length Bar,' by H. H. Wintersgill, *Music & Letters*, vol. xvii, No. 1 (January 1936).

[6] Op. cit., vol. ii, p. 513.   Don Juan here employs the little Mozartian Salzburg orchestra of oboes, horns and strings; in the supper scene in the second finale he sports a wind octet.

hurdy-gurdy (the French *vielle*, called *Leier* by Mozart), the timbrel, the side-drum, cymbals, the piccolo (in one case called *Pickelflöte*), the posthorn and a set of jingles tuned to play notes of actual pitch. The trio of the last of the three *Deutsche* K.605, entitled 'Die Schlitten-fahrt,' which is in the descriptive manner favoured a generation earlier by Mozart's father, ends with posthorns and jingles fading away in the distance, and the conclusion of K.571, one of the more organic sets held together by a coda in which all the instruments join after taking their separate turns in the preceding dances, is scored in an erratic manner not found in the well-conducted minuets:

K. 571 (Conclusion of Coda)
Ex. 2

It is not only the orchestration, however, which shows Mozart's intention of differentiating *Deutsche* sharply from minuets by a sort of musical class distinction: the difference extends very conspicuously to the material itself. Popular melodic forms, unusual in Mozart, who in spite of the stories about 'Non più andrai' in Prague is not the sort of composer whose tunes haunt streets and bath-rooms, are surprisingly frequent in these dance sets. Here, for example, is a tune so unlike him that one might well suspect it to have been lifted from a folksong:

K. 567, No. 2 (Trio)
Ex. 3

and its accompaniment is of a kind often found in his trios in sonata-form works, but not in any minuet one can readily think of. Neither are such tunes as the following imaginable as material for his minuets, though they look very much like the openings of any number of trios:

K. 567, No. 5
Ex. 4

K. 586, No. 1

It will be asked whether in Mozart's sets of minuets there are no trios. There are; but the curious fact is that they rarely, if ever, differ in style from the courtly manner of their main sections. What is more remarkable still, the *Deutsche*, which also have their trios, show the same consistency, the character of both sections being in this case distinctly popular or rustic. Most extraordinary of all, in the sonata-form works we again and again find minuet-and-trio movements the first section of which resembles in style both the main sections and the trios of the consistently aristocratic separate sets of minuets, while the same is true of the trios in the sonata-form works and both sections of the *Deutsche*. Here is a specimen, in skeleton short score, of the first section and of the trio (same number) in one of the sets of *Deutsche*, which not only shows the unusual quality of Mozart's 'plebeian' manner, but also the similarity of style between the two sections, which persists with a curious uniformity throughout all the sets of dances of this type:

K. 509, No. 4
Ex. 5

K. 509, No. 4 (Trio)

Jahn-Abert lay stress on this difference of character between the two species.[7]   They say of the minuets that

> they are more artful in texture, and especially in their orchestration display all the charm of Mozart's orchestral treatment at that time; many of them changing their instrumental garb at the repeats.   The *Deutsche*, on the other hand, aim above all at preserving the popular tone, and they do so by considering its sentimental (especially in the minor-key trios) as well as its coarse aspects.

But this consistency of Mozart's separate dances in triple time once established, how do we account for the frequent glaring contrasts between his minuets and trios in his more important works?   And why do we not find the same thing to anything like the same extent in Haydn?   As to that, the answer is surely that, whatever else one may prefer in Mozart, Haydn is a composer far less bound by tradition, far more ready to use accepted forms and devices wilfully in his own way. He may start a trio in a popular vein and then expand and develop its second part to a very much larger size, so that the treatment becomes symphonic.   He was followed in that practice by Beethoven, who quite early in his career had not only taken Haydn's cue to cultivate the scherzo at the expense of the minuet[8], but made much of that expansion of the second part of the trio.[9]

Mozart, then, was bound by tradition, as indeed we know from his infallible way of always knowing exactly, from his boyhood onward, what was required of a composer brought up as he was in his handling of this, that and the other musical species.   But if there was a tradition even at the bottom of his habit of frequently combining the aristocratic and popular elements of triple-time dances in his sonata-form works, elements he so strictly kept apart in his separate dances, what was that tradition?   That, indeed, is the question now to be examined.

Two hints have already been thrown out.   Mozart knew the custom of mixing different classes of society at the court balls, of

[7] Op. cit., vol. ii, p. 615.   The older spelling of *Teutsche* is used by the authors.
[8] The third movement of Beethoven's first Symphony, though still called a minuet, is an out-and-out scherzo.
[9] In the second Symphony, where the eight-bar first section of the scherzo might have been the tune from one of Mozart's *Deutsche*, the second part, extended to thirty-six bars, could have been nothing else than a piece of Beethovenian symphonic writing.

giving them different dances to dance and of providing music for these dances that differed in character; and secondly he musically symbolized that custom with inimitable skill and humour in *Don Giovanni*, the idea of combining the dances contrapuntally being, of course, his own.   Da Ponte could never have conceived it alone, for it is purely a musician's notion, and one, moreover, such as only a very great master could have dared to entertain, since it involved a technical problem of hair-raising difficulty.

However, Mozart had mixed aristocratic and popular music in the minuet movements of his instrumental works long before he knew anything of the Viennese court at first hand and long before the Don Juan subject came his way: the 'Haffner' Serenade, which dates from the second Salzburg period, is only one isolated instance of his early practice with that kind of thing.   He was twenty when he wrote it, and the tradition had been in his blood long before that age.   It was in fact a very old tradition—much older than he knew, no doubt. Let us trace it back.

According to the *Encyclopaedia Britannica* [10]:

> The earliest dances that bear any relation to the modern art are probably the *danses basses* and *danses hautes* of the 16th century.   The *danse basse* was the dance of the court of Charles IX and of good society, the steps being very grave and dignified, not to say solemn, and the accompaniment a psalm tune.   The *danses hautes* or *baladines* had a skipping step, and were practised only by clowns and country people. [11]

In England it was the country dance which performed a similar function of social equalization—so long as a festivity lasted.   In the Elizabethan era it was on certain occasions danced by masters and servants together; and Playford, writing during the Commonwealth, when 'these Times and the Nature of it [the dance] do not agree,' shows the country dance introduced to good society on the charming title-page of his *Dancing-Master* [12] and in his preface recommends it to 'young Gentlemen.' [13]   Goethe says late in the eighteenth century that in Rome the minuet is ceremonious and that not everybody

[10] Art. 'Dance,' 13th ed., vol. vii, p. 797.

[11] It is an unfortunate accident of terminology that the 'low dance' should be that of the upper classes and the 'high' that of the lower orders.   The adjectives are due, of course, to the nature of the steps: the mincing *pas menus* (hence *menuet*) of the courtiers and gentry, and the strides and leaps of the servants and country folk.

[12] John Playford, *The English Dancing-Master* (1651).   Facsimile reprint edited by Margaret Dean-Smith (London, 1957).

[13] The country dance too was cultivated by the classics, particularly by Mozart in his *Contretänze*, a designation derived from the French *contredanse*, which in turn was simply a phonetic perversion of the English 'country dance,' exactly as *redingote* is of 'riding-coat,' *boulingrin* of 'bowling-green' and *moleskine* of 'moleskin.'   Goethe (*Aus meinem Leben*) writes of the 'English *contre*.'   In the English catalogue of Breitkopf & Härtel's collected edition of Mozart the composer's title, instead of being simply turned back into its original, is translated as 'Contra-Dances.'

(indeed few people) can dance it, or can obtain permission to do so. The country dance, on the other hand, he describes as haphazard and danced by all and sundry.[14]   But from an earlier German writer, an expert, we learn that the country dance was refined by the English aristocracy until it had become 'both a pleasure to dance and lovely to look at,' and was accepted almost everywhere.[15]

No such refinement came over dances of the *Ländler* and *Deutsche* type until they went to town to merge into the Viennese waltz, and that, of course, belonged as much to the middle classes as to the aristocracy.   Until then the music of these countrified dances retained its rustic character even in the work of so civilized a composer as Mozart, and there is no doubt that it did so because its divergence from such a courtly dance as the minuet, to which it was otherwise closely linked by its binary form, its square metres and its triple measure, was founded on a long-standing tradition.   The close association dates from a common origin in a much older dance, the *branle*.   The minuet itself is not very old.   The earliest mention of it Sachs can find [16] was made in 1664, by G. du Manoir, who was 'Roi des Joueurs d'Instruments et des Maîtres à Danser en France.'   According to Grove it did not appear in English publications until the second half of the seventeenth century [17], and the *Encyclopaedia Britannica*, in the article already quoted from, informs us that it came to Paris not much earlier, in 1650, when it 'was first set to music by Lully,' which of course means merely that this was its first introduction to music as a higher art, or, if we prefer it that way, that it was then first deemed worthy of becoming a vehicle for composition.   The French clavecinists, from Chambonnières onward (1670), have it sometimes, and d'Anglebert has a 'Menuet de Poitou' (1689)—a title that will become interesting presently.   Attaignant (*c.* 1530) has only *basses danses*, *branles*, *pavanes* and *gaillardes* in his collections, and there are no minuets in Praetorius's *Terpsichore* (1612).   On the other hand —and this is significant as pointing to the process of a more rustic species detaching itself from the minuet—that dance begins to take on a *Ländler*-like tone in the eight suites of Johann Caspar Fischer's *Blumenbüchlein* of 1698.[18]

In the same year appeared Georg Muffat's *Florilegium secundum*, a collection of keyboard pieces in which the composer put together festive dances in the form of suites, the fourth of which, 'Splendidae

[14] *Italien: Zweiter Aufenthalt in Rom* (1788).
[15] Gottfried Taubert, *Der rechtschaffene Tanzmeister* (Leipzig, 1717).
[16] Op. cit.
[11] Art. 'Minuet,' 5th ed., vol. v, p. 789.
[18] Oscar Bie, *Tanzmusik* ('Die Musik' series, edited by Richard Strauss) (Berlin, 1905), p. 33.

nuptiae,' depicts a wedding-feast at which cavaliers and their ladies are given courtly dances and maidens of Poitou countrified ones.

Poitou again! Why should Poitou have a special dance of its own? But it did have one. Authorities like Dufort [19] and Czerwinski [20], apart from others already cited, make it clear that the minuet originated from a *branle* danced in that province, derived still farther back from the *courante*, which was a lively, running and anything but courtly dance, at first in duple time, unlike the form made familiar by classical suites. Indeed it is perhaps through its transformation into the *branle de Poitou* that it acquired its triple measure, which it handed on to the minuet. Arbeau, whose invaluable book on the dance, the *Orchésographie* of 1588 [21], gives us so much information on the dances of the sixteenth century, and most fortunately quotes a great deal of their music, gives the first part of the tune of a *branle de Poitou* which many a reader would find to his surprise that he knows perfectly well, for it is the theme of the piece called 'Pieds-en-l'air' in Peter Warlock's *Capriol* Suite, based on tunes from Arbeau. It is tender, leisurely in pace and minuet-like, though in a three-times-three motion, not the square arrangement of 3–4 bars the minuet as a dance acquired later but did not by any means impose on its higher musical forms, where metrical irregularity—in Haydn especially—is often its greatest fascination. Unfortunately Arbeau gives no other examples of the Poitou *branle*, and indeed not the whole of this one. 'I will give you only the beginning of the air,' he says, 'because the rest of it, and all the other *branles*, of which there are a great number, have the same movement.' All the other Poitou specimens, he obviously means, for the numerous other kinds of *branle* have not by any means the same movement. It was in fact 'a kind of generic dance which was capable of an almost infinite amount of variety.' [22] Arbeau gives twenty-three varieties and, as we have just seen, tunes for each of them could have been found in profusion.

What interests us especially at the moment, however, is the fact that already in the sixteenth century different types of this forerunner of the minuet were danced by different people according to quite definite rules. Arbeau shows that four of the important varieties of the species were assigned to three different groups of people taking part in the dance: 'The old people gravely dance the *branles doubles* and

---

[19] Giambattista Dufort, *Trattato del ballo mobile* (Naples, 1728).

[20] Albert Czerwinski, *Die Tänze des XVI. Jahrhunderts und die alte französische Tanzschule vor Einführung des Menuett* (Danzig, 1878).

[21] Thoinot Arbeau, *Orchesography: a Treatise in the Form of Dialogue, whereby all Manner of Persons may easily acquire and practise the Honourable Exercise of Dancing.* Now first translated from the Original Edition published at Langres, 1588, by Cyril W. Beaumont. With a Preface by Peter Warlock (London, 1925).

[22] *Encyclopaedia Britannica*, article cited above.

branles simples, the young married ones dance the *branles gais*, and the youngest of all dance the *branles de Bourgogne*.' Sachs (op. cit.) gives similar information, evidently taken from Arbeau, though he does not reproduce it accurately: he assigns the *branle double* to the older people, the 'more lively' *branle simple* to the younger married couples and the 'rapid' *branle gay* [*sic*] to the youngest people.   Of these the *branle gai* is in triple time; the double, simple and Burgundian types were in duple time, noted in four crotchets to the bar, *alla breve*, by Warlock, the piece called 'Bransles' in whose *Capriol* is a compound of the scraps of tune given by Arbeau for these three dances.   Morley adds to the confusion by saying that

the vsuall *Almaine* containeth the time of eight, and most commonlie in short notes.   Like vnto this is the French *bransle* (which they call *bransle simple*) which goeth somwhat rounder in time then this, otherwise the measure is all one.   The *bransle de poictou* or *bransle double* is more quick in time (as being in a rounde Tripla) but the straine is longer, containing most vsually twelue whole strokes.[23]

There is no evidence in these early authorities of any mixing of social classes similar to that encouraged at the Viennese court balls of the eighteenth century, if not in actual fact in the seventeenth-century Spain that is the usual setting for *Don Giovanni*; but the sixteenth century was aware of the striking contrast between coarse peasants dancing and the decorous performances of good society.   Sachs reproduces a serial engraving by Hakluyt's illustrator, Theodorus de Bry (1528–98), the pictorial representation and Latin text of which both prove this awareness; and there can be no doubt that these social divergencies were reflected in the music of the dances, if only at first by the instruments on which they were played: bagpipes, shawms, hurdy-gurdies and what not on the one hand, lutes, viols, oboes and flutes on the other, let us say.   Rustic instrumental sounds, we have seen, are often a feature of the classical minuet-trio, even sometimes where the actual musical stuff does not suggest rusticity.

There is no doubt, then, that a mixture of styles in dance music was a feature of the ballroom from at least the sixteenth century onward, and although the affectation of introducing bucolic elements into it in professional composition may be no older than the 'back to nature' movement advocated by Rousseau, the tendency to level out social differences at festivities at which dancing was the chief enjoyment must itself have had some influence on the music used for the dances assigned to different classes.   We may safely take it that the tradition

[23] Thomas Morley, *A Plaine and Easie Introduction to Practicall Musicke*.   Facsimile, with an Introduction by Edmund H. Fellowes, published for the Shakespeare Association (London, 1937); modern reprint, ed. by Alec Harman (London, 1952).

which led to the curious differentiation between the minuet and its trio
in classical works of the sonata type dates a long way back, so far as
dancing is concerned. The reason why it should ever have been
introduced into absolute music is, of course, not easily discoverable,
if at all; but it is quite readily imaginable, if imagination may be
allowed—and why should it not?—to help us in such an investigation.
A composer like Mozart, trained from infancy to cling to precedent by
instinct as much as by reasoning, and accustomed all his life to apply
his genius to artistic procedures sanctioned by usage, which he could
nevertheless bend to his will as enterprisingly as anybody, but never
thought of breaking, could not fail to hark back unconsciously to old
habits the minuet had inherited from the *branle* when he used the
former according to the accepted practice that had somehow or other
handed it on from the older suite to the sonata form. A contrast was
clearly wanted between the minuet and its trio; Mozart was just the
man to obtain that contrast in much the same way as the customs of
the ballroom had already done by at once opposing and reconciling
different social classes and their dances to each other. While Haydn
was more intent on expanding the minuet as a form, Mozart heightened
what we may call its social significance. Not by any means always;
but he did it often enough by placing aristocratic and popular music
side by side to set us wondering. And to wonder is to seek for an
explanation. Let us hope we have found it.

The trio, not only of the minuet but of its descendant, the scherzo,
is so often more songful than the main section that here again we are
urged to speculate. And again we more than suspect that old tradi-
tions are at the bottom of this phenomenon, for which sonata-form
music in itself offers no explanation. Well, the nobles, always
anxious to be in the fashion, more than probably hugged tradition far
less closely than the people, and their dance, the fashionable minuet,
far more readily followed newer trends. Instrumental music was
more modern than vocal during the time the minuet as a dance for
good society formed itself, and the newer dances, the minuet included,
were never performed to song-tunes, as Peter Warlock in his preface
to the English edition of Arbeau reminds us the older dances were 'as
often as not.' [24] Popular vocal music being much older than instrumental dance music, we should have no difficulty in understanding the
strikingly vocal type of so many classical trios (often taking the form
of a tune with a simple accompaniment) if we are ready to believe that

[24] The 'Basse-Danse,' No. 1 in Warlock's *Capriol* suite, is a transformation of the tenor
part in Claudin de Sermisy's four-part chanson *Jouyssance vous donneray*, and is given that
title by Arbeau. See *A Chanson by Claudin de Sermisy*, by John A Parkinson (*Music &
Letters*, vol. xxxix, April 1958). This chanson is the piece performed by 'The Three
Musical Ladies' in the well-known sixteenth-century picture by the unknown painter
called 'The Master of the Half-lengths.'

they are a sort of unpremeditated survival of dances older than the minuet.

The fact, too, that the trio derives its name from pieces really played by three instruments, a practice still reflected in later music at times[25], indicates an influence of songfulness, for early music written in three parts is almost sure to be in the nature of vocal counterpoint, even if written for instruments. Anything like a solo part, moreover, will there resemble a song, and it is more than probable that the frequent soloistic treatment of melody in classical trios comes from an old custom current when the *branle* was still danced by the nobility and the minuet as yet undeveloped as a special ceremonial function of their own. According to Sachs, 'we know that in the French court dance (from Henry III to Louis XIV[26]) that form of the *branle* predominated in which after one or two rounds one couple left the chain, danced briefly together, and took up their position in the rear . . .' As one visualizes this, one can almost hear the trio of a classical minuet, but not the minuet itself, which one always thinks of not only as a ceremonial but also as a choric dance. And one thinks so because the classics have fixed that association in one's mind.

The aristocratic minuet received its death-blow from the French Revolution—or, to avoid the charge of being all too rashly wise about cause and effect after the event, let us say it came to an end as a fashionable pastime and grew into a quaint relic of the past at the time of the Revolution. Early in the nineteenth century a writer could deplore 'la sévérité, avec laquelle on s'est accoutumé à juger le menuet depuis quelques années.'[27] The *Ländler*, on the other hand, because it was anything but aristocratic, survived and changed comparatively little on merging into the urban and middle-class waltz. The early waltzes, up to and including the elder Johann Strauss, could be remarkably rustic, square-cut and jolting still. Diabelli's 'waltz,' which Beethoven with rude justice called a *Schusterfleck*, but on which he nevertheless wrote one of the grandest variation works in existence, was still very much of a *Ländler*, and with all his elegance the Viennese 'waltz king,' if never countrified, is at least often sentimental about the country. The quicker pace of the waltz is attributed by Sachs to the abandonment of hobnailed shoes and the introduction of the dancers to polished floors; but this seems far-fetched when we remember that the leisurely minuet had long before that been danced in palaces. What is much more likely is that the speeding-up of the *Ländler* into the waltz was a sort of parallel movement to that of the faster scherzo's

[25] e.g. the minuets in Bach's third French Suite and in Haydn's string Quartet, Op. 9 No. 4, where it is given to the two violins alone, the first playing in double stopping.
[26] Only the earliest years of Louis XIV's reign can be meant, of course.
[27] Moreau de Saint-Méry, *De la danse* (Parma, 1803).

N

growth out of the minuet; and it seems to have been dancing which once more influenced the masters who brought the scherzo to perfection, Beethoven and Schubert, just as it had influenced those for whom the minuet assumed the significance of a sonata-form movement, fit for symphony and chamber music at its greatest.   Speaking more generally for a moment, we find the influence of the rustic dance as strong still in Beethoven and Schubert as it was in Haydn and Mozart.   The *Alla danza tedesca* in the former's B♭ major Quartet, Op. 130, was no doubt so called by the composer when he had realized that the theme he had devised for it was that of a typical *Ländler*. The scherzo in the 'Pastoral' Symphony, the 'Peasants' Merry Gathering,' is the ideal bucolic music without being as a matter of fact very much idealized: it is thoroughly folky in character, though not Austrian so much as Flemish in its racily realistic, Teniers-like quality —an impression I had formed years before it was found to be confirmed by a Belgian authority.[28]   In the eighth Symphony all is countrified or domesticated, and the trio is akin to folksong rather than folk-dance, the kind of song founded on the natural open notes of horn music so often cultivated by Germanic composers.   And this is a real minuet-trio, not at all in the scherzo manner.   This is rare in Beethoven (three minuets only in his piano sonatas, again not counting such a movement in *tempo di minuetto* as the first of Op. 54), and rarer still in the town-and-country, aristocratic-plebeian contrast between main section and trio, though there is a goodish example of it in the A major Quartet, Op. 18 No. 5, and a violent revulsion from courtliness to rebellion in the minuet of the B♭ major piano Sonata, Op. 22.

A closer follower of Mozart in this respect was Schubert, for all that scherzos predominate vastly over minuets in his work.   In two chamber works that do contain the latter, the Octet and the A minor string Quartet, as well as in the piano Sonata in G major, Op. 78, which publishers would for long insist on issuing, for some unaccountable reason, as a set of four pieces including a 'Minuet,' the trios are distinctly more 'popular,' more vocal and folksong-like, though with an urban, Viennese tinge, than the principal sections, while the trio in the great C major Symphony is a heavenly *Ländler* spun out to the proportions of an important composition, an exaltation of the common people's music into regions of eternal bliss.   The scherzo-trios of at least five other of Schubert's piano sonatas are rustic in various ways, and though they differ from Mozart as one great creative individuality must needs differ from another, the ultimate influence is surely the same.   The trio of the C major Sonata of 1815 yodels at the beginning; that of the A minor, Op. 42,

[28] Ernest Closson, *L'Élément flamand dans Beethoven* (Brussels, 1929).   English translation, *The Fleming in Beethoven*, by Muriel Fuller (Oxford, 1936).

is delicately but not too delicately pastoral; those of Op. 53, in D major, and Op. 122, in E♭ major, are strikingly *Ländler*-like; and that of Op. 147, in B major, suggests our most bucolic instrument—the bagpipe. And one need only compare these trios with Schubert's waltzes and *Ländler* to find that they have arisen from moods similar to those which engendered these separate dances. The relationship is, in fact, precisely the same as that between the minuets in Mozart's sonata-form works and his *Deutsche*, which greatly strengthen one's belief that ancient precedent accounts for the recurrent similarity of the contrasts between the classical masters' minuets and trios.

Key Heredity

(*The Musical Times*, September 1942)

ONE should never, I suppose, presume to write articles on any subject unless one has some definite point to make. I confess that I have none, or if I have, it will doubtless resemble the one a certain lady is said to have described as being 'very moot indeed.' Nevertheless, I shall be surprised if what I am going to set forth will fail to be thought at least as interesting as it is pointless, strange as such a situation may appear. If I had any pretensions to be a philosopher, I could perhaps suggest that it may prove speculative, but nothing of a philosophical nature will be found here. What I wish to expound is merely a small technical matter.

It has never been raised before, so far as I am aware; on the other hand, it may quite possibly be taken up by others, who may bring forward a theory where I confine myself mainly to raising a question. It is this: Do keys call forth similar ideas in composers at different times? There is little doubt that they suggest certain moods—or that certain moods suggest them. One can think of a type of sustained sentimental melody, for instance, which many composers have been tempted to set down in D♭ major, almost as a matter of course. That may perhaps be accounted for by convention. What I want to discuss, however, is much more mysterious. Let me come to it at once.

Tovey, in his analysis of the *Midsummer Night's Dream* Overture [1], pointed out a mysterious chord that occasionally interrupts the fairies' dance and said that it 'is not over-familiar, even in more recent harmonic styles, and (though easily explained by classical theory) was far beyond the scope of any of Mendelssohn's contemporaries.' In my review of the volume in question I drew attention to the fact that this very chord had been used by Mozart in *Così fan tutte*, in the trio (No. 10) in Act I. [2] In his later 'Retrospect and Corrigenda' [3] Tovey handsomely acknowledged that he had overlooked this classical precedent. What was interesting is not that Tovey was wrong for

---

[1] *Essays in Musical Analysis*, vol. iv, p. 99 (1936).
[2] See musical quotations, Exx. in the chapter on *Così*, p. 40.
[3] *Essays in Musical Analysis*, vol. vi, p. 148 (1939).

once, but that apart from this one slip of his extraordinary memory he seems to have been right in saying that this chord is and has remained unfamiliar. A correspondent pointed out in the *Musical Times*, two months after the original appearance of this essay there, that the chord does occasionally appear in the Viennese classics, but the instances he mentions show it inconspicuously as a passing chord or suspension, not as a dissonance deliberately arrived at as a substitute for a point of harmonic repose, as in the Mozart and Mendelssohn instances.

Let us, then, accept the hypothesis that this chord was handed down, in that particular presentation, straight from Mozart to Mendelssohn. We do not know, of course, whether the younger master was aware of the provenance of his heritage. He was in the fortunate position to have access to an enormous amount of music before the age of seventeen, at which he wrote the Overture, an advantage perhaps never before or since enjoyed by any great composer with the single exception of Elgar, who had at his disposal his father's music shop as Mendelssohn had the paternal library. Still, *Così fan tutte*, which was neglected and rather despised in those days, is not one of the more likely Mozartian works to have come into his hands. He may perfectly well have invented that chord for himself, unaware of the 1790 patent. It does not greatly matter. What does seem remarkable is that it should not only be the very same chord which Mendelssohn chose, but the very same notes: in other words, he used the chord in the same key. His Overture, like Mozart's trio, is in E major, and if the chord really never was used in this particular way by any composer in the intervening thirty-six years, it is more than extraordinary that the only two instances of its employment should make the second look like a direct quotation.

It may be such a quotation, of course, but that is extremely improbable. It would be too flagrant a plagiarism. Composers, even great composers, are not above borrowing from each other, but they do not deliberately borrow quite as conspicuously as all that. It is more than doubtful whether Mendelssohn at seventeen could have been quite so shameless, and we know that he was at that time anything but hard pressed for ideas of his own. If he had helped himself to this chord from Mozart, we may be pretty sure that he would at least have disguised it by means of transposition. The very fact that it appears so boldly in the same key argues that he is innocent of theft. Robbers wrap up the goods they have stolen before they carry them through the streets.

What then? Is there some sort of suggestion about E major which in an unaccountable way lures similar music from different composers, in different countries and at different times? Or have we simply a case of unconscious plagiarism? Had Mendelssohn the

Così fan tutte trio in his mind without being aware of the fact or realizing where he had come across that 'mysterious chord' (doubly mysterious now)?   Did it, when he had chosen to write his Overture in the key of E major, come to confront him as a not fully identified memory, as it would not have done had he happened to use another key?   An affirmative answer to these last three questions certainly looks like the most rational explanation.   But let us go a step farther, at the risk of finding the matter rather less simple after all.

There are other chords in Mendelssohn's Overture which now also become something of a mystery, from our point of view.   Familiar as they are, I had better quote them (Ex. 1) if only for comparison with another series of chords, found elsewhere, which are strikingly similar and, in orchestral performance, very much the same in tone-quality (Ex. 2):

Concert-goers will know them almost as well as Mendelssohn's, for they occur in a fairly popular work—Rimsky-Korsakov's *Scheherazade*. And behold! not only have we once again precisely the same sort of music, but the same key.   True, the signature is for the moment that of E minor, not major; but there is nothing in that, for both the first and last movements in *Scheherazade*, though beginning in minor, decidedly centre in E major, which they establish quite firmly some time before the end, whereas the Mendelssohn chords tend towards E minor, in which key, in fact, the rapid figuration of the fairy music begins.

Well now, did Rimsky-Korsakov too hark back unconsciously to another work in E major and borrow something from it because that key put him in mind of a passage of whose origin he was not at the moment clearly aware?   It is quite possible, of course.   What does not seem to be possible, however, is that he could have remained unaware of the resemblance later.   We know from his memoirs that he knew the Mendelssohn Overture well and that, in fact, he admired it as a boy.   So we can only think that, had he regarded this passage as a plagiarism, even an unconscious one, he would never have let it stand, any more than he would have written it down had he recognized it at once as not genuinely his own.   Since he did let it stand, probably deciding that it would do as a kind of quotation, or perhaps as an allusion to an earlier work with the 'once upon a time opening' he desired, it seems likely that recollection, conscious or unconscious, had nothing to do with the actual process of composition.   The similarity was purely accidental, even more probably than in the Mozart-Mendelssohn case.   But then why did such an accident occur twice over with music in the same key?   'Twice over,' I said, but another correspondent furnished the *Musical Times* with a third example, which occurs in the first act of Gounod's *Faust*.   Again we have E major, and what is more, the passage reproduces Mendelssohn's harmony exactly in the treble, but for two inversions which make no essential difference:

Ex. 3

The question insists on arising again: is there something about the feeling of this or that key which engenders the same notions in more than one composer?   One might ask it generally, whatever tonality one may have in mind, and no doubt one could find examples for each.

I can think of two very striking coincidences of this kind in D minor, for instance: the descending phrase at the point in Mozart's *Don Giovanni* where Don Juan goes down to hell is always called to mind by a very similar passage at the end of Dvořák's Symphony Op. 70; and the spinning-chorus in Haydn's *Seasons* ('Winter') must surely have haunted Schubert's mind when he suggested the spinning-wheel in *Gretchen am Spinnrade* with very similar 6–8 semiquaver figures.   D minor, I repeat, is the key in all these instances.   Then there is an instance in F major which suggests a subconscious recollection rather than a case of deliberate imitation, which surely the later composer would have felt to be too blatant to be allowed; and it can hardly be just a coincidence that the same harmonic progression and almost the same type of accompaniment should have occurred to Sullivan for

H.M.S. Pinafore as it did to Schumann for the children's song *Marien-würmchen*, and, once more, in the same key:

Ex. 4

Since I have been occupied mainly with E major, however, I now revert to that key for my final curiosity, which is, indeed, curiouser and curiouser, and again brings in Sullivan, as it happens. Everybody knows Richard Strauss's way of writing a passage as though it were all in one key and then inserting accidentals in front of two or three chords in the middle which wrench it momentarily out of that key into a distant one. The *locus classicus* is the opening of *Der Rosenkavalier*, and if ever one would have granted a composer the monopoly for a characteristic trick, one would have been inclined to say that Strauss holds it for this:

Ex. 5

But not a bit of it: most readers will be surprised to find that the very same thing can be found in *Utopia Limited*:

Ex. 6

The procedure is exactly the same—and once again both pieces are in E major. No doubt Strauss would have been more surprised than anyone else, for surely here at least we can be perfectly certain that we are not faced with a case of recollection. If anybody can prove to me that Strauss ever knew *Utopia Limited* I will cheerfully undertake to eat, not only my own hat, but Sullivan's Victorian topper and Strauss's green Bavarian holiday *Hüterl* into the bargain.

Phrase-lengths

(*The Musical Times*, March 1954)

AMONG the principles a composition student cannot be taught systematically, but should, if his teacher is wise, be made fully aware of incidentally, is the importance of varying the length of his melodic phrases or, to be perhaps more to the point, his rhythmic periods. Metrical squareness is a fault too easily overlooked in the process of composition and far too apt to spoil a listener's enjoyment of a work of any length which may have many other qualities to recommend it. I was twice reminded of this one season at Covent Garden, where two of the most square-cut operas happened to be given in close proximity: *Lohengrin* and *The Golden Weathercock*. Each has, of course, plenty of attraction and interest. Wagner's work falls short in stature only in comparison with his own later masterpieces, and it has amplitude and coherence of build as well as moments of lambent poetry; Rimsky-Korsakov's enchants with dazzling orchestration and with many magical or witty incidents. But both operas are apt to grow tiresome in the long run—and the run of *Lohengrin* is very long, while that of *The Golden Weathercock*, especially in its second act, *seems* so. What produces weariness, even if the hearer is not aware of the cause, and more so once he has discovered it, is the even tread of 4-bar and 8-bar phrases with far too little relief. One is left after a performance of either work in a state not unlike that of the Shakespearean actor who has been so saturated in all-too-mechanical declamation that he orders his late-night beer and kipper in blank verse.

A composer too, in the case of a vocal work, may have allowed himself to fall into rhythmic monotony by a librettist's words or, as with *Lohengrin*, his own. All too often in that work the musical rhythm simply follows the unremitting 4-line stanzas with their alternate feminine and masculine end-rhymes. Wagner himself said that whatever was new in his music, it did not lie in the direction of rhythm. Nevertheless, he had learnt by the time he came to *Tristan* that if it was too difficult to avoid matching a uniform verbal rhythm with monotonous musical phrasing, then the verbal rhythm had better be varied to begin with; and with this he had no difficulty, once the principle had occurred to him, since he was his own librettist.

Rimsky-Korsakov accepted ready-made words from others, apparently without protest if they set him traps in the shape of rhythmically unvaried rhyming couplets. There are too many phrases in *The Golden Weathercock* which remind one irresistibly of Thackeray's little comic rhymed page-headings in *The Rose and the Ring*:

> Ah, I fear, King Valoroso,
> That your conduct is but so-so.

This is all very well for a children's book, and perhaps we may say, if we are sufficiently indulgent, that it will do well enough for several of Rimsky-Korsakov's operas, which are in the nature of children's books, picturesquely, lavishly and charmingly illustrated. *Tsar Saltan* is especially obsessed with these babyish rhymes, set in quasi-recitative. This sort of thing goes on intermittently all the evening (I translate roughly):

> There would be no wonder in it,
> Should she wed the Tsar this minute,
> If before the year is done
> She presented him a son.

Such rhymes are sometimes set in even quavers throughout, and somehow it fails to bring relief even if the composer decides to try variety by extending the last line to twice its length (crotchets instead of quavers), or even if he drives adventurousness as far as

$$\frac{3}{4} \quad \flat \; \flat | \; \flat \cdot \; \flat \; \flat \; \flat | \; \flat$$

If be-fore the year is done

Squareness of phrasing even in instrumental music is often to be accounted for by the influence of words. This is not to suggest that composers write with any particular poem in mind, but that they remember certain unenterprising conventions of word-setting. Symmetrical sections of music have so often been associated with the regular footfalls of verse (melodies have thus again and again taken the shape of phrase-groups divisible by 4), that it was only too easy for the feeling to take root that such melodic shapes, often pairing phrases in tonic harmony against others of similar length on dominant or subdominant harmony, like rhymes in alternate lines, were the norm of all music, every departure being abnormal and therefore, to certain minds, reprehensible.

It is tempting to say simple minds, but since such a scholar as Hugo Riemann was notoriously so inclined, one must hesitate and seek for another adjective. 'Honest' is perhaps the word, as it is understood by those who think of themselves as liking everything to be forthright and unequivocal, who regard simplicity as such as a virtue and

mistrust all subtlety as concealing falsehood.   This is the type of mind
that likes folksong, for instance, when it is perfectly balanced in 4-bar
phrases, as it often is, though by no means always and not to the same
extent in every country; the type which responds most readily, too, to
old dances and their cultivated descendants in the suite form, the
original reason for whose squareness is, needless to say, to be sought
in the figures performed by the dancers, which had to be regularly
repetitive.   Not for nothing was the outstanding champion of
regular musical phrasing a German scholar, for no species of music
has been more favoured for that very attribute than the German
Volkslied—so called—the kind of popular song that has become
volkstümlich to such an extent that most Germans cannot distinguish
between it and the real thing.   It may be a song from a *Singspiel*
by J. A. Hiller, from a Viennese pantomime by Wenzel Müller or
Drechsler, or one of those sentimental ditties by Silcher, Kücken or
Himmel—the less subtle, the more foursquare, the better.

Even Schubert's *Heidenröslein* is said to have become a folksong—
as if anything of which the composer is known could do that—and it
is true that it has the kind of simplicity that would recommend it to
Germans who, while appreciating the most elaborate feats of symphonic construction, also like to see themselves touched by extreme
artlessness (shades of Mahler!).   But actually this little tune of
Schubert's is not quite as ingenuous as it seems, if not nearly as slyly
allusive as Goethe's poem.   If we just think casually about this song,
we are sure to say that it is a multiple of fours; but working it out on
our fingers, we find that it comes to 4+6+4, or if we like to be
particular, 4+2+2+2+4.

Schubert's melodies often are divisible by 4, but he can also be very
cunning in the management of his phrase-lengths, even where a poem
may tempt him to pedestrian progress.   The delicious 'Fischer-
weise' might serve as an example, but the less familiar and no less
delicious 'Das Lied im Grünen' shall do so here.   This setting
improves vastly on an amiable but indifferent poem by Friedrich Reil,
which Schubert could quite easily have turned into a strophic song,
with the tune appearing eight times in exactly the same form; for there
is nothing in the friendly, cheerful words on the theme of 'gather ye
rosebuds while ye may' to call for any change of mood.   Nor did
they perhaps deserve any subtleties of declamation, for they contain
faults and ineptitudes enough: superfluous words added merely for
the sake of scansion ('Da streichen die Wölkchen so zart *uns* dahin')
and artificial diction of which not even a German can be expected to
catch the sense in the course of a song that goes by at a moderately
rapid pace ('Die Zukunft der grämlichen Ansicht entschlagen').   But
what enchantments await the hearer, thanks to Schubert's decision not

to make a strictly strophic song of this! I say 'strictly' because basically 'Das Lied im Grünen' *is* strophic.   We are kept well aware of the beginnings and endings of the eight verses, and all the music quite clearly springs from the same well of invention.   The verses are most artfully varied musically, just enough to keep interest and delight on the stretch during what turns into a fairly lengthy song and remains, in emotional expression, almost monotonous and at a comfortably low tension.   The first verse calls for what the music fundamentally consists of: three 4-bar phrases.   But already there is a small departure to embarrass the Riemanns of this world.   These phrases, which should normally occupy twelve bars, actually take thirteen. For Schubert naughtily inserts an extra bar after the first group and then refrains from doing the same thing again after the second group, where the third joins straight on.   In the third verse, apart from one of those characteristically abrupt modulations, which takes the music from the key of the subdominant into that of the flat supertonic and immediately back again (twice), there are more pauses between phrases, so that this verse, with some repetitions, now takes twenty-four bars instead of thirteen.   Later on we have two identical verses, where apart from a new surprise (an excursion into the submediant minor), there are now pauses both after the first and the second phrase, so that the two between them take up fourteen bars.   Then follows the most astonishing device to get away from phrases cut to the same length, and here Schubert breaks with the poet and at the same time makes his sense clearer by allowing his own musical phrases to depart from the verbal lines and letting these overlap.   Reil has this:

> Grünt einst uns das Leben nicht fürder, so haben
> Wir klüglich die grünende Zeit nicht versäumt.

What Schubert does with this is best shown in music type:

It will be seen that these words, which appear above the stave and are set to the notes shown with their tails turned up, could quite easily have been treated like those of the first verse, shown below the music (turned-down tails). But Schubert's breaking of the line is vastly preferable, for more reasons than one: it varies the music without actually departing from the original conception; it treats the poet's jog-trot words with a sense of proper declamation; it makes a very pretty surprise; above all it once again avoids regularity of phrase-lengths in a tune that keeps dropping into the same end-line (with a top note for climax the last time only) and could so easily have remained rhythmically quite uneventful. A rather mild song, that might also have been just dully repetitive and plodding, has instead been made exquisite by nothing more than a charming tune and a very cunning avoidance of the squareness inherent in it.

What Riemann would have said to all this does not bear thinking about. Or rather, what he would have made of it. For he was capable of some astonishing feats of juggling with musical phrases if they refused to fit into the 8-bar lengths he thought were fundamental to all music; and he indulged in extraordinary arguments to 'justify' composers for whom he had sufficient regard, if they showed any reluctance to conform. I have an old Steingräber edition of a selection from Tchaikovsky's piano works in a *Phrasierungsausgabe mit Fingersatz von Dr Hugo Riemann*. Under the music appear figures in brackets which show how the musical periods run, according to Riemann's idea, in groups of eight bars, or sometimes four, when it seems quite unavoidable. Unfortunately, Tchaikovsky's music refuses to play this pretty game (on a chessboard, presumably) as Riemann wants it played, and it is amusing to see the shifts the editor is put to in trying to make it appear as though all were going well.

One oddity, to begin with, is that Riemann will count an upbeat as a first bar, with the result that at the end of the eighth, or perhaps the sixteenth, he finds himself with an extra bar on hand, which has then to be disposed of by numbering a whole following section out of step, in the hope that by some lucky chance or some glorious rule of compensation things will come right again later on. Sometimes they do; but if not, the artful Riemann is equal to the emergency, to his own satisfaction, anyway. An odd bar which he doubtless wished the composer had allowed to drop under the table is then calmly marked (8a), and all is well. It has not become a ninth bar, for that would never have done: it is still an eighth bar, and thanks to the 'a' it doesn't really count. In another place we may find a period that is quite plainly ten bars in length marked (1) to (6), (7), (7a), (7b), (8): the eighth bar has thus fallen into its proper place, the odd sevens are forgotten, and all is as it should be once more. Here, in case anybody should think all this unbelievable, is a specimen of Riemann's phrasing from Tchaikovsky's Polka, Op. 9 No. 2 (treble line only quoted):

It will be seen that after the upbeat which, of course, belongs to the rhythmic period preceding the quotation, we have in the first place a regular four-bar phrase, with which Riemann can be perfectly happy. I have marked it 1 = 5, 2 = 6, 3 = 7 (the later figures standing for the repeat of bars 1–3) and 4 and 8 respectively for the alternative bars. Then comes what to any reasonable being who is not wedded to the notion that all music proceeds by fours or eights and their multiples is quite plainly a bridge-passage taking the form of a rhythmic period in three bars. I have accordingly marked it 1–3. But this will not do for Riemann, who can only get over it by ignoring it as a rhythmic constituent and thus marking it as a mere appendage of bar 8; and since there are three bars, one would think he would have resorted to the expedient of calling them 8a, 8b and 8c. But even that is too simple for him: his phrasing is labelled as shown by my figures in brackets, and thus the first bar becomes for him 8a, the *third* 8b, and the second he does not mark at all. We are thus faced not only with the phenomenon of two bars which, considered as metrical units are to be regarded as not counting, but with the even greater marvel of yet another middle bar that has no sort of existence at all, so far as compatibility with Riemann's theories is concerned.

Unhappy Riemann! But perhaps he was more at ease than with Tchaikovsky with such a thing as the opening of the minuet in Mozart's B♭ major Quartet, K.458:

There he would have found eight bars and need have looked no farther. But even here, if he had really looked at the music, his notion would have fallen to the ground; and if he had refused to make a closer examination, he would have had to be told, though he would never have believed it, that it is not twice 4 alone that makes 8, but also, for instance, $3+5$ and, in this unfortunate instance, $2\frac{2}{3}+5\frac{1}{3}$.

The Happy Ending

(*The Monthly Musical Record*, May 1940)

FREQUENTERS of circulating libraries may still occasionally see a lady looking furtively at the final pages of a novel before she decides to take it out. She wants to make sure of a satisfactory 'all's-well-that-ends-well' before venturing to put her sentiments to too acid a test; and she knows, no doubt, that happy endings in fiction, taken for granted years ago by those who instinctively avoided such inconsiderate authors as Meredith or Hardy, have been made all too scarce for the average reader's comfort by the general scepsis attendant on modern psychology. But surely the library subscriber's comfort was always something of a delusion. Long before psychology became a popular parlour-game she must have known, in her heart of hearts, that a novel's finishing with wedding-bells meant as likely as not the opening of new chapters filled with matrimonial knells, even if she was not warned by Hardy's relatively happy ending of *Under the Greenwood Tree*, where the blissfully betrothed heroine finds herself thinking of 'a secret she would never tell.' The truth is that there is always something vaguely disquieting about a story which on the face of it comes to a joyful conclusion, whether we look at it artistically or only sentimentally. The difference between these two viewpoints is merely that to the reader's sentiments the reason for this dissatisfaction remains obscure, whereas artistic perception is capable of analysing it to some extent.

The obvious thing to say is that a tragic conclusion elevates the reader if the work is one achieving or approaching greatness, and makes him feel that an artistic plan has been conclusively rounded off even if it has been unimportant or sordid or paltry; on the other hand the conventional marriage-bell final cadence leaves everything in the air. We are left uncomfortably apprehensive as to what will happen to the lovers in *Under the Greenwood Tree*, while the unbearably grim and tear-compelling end of *Tess of the D'Urbervilles* leaves us not only stirred to the depths but somehow curiously elated. Both the destruction and the consummation of love in death make for a satisfying finality at worst and for the greatest artistic worth at best; its happy fulfilment leaves the receptive artist in us emotionally as

O

197

frustrated as its mere coming to nothing.   Can it be denied that the tragic end of *Tristan and Isolde* leaves us aesthetically happier than the betrothal festivities at the close of *The Mastersingers?*   It certainly does so if we reflect for a moment what the married life of Walther and Eva—a prig and a minx—is likely to turn into.   Which brings us to opera, the immediate topic of this sketch, and to music in general, on which a brief discussion of that topic may throw some light.

Let us not indulge in futile statistics of the relative numbers of operas with happy and with tragic endings; but it is, I think, indisputable that the number of artistically satisfying tragic operas is incomparably greater.   That is to say, operas successful from first to last, though our topic demands special attention to the 'last.'   It is curious how many musical works for the stage devised by librettists to end emotionally to our satisfaction refuse to do so artistically just at the very point where we should begin to feel really contented, where all problems and anxieties have at last resolved themselves.   Again and again composers have failed at this point.   The failure may be only comparative—a falling off from great heights to normal elevations; or it may be absolute—the result of an utter inability on the composer's part to screw himself up for the sake of a mere unravelling of the plot to an emotional pitch equal to that demanded of him by dramatic action or conflict.

This inability is natural.   In the eyes of an artist of wide-awake sensibilities a happy ending is not the conclusive event it has become by convention in the minds of the manufacturers of entertaining novels and their thoughtless readers.   He knows, or feels instinctively, that it is only the prelude to new problems.   He is thus not interested in it as a vital part of his work, but deals with it in the spirit of what detective stories call 'routine work.'   He performs a function that is necessary to the rounding-off of works of art conforming to a certain type but, calling for no special imaginative effort, hardly more attractive or stimulating to the creative artist than the writing of the concluding formula in a letter or the spreading out of a final cadence or common chord on which the curtain may be brought down at the end of an operatic act.   The whole of a happy final scene in an opera, in fact, is too often no more than a kind of extension of this concluding gesture.   The crisis is past, and with it the heightened emotion that has kept invention astir at earlier stages of the work.   The final E♭ major chorus in *The Magic Flute*, for instance, though strikingly original compared with a hundred similar 'curtains' in other operas, is not an interesting piece of music considered in relation to what has gone before.   And why should Mozart himself have been interested?   The libretto demanded that the lovers should be united at the end of their trials, but it was the trials that heated the composer's imagination. The final pages are 'routine work,' and could hardly have been anything else.

I say 'hardly' because it is by no means impossible for such perorations to be something else, something that can actually save a happy ending from unhappily deteriorating in musical quality. What that something is I shall try to show in a moment. First, however, it may be useful to prove with the aid of several other examples how well the assertion that happy endings do not as a rule stir even the greatest composers to their depths is founded. The axiom applies equally to cases where the unravelling of a plot towards a 'satisfactory' conclusion forms part of the last-act finale, as in Weber's *Freischütz*, the final scene of which lamentably fails to maintain the musical qualities of the earlier scenes, and to those in which the solution of the problems has occurred too soon, as in Beethoven's *Fidelio*, where a complete scene without a single important dramatic incident is left to be filled with prolonged jubilations leaving the composer nothing to say that is comparable in significance to the music through which he had expressed conflict and aspiration, suffering and heroism, in the noblest strains and the most convincing forms of which he was capable. Both *Freischütz* and *Fidelio*, it is true, are to a certain extent saved as wholes by describing a kind of arc in which the dramatic tension and the musical climax are approached from a lower level, to which they symmetrically descend again towards the end. Still, the descent is too steep not to leave us disillusioned. We are not even, we feel, left in ignorance of a secret the composers will never tell: we are simply aware that they had nothing more to say while their librettists still compelled them to go on saying something.

One cannot be sure about Weber, who was a naïve artist; but can it be doubted that, had *Fidelio* ended tragically, Beethoven would have risen to the situation in his grandest manner? Is it to be denied that Gluck's *Orfeo* and *Alceste* would be more complete masterpieces if neither Eurydice nor Alcestis were allowed to come to life again for the sake of the conventional reunion with their husbands which drew music of little character from the composer? Whatever subscribers to circulating libraries might feel, tragic operas end nearly always more satisfactorily if they keep to tragedy, and although they may not be intrinsically better than comic ones, the latter are much more likely to fall flat at the end. The exceptions are special phenomena, as we shall see.

The case of Puccini happens to be instructive. His *Girl of the Golden West*, which has had no success at all comparable with that of his three universally popular tragic operas, is not musically so vastly inferior as to deserve such utter neglect. It has, indeed, some features of local colour which need not be regarded as noticeably less interesting than those of *Madame Butterfly*. The real reason for its disappointing career is that the lovers, instead of wringing our hearts to the last, as those in *Bohème, Tosca* and *Butterfly* do, free themselves from their appalling trials and tribulations to experience a spell of felicity. It is the composer's own disappointment mainly, we feel, for he can make nothing of the final scene to satisfy us. Not that he ever elevates us in his tragedies, but he does go on keeping us excited there, whereas the escape of Johnson and Minnie was not to be made musically stirring, for all that the plot has been kept at boiling-point as long as possible. *Gianni Schicchi* might be cited, in refutation of my argument, as Puccini's best musical work in spite of its happy ending; but it ends happily only for three of the characters and leaves satisfaction mingled with a bitter taste of defeat and cruel mockery. As for *Turandot*, we need surely not think that its very poor close is due only to its completion by another hand. It is more reasonable to suppose that Puccini would not have delayed the work so as to leave it unfinished at his death had he not felt the conclusion of the opera to be lame and depressing, just because on the face of it all ends well. Calaf wins the Princess at the price of his human decency. If he had turned and left her, scorning a love she had sacrificed countless lives to keep locked out of her heart, and she had thereupon committed suicide in despair, everybody would have been happy and the composer could have finished his finest score worthily. As it is, there has never been an unhappier happy ending, and he could not bring himself to finish what is musically his finest work at all.

Not only tragic operas with a twist of good fortune at the end suffer the fate of being too often negligently finished by their composers. The same is true of comic operas and other works intended to give pleasure rather than pain, from *Figaro*, which finishes well only because the unravelling comes so near the end that there is room only for a kind of extended festive flourish, down to the Viennese operettas, the last acts of which, including that of the classic of the species, *Die Fledermaus*, are musically always deplorably flimsy. The best thing in the third act of Johann Strauss's piece—indeed almost the only good thing—is a recall from the second act, a means of sending us out of the theatre in a happy frame of mind that is not quite fair, because it never taxed the composer's invention at all at this most difficult juncture. The same expedient was habitually used by Sullivan, and it was moreover imposed on him in *Ruddigore*, the original second finale of which was so poor that it is neither used in performance nor even published in the vocal score. It has often struck critics, and even unprofessional Gilbert and Sullivan devotees, that the first-act finales in the Savoy operas are almost without exception musical masterpieces, whereas those at the end are perfunctory; but I am not sure that the true reason has ever been shown. It is not, of course, that Sullivan tired of a piece before it was finished or was in an undue hurry to complete it, but simply that his first-act finales coincide with a dramatic crisis of Gilbertian craziness, whereas at the close Gilbert's fancy forsook him and he resorted to disentanglements he did not mind making as feeble as possible, as long as they led to happiness. (The semi-tragic close of *The Yeomen of the Guard* is an exception, but it failed to draw the best out of Sullivan because of its obvious insincerity and its tasteless disregard of style.)

Let us now ask ourselves whether we cannot find any operas at all that can send us home after a happy conclusion as profoundly stirred as we are by the greatest tragic closes—those of *Tristan*, *Aida*, *Othello*, *Pelléas and Mélisande* and *Boris Godunov*, for example. Stirred, not merely pleased, as we may well be by the sprightly polacca at the end of *The Barber of Seville*, the catchy tune that brings down the curtain on *The Bartered Bride*, the festive and friendly celebrations at the end of Rimsky-Korsakov's fairy-tale operas or the jolly dance that promises the children happiness for ever after the curtain-fall in *Hänsel and Gretel*. We must except, too, closes that intentionally leave us with mixed feelings, like those of *Don Giovanni* or *Rosenkavalier*, though the former's case will be worth recalling presently. There are a few —a very few—however, which do match fairly extended scenes of final felicity with music that fills us with complete satisfaction. The most exhilarating of them all, it will probably be almost universally conceded, is that of Verdi's *Falstaff*, the work of a man who had written only one opera with a happy ending—and that a dismal failure—until he was nearly eighty. Which seems to show how difficult such a task is, and that is indeed perfectly true. The musician may not dismiss a happy ending cursorily. It demands the most concentrated attention and labour if it is to succeed. Observe that the final pages of *Falstaff* are a fugue, and note particularly that they are so successful for that very reason. We are left in a sort of paroxysm of pleasure, too excited to sleep for hours, after a performance of *Falstaff*, not by any means because we are glad that the piece ended well, but because we have been listening to great music crowned by a still greater purely musical climax. Verdi knew that our interest as play-goers would be dead from the moment Falstaff realizes that he has been hoaxed, and that he must therefore do his utmost to keep our interest as musicians awake.

This is, of course, an immense advantage to tragic opera as well: witness the stirring effect of a song based on the rigid formula of the ground-bass at the end of Purcell's *Dido and Aeneas* or the close symphonic workmanship of the *Liebestod* in *Tristan*. But it is not essential in tragic opera: *Traviata* and *Carmen* and many others do very well without it.   In comic opera or in serious opera with a happy end, on the other hand, this special application of craftsmanship is indispensable if the hearer is to be thrilled at the last, for it is really as hearers that the composer must here appeal to us, since as spectators we are no longer deeply interested.   The happy, if only temporarily happy, close of *Siegfried* is dramatically an unbearably dull love duet; but it is made exciting by Wagner by being fashioned into a shapely, formal piece of music on a vast scale.   Mozart's *Seraglio* finishes very exhilaratingly because the concluding *vaudeville* is not only a good tune we can hum contentedly on coming out of the theatre, but an admirably constructed piece of music partaking of elements of the rondo and variation forms.   The final sextet in *Così fan tutte*, which is as enlivening as the *Falstaff* fugue, sends shivers of delight down one's back because its musical texture is handled with superb skill, not because the fickle lovers have made a reconciliation we do not care whether we can believe in or not.   The conventional operatic ensemble which Ravel deliberately introduced into the close of *L'Heure espagnole* yields a purely musical delight, coming as a touch of heightened artifice in a score that is at its best when it is most artificial.   The quasi-fugue at the end of the final sextet in *Don Giovanni* has much the same effect as the true fugue in *Falstaff*.

And here we come upon the most enlightening case.   It used to be the almost universal practice to omit this sextet and to close the opera with Don Juan's descent to hell.   This was found to be dramatically more satisfactory, simply because a tragic close is apt to be felt as a stronger and more conclusive finish to a great work; and, as it happened, it was also musically quite satisfying, because the opera thus ended, as the overture began, in D minor.   But the overture goes on, after the gloomy D minor introduction, in a vivacious *Allegro* in D major, so that the ideal symmetry is attained only if the whole opera finishes brightly in that key.   Still, the sextet is only just saved from being an anticlimax by the mock-fugue that forms its third section, like the *presto* finale of a sonata in three movements, and saved undoubtedly by its great technical interest.   For it is not to be denied that the *allegro assai* and *larghetto* sections somewhat fall off in quality against the passion, the solemnity and the cold horror of the scene of the stone guest's visitation.   The frequent cutting of the sextet was thus understandable enough, not only from a dramatic but to some extent from a musical point of view, until the modern conception of *Don Giovanni*—which is undoubtedly the right one—as a work of a curiously and disquietingly dual nature, as the great classic tragi-comedy in music, had gained a firm hold.   And since it is also the most profoundly musical and musicianly of operas, that purely musical extra finale, that incomparably shaped sonata, has after all become indispensable.   It is, with that of *Falstaff*, the greatest happy ending in dramatic music, the greater because it follows without anticlimax what is still one of the greatest tragic endings.

It was convenient to confine this argument mainly to opera, which happens to furnish the most obvious and convincing illustrations; but it is, I think, true of all music that a grave conclusion to any work is easier for the composer to deal with than a joyful one, and that in the latter case he cannot hope to produce an impression of greatness unless he makes some special technical effort.   Mozart, for instance, became more readily engrossed in tragic closes.   Professor Girdlestone has pointed out in his book on Mozart's piano concertos that the greatest and most extensive codas occur as a rule in the works in minor keys, which we all know to be generally his most impressive.   But Mozart also knew what he was about when he made the finale of the 'Jupiter' symphony, which is one of the most thrillingly joyous movements in all music, a staggering feat of polyphonic writing; and two of his quartet finales, in G major (K. 387) and A major (K. 464), produce sensations of almost unearthly pleasure by an application at full pressure of the composer's astounding mental lucidity.

Haydn's playful, witty and heart-easing finales, especially in the quartets and symphonies, are most successful where the greatest contrapuntal dexterity is expended on them, while Schubert, on the other hand, whose great virtues are not primarily those of close workmanship, too often gives his joyful finales too flimsy a texture to save them from falling off against the earlier movements—which, incidentally, may well be the reason why, obscurely aware of this deficiency, he left a great symphony, a great string quartet and more than one fine piano sonata unfinished.   And it is no accident, of course, Beethoven being Beethoven, that his *Hymn to Joy* is a scheme of musical organization of enormous complexity, including devices of the rondo and variation forms as well as of the double fugue, treated in the most extensive and elaborate way.   If profound artistic, not mere hedonistic, joy is the creative musician's aim, he can attain it only by letting the art of composition take masterful control.

Index